MAY '89

Dear Howard,

You bring so much love &
joy into my life.
May we always celebrate
being together

With deep love.

Kim

skye

Ralph Storer

skye

Walking, Scrambling and Exploring

Lovest thou mountains great,
Peaks to the clouds that soar,
Corrie and fell where eagle dwell,
And cataracts rush evermore?
Lovest thou green grassy glades,
By the sunshine sweetly kist,
Murmuring waves and echoing caves?
Then go to the Isle of Mist.

from *The Isle of Skye*
by Alexander Nicolson

DAVID & CHARLES
Newton Abbot   London

To the people of Skye

Page 2:
Loch Coruisk from Sgurr na Stri

British Library Cataloguing in Publication Data

Storer, Ralph
  Skye, walking, scrambling and exploring
  1. Scotland. Highland regions. Skye –
  Visitors' guides
  I. Title
  914.11'82

  ISBN 0-7153-9223-9

Typeset by ABM Typographics Limited, Hull
and printed in Great Britain
by Butler & Tanner Limited, Frome and London
for David & Charles Publishers plc
Brunel House   Newton Abbot   Devon

contents

Stunning coastal scenery between Idrigill and Lorgill

pReface

Summer usually finds me on Skye. Since my first visit to the Cuillin more than twenty years ago I have been under the spell of those magic mountains, which are justly famed worldwide. The diversity of mountain forms on the island never ceases to amaze me, from the jagged Cuillin ridge to the unique flat-topped MacLeod's Tables and the fantastic eroded pinnacles of Trotternish. In addition, the coastal architecture is the most Gothic and exciting in the British Isles, with a host of spectacular sea caves and stacks, and cliffs rising to more than 300m (1,000ft) above Atlantic breakers, while underground lie some of the most sporting caves in Scotland.

It is not just the existence of these varied landforms that makes the exploration of Skye on foot such a pleasure, but a combination of all of them in close proximity in an island setting. At every turn the eye is stimulated by remarkable and contrasting forms, and forming a perfect backdrop to every view is the endless sea. To this is added another dimension, that of time, for one cannot walk on Skye without being made constantly aware of its bloody history. Yet, even more than this, there is an indefinable quality about the island that induces a love bordering on addiction. Some call it the magic of Skye, others Skye-fever. Perhaps it has something to do with the purity of the atmosphere or the quality of the light, which here has a soft brilliance like nowhere else.

Many visitors to Skye, however, remain blissfully ignorant of many of its attractions. There are obvious landmarks, such as the Cuillin and The Storr, to be climbed or photographed, but how many of those who stay at Sligachan or Glen Brittle year after year know of the beautiful natural arches near Idrigill Point, or the perfectly formed basalt columns of Preshal Beg, or the 40m (130ft) archway cave of Meall Greepa, or of scramblers' playgrounds just a few minutes' walk from the road? I choose these examples at random from a list that seems almost endless. Of course, all these places are known, or were known in more populous times, to the inhabitants of Skye. Many were also known to visitors of old, who travelled by boat before

Storm clouds over Sgurr an Fheadain

motorised transport was invented. Yet to most modern visitors the secret places of Skye will be a revelation.

There are some who would keep the secrets of Skye to themselves, but I believe there is no place for elitism where our national heritage is concerned and I have faith that visitors will be aware of their responsibilities to the land upon which they walk. My aim in writing this book is to promote a rediscovery of the island, to share with you the fruits of many years of exploration and so bring about a greater appreciation of what Skye has to offer to those prepared to leave the roadside. All manner of walks will be found herein, from short roadside strolls to hard Cuillin scrambles and long serious coast walks. I wish you well in your explorations and as many hours of contentment as I have enjoyed walking, scrambling and exploring on Skye.

1 introduction

1.1 General Description

With an area of nearly 700sq miles (18,000sq km), Skye is the second largest of the Hebridean islands lying off the west coast of Scotland. As the eagle flies it is approximately 50 miles (80km) long by 7 miles (12km) to 25 miles (40km) wide, yet such are the contortions of its shape that road distances are always greater than expected and the coastline is many hundreds of miles long.

So indented is the coastline that on the map the island looks like a group of peninsulas joined together in the middle. No place is more than 5 miles (8km) from the sea, and the nearness of the sea makes walking on Skye a quite different experience from walking in the mainland Highlands. Some say that Skye derives its name from its shape, the name being a modern version of the Celtic *skeitos* or Gaelic *sgiath* (meaning wing). Others derive the name from the Celtic *sci* (cut or indented), the old Gaelic *sgith* (Scots), the Celtic *skia* and *neach* (sword people), the Norse *skith* (a tablet or log used during the Norse occupation) and the Norse *sky* and *ey* (cloud island). Take your choice.

In broad geographical terms there are five peninsulas radiating from the central part of Skye: Duirinish, Waternish and Trotternish to the north, stocky Minginish to the west and the fish-tail of Sleat to the south. The first four of these names are Norse district names, whereas Sleat is a parish name. Neither the Norse nor parish divisions satisfactorily describe the distinct geographical units that are obvious to the Skye visitor, and so, for the purposes of this book, the following divisions (shown on the accompanying map) are used: Sleat, Strath, Minginish, Duirinish, Waternish and Trotternish. Part of the magic of Skye lies in the fact that each of these areas has a character all of its own enhanced by the contrasting character of its neighbours.

Most walkers and climbers are attracted to Skye by the Minginish peninsula, for it is here that the Cuillin are to be found. This supreme mountain range contains no less than eleven Munros and dominates the island from all angles. The rough gabbro rock of which the mountains are largely composed is like something out of a climber's dream, and the sharp summit arêtes and fantastic rock shapes it has formed makes walking and scrambling in the Cuillin more exciting, challenging and rewarding than anywhere else in the British Isles.

Less well known than the Cuillin, but equally spectacular in its own way, is the Minginish coastline where mile upon mile of vertiginous cliff top provides magnificent walks of testing length and remoteness.

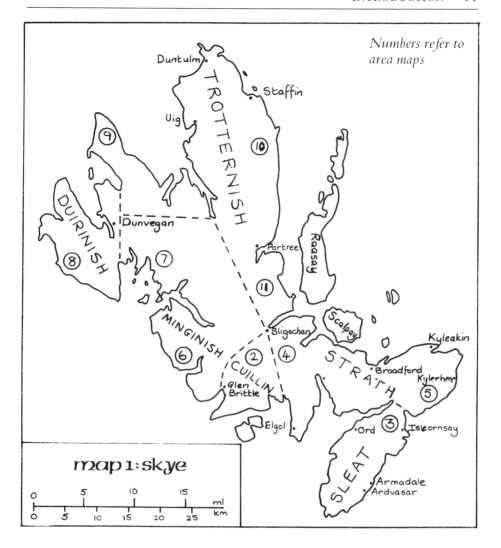

Numbers refer to area maps

Duntulm
Staffin
Uig
TROTTERNISH
⑨
⑩
DUIRINISH
Dunvegan
⑧
⑦
Portree
Raasay
⑪
Sligachan
Scalpay
Kyleakin
MINGINISH
⑥
② ④
CUILLIN
STRATH
Broadford
Kylerhea
Glen
Brittle
⑤
Elgol
Ord ③ Isleornsay
SLEAT
Armadale
Ardvasar

map 1: skye

0 ... 5 ... 10 ... 15 ml

0 ... 5 ... 10 ... 15 ... 20 ... 25 km

Minginish is bounded on the south by Loch Scavaig and on the north by Loch Bracadale, but for the purposes of this book the adjoining areas of central Skye and the Bracadale and Scavaig coastlines have also been included in the Minginish chapter. The bleak moors of central Skye are mainly given over to sheep, cattle and forestry plantations and have little of interest to offer the walker, but the many small peninsulas of beautiful Loch Bracadale contain some fascinating coastal scenery and are a delight to explore.

After Minginish the second most popular walking area is Trotternish, the most northerly of Skye's peninsulas, where a high mountain backbone running the length of the peninsula erupts on its eastern side into a succession of weird pinnacles and basins. The highest and most popular hill is The Storr (719m/2,358ft) and the most famous pinnacles are those of The Storr and The Quiraing, but off the beaten track other equally fascinating hills and rock basins await the explorer. In addition, an extremely varied coastline on each side of the mountains provides innumerable short but exciting excursions to rocky headlands, sea stacks, caves, natural arches, waterfalls and abandoned castles. The similar adjoining area south of Portree has also been included in the Trotternish chapter.

The prize for the most dramatic coastal scenery goes to the Duirinish peninsula in the north-west. Here is to be found the highest sea cliff on the island (Biod an Athair, 313m/1,028ft), the tallest sea stack (the Mother stack at MacLeod's Maidens, 63m/207ft) and the most beautiful and intricate series of coastal formations to be found anywhere in the British Isles. Inland the remarkable flat tops of MacLeod's Tables dominate the landscape and provide a curious hill walk. The adjoining countryside around Dunvegan has also been included in the Duirinish chapter.

Between Trotternish and Duirinish is the least accessible and least frequented of all Skye peninsulas: Waternish. This is a land of empty moors and remote shorelines that appears uninteresting on the map yet on closer investigation reveals many hidden gems, including some fine sea cliffs, stacks and duns. The interesting smaller peninsulas of inner Loch Snizort to the east have also been included in the Waternish chapter.

In the south, the Sleat peninsula makes a dramatic contrast to its northern neighbours. This is 'the garden of Skye', a landscape without mountains where gentle wave-lapped shores are backed by green fields and woods. As with Waternish a glance at the map of Sleat reveals little of interest to the walker, but those who explore on foot will here discover some of the island's most beautiful coastal scenery, including the untracked shores of the rocky west coast, and some remarkable old castles.

Between Minginish and Sleat the old parish of Strath sprawls across the southern part of the island with a tremendous variety of scenery, as though trying to incorporate something of all the other areas. After the Cuillin this is the second most mountainous area on Skye, where Cuillin outliers such as Bla Bheinn (considered by many to be the most beautiful of the mountains), contrast with the crumbling Red Hills, which provide more relaxed high-level walking. Here also there is limestone country to explore and a coastline that includes some notable caves (including the wondrous Spar Cave) and some alarmingly weathered sandstone sea cliffs.

In all, the walker on Skye is spoiled for choice. The many and varied districts provide a wealth of interesting and exciting walking experiences unequalled in the British Isles. Add to this the island setting, the magnificent seascapes and the quality of Skye light and there is something here for everyone, enough for anyone.

1.2 GEOLOGY

The tremendously varied scenery of Skye reflects a complex geology that has made the island a classic centre for geological study. What follows is a brief walker's guide to this geology, avoiding specialist terms where possible.

The oldest rocks on Skye are found in Sleat, whose surface geology produces low-lying moorland that is more characteristic of the Northern Highlands than the rest of Skye. The oldest rock is Lewissian gneiss, a coarse-grained grey rock easily recognised by its gnarled and banded appearance. It was formed up to 3,000 million years ago and today reaches the surface along the east coast of Sleat from Isleornsay to Aird of Sleat, beyond Ardvasar.

Over the course of time the gneiss landscape was eroded by rivers whose alluvial deposits formed the Torridonian sandstones and whose deltaic deposits formed the Moine schists of some 800 to 1,000 million years ago. Schist is recognisable by its thin bands of flaky material, treacherous for climbing but attractive when reflecting the light; it occurs mainly in the south-west of Sleat. The sandstone has a much rougher feel and forms the backbone of the Sleat peninsula.

Between 450 and 600 million years ago the sea-level rose, the land that is now Skye was under water and sedimentary rocks were formed on the sea bed: quartzites, shales, grits and limestones. Today these rocks reach the surface in the Ord district of Sleat and on the east side of Strath Suardal south of Broadford, where porous limestone provides dry terrain and lush green grass. The limestone contains the earliest fossils found on Skye. Some of the limestone was later metamorphosed into marble, which is still quarried near Torrin.

There is then a gap in the geological history of Skye until the sandstones and conglomerates of 225 million years ago, formed on river flood plains, and the limestones, sandstones and shales of 135 to 195 million years ago, formed when Skye was again under water. Today these rocks occur around Broadford, in the Strathaird district and around the coast of Trotternish; the younger rocks are abundant in fossils and form the best soils on Skye.

The greatest geological upheaval was still to come, for 60 million years ago the land was covered by vast outpourings of lava from fissures in the earth's surface. In the north of Skye wave upon wave of lava flowed to the surface, cooling quickly to form great sheets of fine-grained basalt that today cover more than half the island.

The horizontal nature of the lava flows gave rise to the flat-topped summits of MacLeod's Tables and the characteristically rolling countryside of Trotternish. Often the hills and cliffs have a terraced appearance, due to weathering between the flows, and this enables individual flows to be traced with ease. The basalt reaches its highest point at The Storr (719m/2,358ft) and also forms the great sea cliffs of the west coast. Cooling fractures often give the cliffs a columnar appearance, as seen most spectacularly at Kilt Rock. On the eastern side of the Trotternish mountains, underlying rocks have been unable to support the weight of the basalt, and some of the largest landslips in Britain have occurred, producing chaotic jumbles of pinnacles such as those at The Storr and The Quiraing.

The Cuillin were formed from the lava reservoir, which cooled very slowly, producing the extremely hard coarse-grained gabbro that has weathered into the fantastic shapes we know today (see page 28 for further description). The granite Red Hills were formed at the same time. One theory says that they were formed from surrounding rocks, which were uplifted, melted and in time eroded uniformly to form the rounded, scree-girt hills of today. Another theory says that they were formed from the cooling of a type of magma different from that which formed the Cuillin.

Since that cataclysmic era the Skye landscape has continued to be changed by weathering and glacial erosion. From 2 million years ago until about 10,000 years ago ice covered most of Britain, scouring the landscape as it moved slowly westwards. The Red Hills were ground down into their rounded forms. On the Cuillin, glaciers flowed down the mountainsides to form bowl-shaped corries of bare rock. Huge rounded slabs of rock, known to the Cuillin climber as 'boiler plates', were left behind. Glens such as Glen Sligachan were chiselled into U-shaped valleys as the ice ground along their bottoms.

After the ice melted the sea-level changed several times, forming 'raised beaches' around Skye at about 7m (25ft), 15m (50ft) and 30m (100ft). Long sea inlets such as Loch Harport are drowned glens. Even today weathering continues to wear down the landscape. As recently as 1987 the famous gendarme on the west ridge of Sgurr nan Gillean disintegrated. The base of the Old Man of Storr is being whittled away piece by piece year after year, until it too will one day topple. Around the coast weathering of sea cliffs has produced the amazing variety of caves, natural arches and stacks that are such a constant source of wonder to the coast walker.

Such is the geological history of Skye, a continuing process but, it is to be hoped, one that will not change drastically during the lifetime of this guidebook.

1.3 HISTORY

History does not determine the form of a landscape to the same extent as geology, yet it leaves its imprint everywhere, and even a superficial historical knowledge can add much to the pleasures of walking. What follows is a brief sketch of the history of Skye that will place into context any detailed historical references in the main text.

Apart from Mesolithic nomads who reached the western isles about 6000BC, archaeological evidence suggests that Skye was first peopled by Neolithic farmers from Europe about 4000BC; the chambered cairns of Skye (drystone-wall burial chambers roofed by a cairn), such as that at Rubh' an Dunain, date from this period. The next settlers, about 2000BC, were the Beaker People, a race of semi-nomadic herdsmen named after their ornate pottery.

In the late first millennium BC the Celts of central Europe reached Skye and fortified the island with more than fifty duns (forts), whose ruins are so conspicuous in the modern landscape. Many of these duns were in the form of a circular drystone tower, known as a broch, which had thick double walls up to 15m (50ft) high. Between inner and outer walls were small rooms or galleries, sometimes five or six storeys high. All Skye brochs are now in a ruinous state, as their stones have been reused over the centuries for later buildings, but some of the best preserved are well worth visiting for an insight into prehistoric life (eg Dun Beag near Struan). Another defensive structure was the souterrain, an underground refuge of which good examples can be seen at Claigan and Tungadal, and also dating from this period are a number of standing stones and other sites, such as at Boreraig in Strath.

In time the Celts became polarised into different groups, such as the Picts of the Highlands and Islands and the Scots of Ireland (*Scotti* was the Roman word for raiders), each group speaking a different language. The Picts have left their mark on the Skye landscape in the form of incised symbol stones (eg Clach Ard). Roman Britain repulsed an invasion of combined Picts and Scots in 367, and there was much fighting between various groups all over the Highlands and Islands throughout the fourth and fifth centuries. In the sixth century the Gaelic-speaking Scots invaded and settled in the Islands, gradually turning Pictland into Scotland. In their wake came St Columba and a number of other (sometimes rival) saints, who converted the people to Christianity.

From the eighth century onwards Vikings began to settle on the west coast of Scotland, and Skye was under Norse occupation as Scandinavian and Scottish kings fought for the upper hand. Norwegian supremacy was ended once and for all when the 120-strong fleet of King Haco was defeated at the Battle of Largs by the Scottish king Alexander III in 1263, and the Western Isles were seceded to Scotland by the Treaty of Perth in 1266.

Even then peace was not to be found. The Isles saw themselves as separate from Scotland, and under the leadership of the Lord of the Isles there were many rebellions against the Scottish crown in the fourteenth and fifteenth centuries. Constant inter-clan feuds also took place; the clan were the children or followers of a chief who placed themselves under his protection in return for serving him. The two major Skye clans were the MacLeods and the MacDonalds (mac = son), who fought innumerable ferocious battles all over the island.

James IV abolished the Lordship of the Isles in 1493, but failed to quell the rebelliousness of the chiefs. In 1540 James V demonstrated his power by taking a great fleet to the Isles. He visited both Duntulm Castle (the MacDonald stronghold) and Dunvegan Castle (the MacLeod stronghold), took hostages and anchored in Portree Bay, where the chiefs came to pay their respects. The ensuing peace lasted no longer than James himself, however, who died two years later, and clan fights and rebellions continued apace into the seventeenth century. The last clan battle fought on Skye soil took place in Coire na Creiche in the Cuillin in 1601.

During the seventeenth and eighteenth centuries island life was much affected by Jacobite attempts to restore the Stuarts to the throne of England and Scotland, culminating in the 1745 Rebellion led by Prince Charles Edward Stuart ('Bonnie Prince Charlie'). After the disastrous defeat at Culloden in 1746, Prince Charlie's wanderings in the Highlands and Islands, in flight from the English redcoats, became the stuff of legend, fêted in story and song, and the few days he spent on Skye have left an indelible mark on the island's folklore.

He arrived in Skye from South Uist on 28 June 1746, accompanied by Flora MacDonald and dressed as her maid. They landed on the Trotternish coastline at the headland now named Prince Charles's Point and went on foot to Portree. From Portree Charlie went to Raasay before returning and heading southwards to the Strathaird coast. To avoid the redcoats he and his guide probably kept well west of Sligachan, forded the River Sligachan below Nead na h-Iolaire, crossed the Mam a' Phobuill beside Marsco, circled round Glas Bheinn Mhor into Srath Mor and followed the shore of Loch Slapin.

Anyone who has undertaken this route will be in no doubt as to Charlie's fitness and hillcraft, especially as he crossed the mountains at night, exclaiming at one point, 'I'm sure the Devil would not find me now'! He was conducted to the cave south of Elgol, now named Prince Charlie's Cave, from where he was rowed over to the mainland, eventually to escape to safety in France. His route on Skye would make an interesting and unusual backpacking route.

Following the '45, Parliament attempted to eradicate the culture that had spawned rebellion by outlawing weapons, Gaelic and even the kilt. The result was peace in the Isles, but the tragic cost was the destruction of a culture that has never really recovered. With peace at last, however, the population grew steadily in the latter half of the eighteenth century, reaching a peak of 23,000 in 1841. In the Napoleonic Wars Skye sent over 10,000 men to Europe, more than the entire population of the island today.

Social and economic disaster struck in the mid-nineteenth century, when the kelp industry collapsed and the potato harvest failed. The people became destitute, the landlords bankrupt. Amid scenes of appalling tragedy and hardship, people all over the Highlands and Islands were cleared from the land, often forcibly, in order to combine small crofts into more profitable larger holdings and make room for sheep, which thrived on the land. One estimate puts the number of people evicted in Skye alone between 1840 and 1883 at 6,940 families; thousands emigrated to the colonies, many to perish during the voyage.

The tragedy of the Clearances continues to arouse emotion even today. Some blame greedy landlords, others farmers who did not pay rent to bankrupt landlords, others overpopulation, others the fungus that blighted the potato crop. Whatever the causes and the rights and wrongs, anyone who walks the Highlands and Islands today and revels in their solitude cannot help but feel pangs of guilt for the historical reasons that have made the land as it is. Wherever you go in Skye you will come across forlorn ruins from the days of the Clearances.

In the late nineteenth century people began to fight against eviction. In 1882 there was a running battle between crofters and police at the Braes. Agitation eventually led to the Napier Commission of 1883 and the first Crofters' Act of 1886, whereby crofters were given security of tenure and fair rents. Successive Crofters' Acts this century have further eased the farmer's lot. Today agriculture remains the main industry, followed by tourism, fishing and forestry. The total population is only about a quarter of its 1841 peak of 23,000. As elsewhere in the Islands, young people quit Skye to pursue mainland careers, and constant effort is required to prevent native Gaelic from dying out.

The major hope for the future welfare of the island appears to be tourism, which has been on the increase ever since the visits of Thomas Pennant in 1772, Dr Samuel Johnson and James Boswell in 1773 and Isobel Murray in 1802, all of whom wrote books about their travels. In 1814 Sir Walter Scott visited Coruisk, and his vivid description of it in *The Lord of the Isles* firmly placed the Cuillin on the tourist map. 'Unclimbable' Sgurr nan Gillean was climbed in 1836, and this paved the way for other first ascents and increasingly difficult rock climbs, a process that continues to this day (see page 32 for a history of Cuillin exploration).

The walker on Skye today follows some of the greatest climbers, writers and artists of their generations, on ground that has more tales to tell than most. While wandering around the island I am often reminded of Dr Johnson's words: 'Far from me be such frigid philosophy as may conduct us indifferent and unmoved over any ground which has been dignified by wisdom, bravery or virtue.'

1.4 NATURAL HISTORY

Skye has an immense variety of flora and fauna, which reflects its varied topography and diverse habitats; there are, for instance, some three hundred common flowering plants and more than three hundred species of butterfly and moth. To do justice to such a natural history would require several volumes, but for this guidebook a brief outline will suffice, together with more specific details on species likely to interest the non-specialist visitor.

The flora of Skye varies from the flowers of the shoreline to mountain-loving Alpine and Arctic plants found especially in the mineral-rich crevices of the Trotternish hills. Strath limestone provides a rich habitat for lime-loving plants, while the moors of Minginish and northern Skye host moorland plants such as heather and bog cotton (at one time collected for filling pillows). Trees are scarce except in coastal Sleat, where birch, oak, hazel and ash are common.

Fauna distribution also varies according to habitat. On the flat coasts herons and orange-beaked oystercatchers are plentiful, while large seabirds, such as shags and cormorants, breed on the sea cliffs. Ravens are common, and you may even see an eagle. At present, more than forty pairs of eagles breed on Skye, but to the untrained eye they are often confused with buzzards; the eagle is larger than the buzzard (about 80–90cm/32–35in long compared to the buzzard's 50–60cm/20–24in), has a 2m (6½ft) wingspan (compared to the buzzard's 1.2m/4ft), is less stocky and is more elegant in flight. Note also that the white-tailed sea eagle, Europe's largest eagle, with a wingspan of almost 2.5m (8ft), may also be seen. This species became extinct in Britain when the last one was shot on Skye in 1916 (they were blamed for taking lambs), but in 1975 they were reintroduced in Rum, with (so far) some success.

Most of the common small animals occur on Skye: mice, voles, hedgehogs etc. Rabbits are abundant on the moors and edges of sea cliffs. There are also foxes, unlike on any other Scottish island. There are no longer any wildcats, although there are feral tabbies. Roe-deer may be seen in the woods of Strath and Sleat, and red deer on the Minginish moors, though not in such great numbers as in the sixteenth century, when it was recorded that a thousand were killed in one hunt alone.

On the coast the doglike head of the common seal can often be seen bobbing in the water just offshore; the bulkier grey seal is rarer. Otters are fairly common but not often seen. In the sea are porpoises, whales, sharks and dolphins.

Reptiles resident on Skye are the lizard, the slow-worm and the adder, although you are unlikely to see them. Insects are abundant, notably the cleg and the midge, which ravage visitors from mid-June to late summer. The cleg is a large, persistent horse-fly with a nasty bite, but it can usually be spotted before it gets you.

Midges are something else; no matter how many are swatted they are never short of kamikaze reinforcements. They prefer boggy ground and damp warm weather, and just love Sligachan and Glen Brittle campsites. As testament to the persistence of the midge, the nineteenth-century geologist John MacCulloch once recorded that despite being anchored in the Sound of Soay 1 mile (2km) from shore the 'light militia of the lower sky' still managed to nose him out. Things are not always so bad; midges hate wind, cold, heat and heavy rain, and (some people claim) certain insect repellents. In exposed places like hills and sea cliffs they are normally no problem.

1.5 WEATHER

Skye has a reputation for bad weather only partly borne out by facts. Rainfall is high, averaging 120+cm (50+in) per annum on the coast and 300+cm (125+in) on the mountains, compared to 95cm (40in) in Glasgow and around 60cm (25in) in London and Edinburgh. Average maximum summer temperatures are around 16°C (60°F) during the hottest months of July and August. Average annual sunshine is around 1,200hr, considerably lower than the south and east of Britain, but only slightly lower than the west. Strong winds and gales are common, Skye being directly in the path of the prevailing southerly and westerly winds that blow off the Atlantic.

These figures support the notion of a more inclement climate than on the mainland, but they are insufficient to account alone for Skye's bad weather reputation. Clearly other factors are at work, one of which is the tendency for visitors to holiday in the late summer, which is nowhere near the driest, brightest and calmest time of the year (see table below).

Another factor is weather variability. Broadford's rainfall, for instance, is about twice that of Staffin, snow is as likely in May as in October, April has been known to be completely dry one year and abnormally wet the next, there may be as much sun in the summer of one year as in the whole of the next. Such variability makes weather prediction difficult, especially as different localities may experience widely differing weather simultaneously. The mountains of Trotternish may be clear when the mountains of Minginish are enveloped in cloud, the Braes bathed in sunlight beside a storm-ridden Glamaig and the high tops of the Cuillin in sunshine above sea-level cloud at Glen Brittle.

It is this very variability and imponderability, however, that gives Skye a unique atmospheric quality that constantly surprises and delights. On a hot day in the Cuillin mist can form in seconds, billowing up from nowhere to engulf a peak; anvil-shaped clouds can form before your eyes and hang threateningly overhead. Double rainbows are not uncommon, and there is one report of a triple rainbow; sunsets may be all colours of the rainbow. Even a dreich drizzly day can have a delicate translucent quality, and after rain the light has a soft brilliance like nowhere else.

The 'misty isle' myth derives from the incidence of hill cloud, but hills attract cloud everywhere, not just in Skye. Sea-level Skye is notable not for its mist but for the pollution-free clarity of its light. On a clear day on the Cuillin it is even possible to see the remote island of St Kilda, 100 miles (160km) away beyond the Outer Hebrides.

The unique quality and delicacy of the weather patterns of Skye contribute much to the magic of the island, and many of us who fall under its spell are quite content to leave things as they are. Or, to put it in the words of an old Skye wish:

> Geamhradh reodhagach, Earrach ceothagach,
> Samhradh breac riabhach, 's Foghar glan grianach.
> (A frosty Winter, a misty Spring,
> a light and shade Summer, and a clear sunny Autumn).

As a rough weather guide, the following table shows a monthly comparison of temperature, rainfall, sunshine and wind. The figures are a ranking from 1 to 12. Figures for temperature (1= hottest, 12=coldest) and wind (1=calmest, 12=windiest) are relatively constant throughout the island. Figures for sunshine (1=brightest, 12=dullest) and rainfall (1=driest, 12=wettest) vary considerably depending on locality. Where months are shown as being of equal rank, this indicates an averaging to reflect the local variation; thus April is normally drier than June in Staffin but the reverse is true in Broadford.

	TEMPERATURE	RAINFALL	SUNSHINE	WIND
JAN	12	8=	11	12
FEB	11	4=	8=	2
MAR	9	4=	6	10
APR	7	2=	3	8
MAY	5	1	1=	1
JUN	3	2=	1=	3
JUL	2	4=	5	6
AUG	1	7	4	4
SEP	4	8=	7	7
OCT	6	8=	8=	9
NOV	8	8=	10	5
DEC	10	8=	12	11

NB A mountain weather forecast can be obtained by phoning 0898-500-441.

1.6 NOTES ON USE OF GUIDE

Grading system

The walks and scrambles in this book are graded for difficulty on a scale of 1 (easiest) to 5 (hardest):

Grade 1: Short and easy walks, usually on paths; the going may sometimes be boggy and wellingtons are advisable, but no special footwear is required

Grade 2: Longer walks of no real difficulty and involving little ascent, although care may be required on cliff-top coast walks and good footwear may be required

Grade 3: Walks involving more difficult going, normally requiring good footwear and care on cliff-top coast walks; a certain amount of climbing (but no scrambling) may be involved

Grade 4: Mountain walks and more difficult coast walks, normally involving appreciable climbing (but no scrambling); good footwear essential

Grade 5: Mountain walks and serious coast walks involving scrambling or difficult terrain; good footwear, fitness and experience essential.

Scrambles are categorised as simple, moderate or hard. A simple scramble involves use of hands for assistance, a moderate scramble has fewer handholds and footholds, and a hard scramble fewer still, while still remaining below the level of what would normally be regarded as a rock climb. Such judgements are necessarily subjective and, although great pains have been taken to ensure that gradings are standard across routes, a simple scramble may seem hard to one person and a hard scramble simple to another, depending on individual factors such as build and response to exposure. Rock climbing grades Easy, Moderate, Difficult, Very Difficult, Severe and Very Severe are also referred to in the text.

Advice to walkers

Route descriptions and gradings are for good summer conditions only; in adverse weather difficulties are compounded and many mountain walks and coast walks are best avoided. In addition, the Cuillin are subject to special considerations that are discussed in section 2.1 (see page 37). Under snow the mountains of Skye should be avoided by those unused to Scottish winter conditions. Snowfall varies greatly from year to year, but in a normal season the hills get their first dusting of snow in October and winter conditions prevail until after Easter, with pockets of snow lasting into June.

Coast walking is not normally regarded as requiring the same degree of fitness, commitment and expertise as mountain walking, yet many Skye coast walks are remote and serious undertakings. The rewards are many, including wild and spectacular coastal scenery and superb views, but there are dangers of which the novice coast walker may be unaware and which he will underestimate at his peril. Much of the Skye coastline is distant from the nearest road. Cliffs often overhang, undercut by the sea. Their vertiginous edges are often crumbling, honeycombed by rabbits and swept by sudden gusts of wind. There is rarely any shelter from the elements.

Cliff-top terrain is often undulating, requiring constant ascent and descent (sometimes on steep exposed hillsides of grass that become slippery when wet) and a different mental attitude from mountain walking; the end point of the walk is hardly ever in view. Cliff-top rivers may cut deep gorges as they fall to the sea, requiring appreciable inland detours to outflank. In spate rivers may be dangerous or impassable (this is true all over Skye, on mountain, moor or coast, and rivers spate quickly after rain). In many places sheep paths at the cliff edge make for excellent going but may also induce a false sense of security, for sheep have small feet and no sense of vertigo (in fact no sense at all) — use their trails with care.

Shoreline coast walks have a different set of dangers from cliff-top coast walks. Shoreline rocks may be greasy and require care if a twisted ankle or worse is to be avoided. Shoreline crags may be awkward to negotiate. Stonefall, sometimes induced by seabirds, is always a danger at the foot of cliffs. And there is the greatest danger of all — becoming trapped at the cliff foot by an incoming tide.

In short, as much preparation and care is required for coast walking as for mountain walking. The longer coast walks should be attempted only in dry weather in good footwear by well equipped walkers. Heed the warnings in the text. Stay away from dangerous cliff edges. Where a torch is required for the exploration of sea caves, this is noted in the text. Sections of walks that are under water at high tide and can be undertaken at low tide only are unmistakably marked in the text: AT LOW TIDE ONLY. A tide timetable is an indispensable item of equipment; tide tables for the west coast of Scotland are produced by Oban Yacht Services and are obtainable from fishermen's shops on the quayside at Portree or from Oban Yacht Services, Oban, Argyll (0631-63666).

This is a guidebook rather than an instruction manual, and it is assumed that for all walks above Grade 1 parties will be suitably equipped (good footwear, waterproofs, map, compass etc) and competent to undertake their chosen itinerary. In case of accident inform the police at Portree (0478) 2888; for mountain rescue in the Cuillin see section 2.1 (page 37).

Note: walking is a non-sexist activity, and in the absence of a suitable personal pronoun, all references in the text to 'he' should be taken as meaning 'he or she'.

Access

There are few access restrictions to the land on Skye and no stalking restrictions as in the mainland highlands. The fact that a route is included in this book, however, does not imply a right of way; respect private property and if in doubt about a path enquire at the nearest house. Please leave the land as you would wish to find it, and in particular do not leave gates open, do not damage farm fences and do not worry livestock. Follow the Country Code. Any specific access problems are noted in the text where appropriate.

Maps

The most suitable maps for walking and touring on Skye outside the Cuillin are the Ordnance Survey (OS) 1:50,000 maps. Two maps cover the whole of Skye except for the extreme eastern tip: number 23 North Skye and number 32 South Skye; number 33 Loch Alsh and Glen Shiel covers the eastern tip. For the complex topography of the Cuillin the larger scale OS 1:25,000 Outdoor Leisure map to the Cuillin and Torridon Hills is recommended. Grid references (GR) given in the text are based on these maps.

Sketch maps in the text should be self-explanatory except for the symbols used to indicate mountain tops:

▲ Munro (ie separate mountain over 914m/3,000ft),
△ Top (subsidiary summit over 914m/3,000ft in Munro's Tables),
● Other summit over 914m (3,000ft),
○ Summit over 762m (2,500ft),
■ Summit over 600m (2,000ft),
□ Summit under 600m (2,000ft).

Note: river directions, left bank and right bank, in accordance with common usage, refer to the direction when facing downstream.

Measurements

Distances in the text are specified in both miles (to the nearest half-mile) and kilometres (to the nearest kilometre); shorter distances are specified in metres (an approximate imperial measurement is yards).

Heights of mountains, hills and cliffs are specified in both metres and feet. Metric heights have been obtained from OS Second Series 1:50,000 maps. Equivalent heights in feet have been obtained by multiplying the height in metres by 3.28 (rounded down); these may not tally with heights on old OS one-inch-to-the-mile maps, which were obtained from an earlier survey.

Total amount of ascent for a route is specified to the nearest 10m/50ft. This is an approximation based on OS map heights and contours, which are shown at 10m intervals and are in many instances omitted because of cartographic complexity.

Route times (to the nearest half-hour) are based on the time it should take a person of reasonable fitness to complete the route in good summer conditions. They take into account length of route, amount of ascent, technical difficulty, type of terrain and short stoppages, but do not make allowances for long stoppages or adverse weather. They are roughly standard between routes for comparison purposes and can be adjusted where necessary by a factor appropriate to the individual.

Names

Most Skye names are of Gaelic or Norse origin and many are unpronounceable to English-speaking visitors, yet an ability to pronounce them and understand their meaning can add much to the pleasure of walking on Skye. To this end a guide to pronunciation and meaning is provided where appropriate. OS spellings have been retained for purposes of standardisation, although they are sometimes incorrect. In addition, some names have become anglicised to such an extent that it would be pedantic to enforce a purist pronunciation on a non-Gaelic speaker; eg the correct pronunciation of Ben is something akin to Pane, with a soft 'n' as in the first syllable of onion. Despite these problems the phonetic guide given in this book (based on Gaelic as spoken on Skye) should enable a good attempt at a pronunciation that would be intelligible to a Gaelic speaker.

In connection with the pronunciation guide the following points should be noted:

Y   before a vowel pronounced as in *you*

OW   as in *town*

CH   as in Scottish *loch* or German *noch*
TCH as in *church*
OE   as in French *œuf* or the *u* in *turn*

Toponymy (the study of place name meanings) is complicated by OS misspellings, changes in spellings and word usage over the centuries, words with more than one meaning and unknown origin of names (Gaelic, Norse, Irish etc). For example, consider the possible meanings of the names Skye (see page 10) and Cuillin (see page 30). Meanings given in the text are the most commonly accepted, even if disputed; some names are too obscure to be given any meaning.

1.7 VISITOR INFORMATION

Information given below is necessarily subject to change and, if vital, should be verified before travelling to Skye.

Car ferries

There are three car ferries from the mainland: Mallaig–Armadale, Glenelg–Kylerhea and Kyle–Kyleakin. Mallaig–Armadale (crossing time 30min) provides the shortest route to Skye when coming from the south, but it is also the most infrequent and expensive. Glenelg–Kylerhea (crossing time 5min) is the oldest and perhaps the most scenic of the three, while Kyle–Kyleakin (crossing time 5min) has the best roads and is the only one that carries cars outside the summer season.

Ferry details (phone numbers for further information are listed in brackets):
Mallaig–Armadale: April to September 4 or 5 ferries daily, excluding Sunday; October to March carries passengers only, 1 or 2 ferries daily, excluding Sunday (Caledonian MacBrayne: Kyle (0599) 4218).
Glenelg–Kylerhea: May to September only, at frequent intervals 9am to 5pm (6pm July and August), excluding Sunday (Glenelg (059982) 224).
Kyle–Kyleakin: daily at frequent intervals from about 6am (10am Sunday) to 11pm (6.30pm Sunday October to March) (Caledonian MacBrayne: Mallaig (0687) 2403).

Should you wish to venture further afield than Skye, CalMac ferries sail from Sconser to Raasay (Raasay (0478) 62226) and from Uig to North Uist and Harris (Uig (047042) 219).

Information on all CalMac ferries (ie all the above ferries except the privately operated Glenelg–Kylerhea) can be obtained from Caledonian MacBrayne Ltd, The Ferry Terminal, Gourock PA19 1QP (0475-33755).

Public transport

The car-free visitor can reach Skye by rail or road; at the time of writing there are no scheduled flights to Broadford Aerodrome (04712-261). By rail, two of the most scenic railway lines in Britain lead to the doorstep of Skye (to meet ferry and bus connections): The Highland Railway from

Inverness to Kyle and the West Highland Railway from Glasgow via Fort William to Mallaig. Though neither line is renowned for its speed, both run through beautiful countryside, and it is to be hoped that they never suffer the closure with which they are often threatened. Further details from British Rail at Glasgow (041-204-2844), Inverness (0463-238924), Kyle (0599-4205), Fort William (0397-3791) or Mallaig (0687-2227). By road, express coaches and buses run from Edinburgh, Glasgow and Inverness; contact tourist offices (phone numbers below) for up-to-date information.

On Skye itself bus services connect all major centres, including Glen Brittle, and post buses serve the more remote villages. There are no services on Sundays and some buses run only Monday to Friday and only during the summer season. For bus timetables enquire at tourist offices.

Note also that there is an infrequent summer (May to October) passenger ferry from Mallaig via Armadale to Kyle; for details phone one of the above CalMac numbers.

A Travelpass is available for all ferry/rail/bus routes in the Highlands and Islands; further details from Hi-Line, Bridgend Road, Dingwall, Ross-shire IV15 9SL (0349-63434).

For further information on travel to and on Skye consult *Getting Around the Highlands and Islands,* published annually by Farm Holiday Guides Ltd in association with the Highlands and Islands Development Board (available from Farm Holiday Guides Ltd, Abbey Mill Centre, Seedhill, Paisley PA1 1JN).

Other information
The annual *Skye Directory,* obtainable from tourist offices for a small price, is full of useful tourist information.
Tourist Offices: Portree (0478-2137), Broadford (May to September only, 04712-361/463).
Hotels, B+B, Restaurants: widely distributed throughout Skye — consult the *Skye Directory*.
Youth Hostels: Armadale, Broadford, Glen Brittle, Kyleakin, Uig.
Mountaineering Club Huts: Coruisk (Junior Mountaineering Club of Scotland), Glen Brittle (British Mountaineering Council).
Caravan and Camping Sites (with facilities): Borve (Loch Greshornish), Broadford, Glen Brittle, Portree, Sligachan, Staffin, Uig.
Petrol Stations: Armadale, Borve crossroads (GR 443481), Broadford★, Carbost, Dunvegan★, Glendale, Isleornsay, Kyleakin★, Portree★. Those marked with an asterisk open on Sundays (mostly with restricted opening times) during the summer season; Broadford and Kyleakin open on Sundays all year round.
Banks: Broadford, Portree.
Shops: Portree is the main shopping centre. Food may also be obtained at stores at Ardvasar, Broadford, Carbost, Dunvegan, Elgol, Glendale, Isleornsay, Kyleakin, Portnalong, Struan.

2 the cuillin

2.1 INTRODUCTION TO THE CUILLIN

General description

The Cuillin are unquestionably the finest mountains in the British Isles. They are the perfect miniature mountain range. The gabbro rock, of which they are largely composed, is universally acknowledged to be the best climbing rock in the world, and nowhere else does it occur in such quantity or form. It is an extraordinarily rough rock, merciless to skin and clothes but supremely adhesive to feet and other useful parts of the anatomy. The geologist John MacCulloch vividly described its 'nutmeg-grater-like surface in contact with which the human body may almost defy the laws of gravity'.

The Cuillin landscape is savage and elemental. There are no hillsides of grass or heather here, no plateau summits; the rock forms vertical faces and narrow ridges, some so sharp that the best means of progress is to sit (carefully) astride them *(à cheval)*. Some summits can only be gained by rock climbing; few can be climbed without putting hand to rock.

In form the range consists of a horseshoe-shaped main ridge some 8 miles (13km) long, with satellite ridges radiating out around deep-cut corries. Along this ridge are strung 11 Munros (separate mountains over 914m/3,000ft), 9 further Munro Tops (lesser peaks over 914m/ 3,000ft, as defined in Munro's Tables) and numerous other lower tops, which give the Cuillin skyline a jagged and dramatic appearance when viewed from afar. Mountaineering here is like nowhere else. To walk and scramble along the narrow ridge from peak to peak through an other-worldly landscape of remarkable rock formations, with island upon island crowding the western horizon and the whole scene bathed in breathtakingly pure light, is a supreme experience.

The Cuillin corries were gouged out by glaciers during the Ice Age, and they typically consist of a flat-bottomed hollow surrounded by steep walls of rock. Sometimes their floors have been scraped smooth by glacial action to form great slabs known as boiler-plate slabs. Boulders removed during this process were sometimes gently deposited elsewhere when the ice melted to form precariously balanced 'erratics'. On a hot day the irresistibly beautiful lochans and streamways that characterise the corries, pure and clear beyond imagining, have put paid to many a well-laid plan.

The faces of the peaks are mainly the preserve of rock climbers. The normal route to the skyline for non-climbers is either via a steeply rising satellite ridge between two corries or via the corrie floor and a

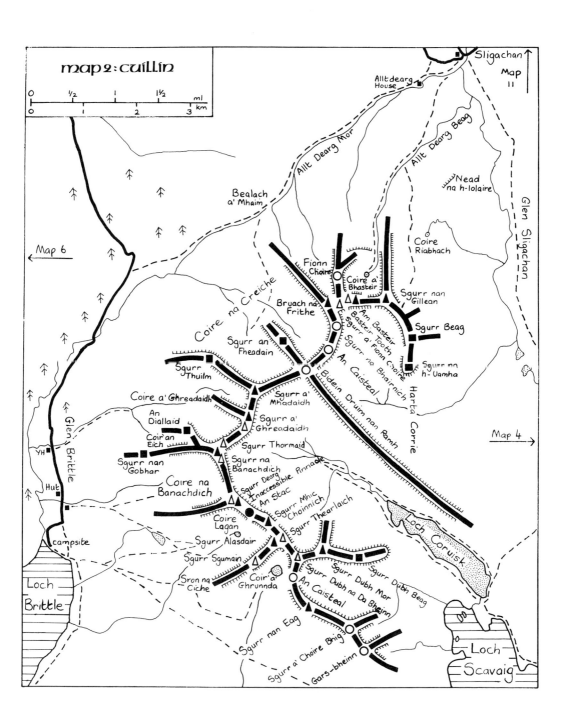

map 2: cuillin

Sligachan

Map 11

Allt dearg House

Allt Dearg Mor

Allt Dearg Beag

Glen Sligachan

Bealach a' Mhaim

Nead na h-Iolaire

Coire Riabhach

Map 6

Coire na Creiche

Fionn Choire

Coire a' Bhasteir

Sgurr nan Gillean

Bruach na Frithe

Am Basteir
Basteir Tooth
Sgurr a' Fionn Choire
Sgurr na Bhairnich

Sgurr Beag

Sgurr nn h-Uamha

Sgurr an Fheadain

An Caisteal

Harta Corrie

Sgurr Thuilm

Bidein Druim nan Ramh

Coire a' Ghreadaidh

Sgurr a' Mhadaidh

An Diallaid

Sgurr a' Ghreadaidh

Map 4

Coir'an Eich

Sgurr Thormaid

YH

Glen Brittle

Sgurr nan Gobhar

Sgurr na Banachdich

Coire na Banachdich

Sgurr Dearg
Inaccessible Pinnacle
An Stac

Sgurr Mhic Choinnich

Loch Coruisk

Hut

Coire Lagan

Sgurr Thearlaich

campsite

Sgurr Alasdair

Sgurr Dubh Beag

Sgurr Sgumain

Sgurr Dubh Mor

Sron na Ciche

Coir'a' Ghrunnda

An Caisteal
Sgurr Dubh na Da Bheinn

Loch Brittle

Sgurr nan Eag

Sgurr a' Choire Bhig

Gars-bheinn

Loch Scavaig

0   ½   1   1½   ml
0   1   2   3   km

stony gully at the back. Good paths up to the corries make for quick descent routes and enable the walker to linger high late into the evening as the sun sets over the Outer Hebrides.

Around the base of the Cuillin is a spongelike moor whose water-retaining properties are almost unnatural. This is a prime candidate for The Plain of Ill Luck that, according to legend, barred the way of Cuchullin on his way to Dunscaith. Cuchullin was able to progress only with the aid of a wheel that, when rolled before him, generated a heat so fierce that the bog dried in its path. Such wheels are unfortunately currently unobtainable on Skye, and a certain degree of humour is a useful asset during the approach to the peaks.

It has long been held by certain tourist guides that it is from Cuchullin that the Cuillin derive their name, but this is unlikely. More likely meanings of the name include High Rocks (from Norse *Kjölen*), Holly (from Gaelic *Cuilion*, referring to the serrated skyline) and Worthless (from the Celtic, referring to the Cuillin's agricultural potential).

The topographical complexity of the Cuillin is such that the descriptions of peaks and walks in the following sections of this chapter will require prolonged study in consultation with a large-scale map (the OS 1:25,000 Outdoor Leisure map is recommended and the Scottish Mountaineering Club 3 inches to 1 mile outline map is also useful). Each section describes a part of the range (beginning in the north) that can be considered as a separate entity for the purposes of a day trip. Fitter individuals can easily combine these parts into longer rounds.

For ease of reference ascents to the main peaks described in the following sections are listed below, in approximate order of increasing difficulty. In addition, peaks that can be reached with no more than simple scrambling are marked in the text with an asterisk. See also: Advice to walkers and scramblers (page 37).

Barely a scramble
Bruach na Frithe, via Bealach nan Lice (page 45)
Sgurr na Banachdich, via Coir' an Eich (page 57)
Sgurr Beag, via Coire Riabhach (page 39)
Sgurr Sgumain, via Sron na Ciche (page 64)
Sgurr Dubh na Da Bheinn, via Bealach Coir' an Lochain (page 70)
Sgurr nan Eag, via Coir' a' Ghrunnda (page 71)
Sgurr Sgumain, via Bealach Coir' a' Ghrunnda (page 64)
Sgurr Dearg, via Bealach na Banachdich (page 61)

Simple scrambles
Sgurr Dubh na Da Bheinn, via Bealach a' Garbh-choire (page 70)
Sgurr a' Bhasteir, all routes (page 44)
Sgurr a' Fhionn Choire, via Bealach nan Lice (page 45)
Sgurr na Banachdich, via Sgurr nan Gobhar (page 56)
Sgurr a' Choire Bhig and Gars-bheinn, from Sgurr nan Eag (page 71)
Bruach na Frithe, north-west ridge (page 45)
Sgurr an Fheadain, south-east ridge (page 51)
Sgurr Alasdair, via Great Stone Shoot (page 63)
Sgurr Dearg, south-west shoulder (page 61)

Moderate scrambles
Sgurr a' Mhadaidh, via An Dorus (page 53)
Bruach na Frithe, descent via Sgurr na Bhairnich (page 48)
Sgurr Mhic Choinnich, via Bealach Coire Lagan (page 62)
Sgurr an Fheadain, north-west spur (page 51)

Hard scrambles
Sgurr Dubh Mor, from Sgurr Dubh na Da Bheinn (page 70)
Sgurr a' Ghreadaidh, traverse (page 55)
Sgurr Alasdair, south-west ridge from Sgurr Sgumain (page 63)
Am Basteir, via Bealach a' Bhasteir (page 43)
Sgurr na Banachdich, via Bealach na Banachdich (page 56)
Sgurr nan Gillean, south-east ridge Tourist Route (page 38)
Sgurr na h-Uamha, via Bealach a' Ghlas-choire (page 39)
An Caisteal, via Bealach Coir' an Tairneilear (page 49)
Sgurr a' Mhadaidh, from Sgurr Thuilm (page 53)

Valley bases and paths
The two main valley bases are Sligachan at the northern end of the range and Glen Brittle at the southern end. Both have seasonal campsites with shops (GR 485301 and GR 412206); Sligachan also has a hotel and Glen Brittle a youth hostel (GR 409225), a British Mountaineering Council (BMC) Hut (GR 411216) and other private accommodation.

Coruisk is a third possible base at the heart of the Cuillin horseshoe, but there is no road access to it and easy routes to the skyline are longer and less numerous. Accommodation is at the Junior Mountaineering Club of Scotland (JMCS) Hut (GR 487196), which is kept locked and can only be used if pre-booked, or by camping wild; all provisions must be carried in. Coruisk is a magnificent spot, but most walkers will prefer to stay at Sligachan or Glen Brittle, or even further away with transport. Routes to Coruisk are described in 2.10 (page 77).

An important path around the foot of the Cuillin links Sligachan and Glen Brittle via the Bealach a' Mhaim (*Byal*och a *Va*-im, Pass of the Rounded Hill, ie Am Mam to the west of the bealach). At the Sligachan end this path has several starting points, the most commonly used of which is the car park on the Dunvegan road beside the access road to Alltdearg House (GR 480297, where a signpost reads 'Footpath to Glen Brittle'). From here walk along the access road and follow the fence right around the house to reach the banks of the Allt Dearg Mor. Other paths begin opposite Sligachan Hotel and along the Dunvegan road and join the main path at the fence.

The path holds to the left bank of the Allt Dearg Mor all the way to the bealach, then descends beside the Allt a' Mhaim and alongside a forestry plantation into Glen Brittle, reaching the roadside at a forest gate (GR 424258) 4 miles/6km from the campsite (campsite to campsite: 8 miles/13km, 360m/1200ft, 4hr). Just beyond the lochan at the bealach another path traverses beneath the north-west ridge of Bruach na Frithe to the foot of Sgurr an Fheadain, thereby making a useful access route from Sligachan to Coire na Creiche.

There is also a useful shortcut in Glen Brittle between Glen Brittle Hut or youth hostel and the campsite. When the road turns sharp right beyond Glenbrittle House, keep straight on past the mountain rescue post along the access road to Cuillin Cottage. At the cottage turn right to pick up a path that skirts the fields to the campsite shop.

History of exploration
The peaks of the Cuillin are the only mountains in Scotland to have been named after the men who first climbed them, and so the history of their exploration is of more than usual interest. Few walkers of today will ever know the excitement of climbing an unnamed and un-trodden peak, yet little more than a century ago the Cuillin were virtually a virgin mountain range. The earliest recorded attempts to climb them were made by the geologist John MacCulloch in the 1810s, but as his favourite mode of ascent was on horseback it is no surprise to learn that he failed seven times in five successive years (blaming the weather, as many still do).

(top right) *The Cuillin from the north;* (right) *The east ridge of Am Basteir from the Bealach a' Bhasteir;* (far right) *Sgurr a' Mhadaidh from Sgurr Thuilm*

The Cuillin remained unclimbed until the physicist and geologist Professor James Forbes persuaded Duncan MacIntyre, a local forester, to guide him up Sgurr nan Gillean on 7 July 1836. The route they pioneered has since become known as the Tourist Route. Forbes returned to Skye again in 1845 and (again with MacIntyre) made the first ascent of Bruach na Frithe. These ascents remained isolated events; other travellers to Skye contented themselves with a boat trip to Loch Coruisk, firmly placed on the tourist map since the visit of Sir Walter Scott in 1814.

The 1850s saw the first guideless ascent of Sgurr nan Gillean by Inglis and party (1857), the first ascent of Bla Bheinn (from Loch Slapin) by Professor John Nicol and the poet Algernon Swinburne (1857) and the first ascent of Sgurr na Stri by Alpine Club member C. R. Weld (1859). But it was fittingly a Skye man, Alexander Nicolson, who took upon himself the fuller exploration of the Cuillin.

Nicolson's first ascent was in 1865, when he was guided up the Sgurr nan Gillean Tourist Route by Duncan MacIntyre's son, then gamekeeper at Sligachan. The subsequent years of adventure culminated in the momentous year of 1873, when Nicolson climbed Sgurr na Banachdich, Sgurr Dearg and Sgurr Alasdair (by the Great Stone Shoot). Before 1873 Sgurr Thearlaich, Sgurr Alasdair and Sgurr Sgumain were all lumped together under the name Sgurr Sgumain, but after Nicolson's feat the highest of the three peaks was named after him.

Nicolson fell in love with the Cuillin and praised them in prose, poem and song. From the late 1860s onwards tourists began to arrive in numbers, with Sligachan Inn as their base and the Sgurr nan Gillean Tourist Route the main attraction. In 1880 brothers Charles and Lawrence Pilkington, two of the greatest mountaineers of their day, climbed The Inaccessible Pinnacle by its east ridge. In 1886 the west ridge fell to Stocker and Parker. In 1887 Charles Pilkington's party climbed the north peak of Sgurr Alasdair, which was named Sgurr Thearlaich after him. In the same year the same party completed the first round of the Coire Lagan skyline, naming the peak south of Sgurr Dearg Pic MacKenzie after one of their number, John MacKenzie; the name survives as Sgurr Mhic Choinnich.

John MacKenzie was the first Cuillin rock-climbing guide. He climbed Sgurr nan Gillean in 1866 at the age of ten, accompanied

(top left) *Looking down over Sgurr Dubh Beag to Coruisk from Sgurr Dubh Mor*
(left) *Garbh-bheinn and Bla Bheinn from the Beinn Deargs*

Tribe on the first ascent of Sgurr a' Ghreadaidh in 1870 and was with Nicolson in 1873. During a climbing career spanning more than fifty years he came to know the Cuillin inside out and was much sought after for his guiding prowess and congenial company.

His great companion was Professor Norman Collie, who was converted to mountaineering while at Sligachan for the fishing in 1886. Collie became famous for his worldwide mountaineering expeditions, but the Cuillin remained his first love and, with MacKenzie, he opened up many new rock faces. They discovered Collie's Ledge on Sgurr Mhic Choinnich in 1888, made the first crossing of the Thearlaich-Dubh gap (with King) in 1891, climbed Sgurr Coir' an Lochain (the last unclimbed peak in the Cuillin, with Howell and Naismith) in 1896 and discovered the Cioch on Sron na Ciche, climbing it in 1906 (MacKenzie named it).

When Collie retired he spent an increasing amount of time at Sligachan, often fishing with his inseparable companion MacKenzie. MacKenzie died in 1934 aged seventy-eight. Collie stayed at Sligachan from 1939 onwards, a rather sad figure haunted by Cuillin memories. He died in 1942 aged eighty-three and at his own request was buried close beside MacKenzie in old Struan cemetary (GR 355388). Their graves, neglected and windswept, can still be visited by all Cuillin lovers with a sense of history. MacKenzie's is marked simply 'Cuillin Guide'. Sgurr Thormaid was named after Collie.

Collie and MacKenzie were part of a new breed of rock climbers who began to appear towards the end of the nineteenth century. In 1889 Swan made the first recorded Cuillin winter ascent (of Bruach na Frithe). In 1895 Kelsall and Hallitt made the first ascent of Waterpipe Gully of Sgurr an Fheadain. In 1898 the last remaining problems on the main ridge were overcome: King's Chimney on Sgurr Mhic Choinnich and the direct ascent of the Basteir Tooth.

The subsequent history of rock climbing in the Cuillin is not really a subject for this book, but walking history continued to be made. In 1911 Shadbolt and MacLaren made the first traverse of the main ridge (The Great Traverse) from Glen Brittle to Sligachan in 16³/4hr. Their fitness can be judged by their ascent time of 2¹/2hr from Glen Brittle to Gars-bheinn. In 1939 The Greater Traverse (including Clach Glas and Bla Bheinn) was accomplished by Charleson and Forde. The first winter Great Traverse took place in 1965. Rock athletes of today have reduced the traverse time from Gars-bheim to Sgurr nan Gillean to under 4hr.

There are no virgin peaks left in the Cuillin for explorers of today, but to follow in the footsteps of the pioneers will be adventure enough for most. For a vivid account of the history of Cuillin exploration consult Ben Humble's classic *The Cuillin of Skye* (1952, republished by The Ernest Press 1986).

Advice to walkers and scramblers
The Cuillin are no place for novice hill walkers and special considerations apply to walking in the range over and above the general advice given in 1.6 (see Advice to walkers, page 22). There are few peaks that can be climbed without putting hand to rock and there are few escape routes. In this three-dimensional labyrinth of rock route-finding is often a problem, to such an extent that in mist the route onwards may be impossible to locate. The problem is compounded by the magnetic nature of the rock, which makes compass readings on the ridge crest dangerously unreliable.

Other problems for the unwary include loose rock and rubble-strewn ledges, which necessitate constant vigilance, and sudden atmospheric changes (cloud can appear from nowhere, literally in seconds). Not all of the rock is gabbro. Considerable quantities of basalt have intruded into the gabbro, often in the form of trap-dykes (eroded ladder-like features that sometimes provide an easy route through otherwise difficult terrain). Basalt is much smoother than gabbro and quickly becomes greasy and slippery when wet; great care is then required, and some routes are best avoided (this is noted in the text where appropriate).

In short, the Cuillin demand great respect and a high level of mountaincraft; they are best tackled in fine weather only. The first-timer would do well to seek out the company of someone with Cuillin experience for his initial forays onto the peaks.

In the following sections all ascents should be regarded as Grade 5, because, even if scrambling is not involved, the terrain is everywhere difficult. Even the easiest routes cross rocky or stony terrain and may involve difficult route-finding, and if a route is described as easy it is only in relative terms. See page 30 for an approximate graded list of ascents of the major peaks.

In an emergency there are public telephones at Sligachan (GR 485299) and Glenbrittle House (GR 412214), or alert someone local; the Skye Mountain Rescue Team is based at Portree Police Station (Portree (0478) 2888 or 999).

2.2 SGURR NAN GILLEAN AND THE NORTH END

Sgurr nan Gillean (965m/3,167ft, Skoor nan *Geel*-yan, Peak of the
  Gullies or Young Men)

Sgurr nan Gillean at the north end of the Cuillin is one of the most
distinctive and difficult mountains in the range. For the non-climber
there is only one way up — the so-called Tourist Route, but do not be
misled by the name into thinking this is a mere stroll, for in its latter
stages it is a hard scramble requiring care and nerve. Should you
decide in your wisdom to leave the last few metres for another day the
ascent is still worthwhile, however, for the typically fine Cuillin
scenery and views. And even if you do not reach the top the day need
not be summitless, for behind Sgurr nan Gillean at the tail-end of the
Cuillin horseshoe are the two smaller peaks of Sgurr Beag and Sgurr
na h-Uamha, the former of which is easily reached.

In the famous view of the northern Cuillin from Sligachan Sgurr
nan Gillean is the peak on the left, a perfect pyramid of rock. The west
ridge (the right-hand skyline) and the north ridge (facing, also known
as Pinnacle Ridge) involve rock climbing (see below). The Tourist
Route goes across the left-hand skyline and climbs the south-east
ridge; it is cairned and has a path most of the way, but it is still difficult
to follow in mist.

The route begins opposite Sligachan Hotel on the Bealach a'
Mhaim path (see page 32). A few hundred metres beyond the hotel the
Sgurr nan Gillean path branches left across the Allt Dearg Mor (Owlt
*Jerra*k Moar, Big Red Stream) and meanders across the almost flat
moor to the Allt Dearg Beag (Bake, Little), whose beautiful pools and
cascades are followed to another bridge.

At this second bridge the path divides. Cross the river and follow
the branch that crosses the broad flat ridge above Nead na h-Iolaire
(Nyett na *Hill*-yera, Eagle's Nest) into Coire Riabhach (*Ree*-avach,
Brindled), an untypical shallow heathery Cuillin corrie. The path
contours well above the lochan in the bowl of the corrie and climbs
steep stony slopes around Sgurr nan Gillean's east face, bearing right
beneath the towering pinnacles of Pinnacle Ridge. Once out of the
corrie the route flattens out and reaches a smaller corrie whose floor
and sides are a chaotic jumble of crags and boulders.

The path becomes indistinct in places but is well cairned. It continues up the gully at the back of the corrie onto the boulderfield
below the south-east ridge, and reaches the skyline halfway between
Sgurr Beag and Sgurr nan Gillean. Turn right to climb the south-east

ridge direct. There are many route options at first but as the steepening summit cone gets nearer the scrambling becomes harder and more exposed. On the last 30m (100ft) there are only two possible routes: the extremely narrow crest of the ridge or sloping rocks to the left, both of about equal standard. It is at this point that those of a nervous disposition may not wish to proceed, and remember that it will be necessary to descend the same way.

The final few metres along the narrow summit ridge are very exposed, especially at a short hiatus where parts of the anatomy other than hands and feet are likely to be put to good use. The summit itself is an eerie platform from which none of the supporting ridges can be seen, as if it were suspended in the sky (3½hr). By scrambling just beyond the summit, views of the west ridge and magnificent Pinnacle Ridge can be obtained. From Sligachan the pinnacles of Pinnacle Ridge cannot be distinguished unless cloud swirls between them and silhouettes them, but from here the ridge is seen in all its splendour — a Difficult rock climb with a real mountaineering flavour, requiring the ability to climb down as well as up during its traverse.

The west ridge is easier than Pinnacle Ridge but should be avoided by non-climbers as it involves Moderate rock climbing towards the foot. Until very recently a gendarme astride the ridge here required a heart-stopping traverse above the abyss, but in the winter of 1986–7, to the dismay of all Cuillin lovers and all previous guidebook writers, the gendarme disappeared. No one without rock-climbing experience should venture here.

Unless you decide to take up permanent residence on the summit of Sgurr nan Gillean, therefore, you must descend via the south-east ridge again. Most walkers are content to retrace the route of ascent all the way to Sligachan (6hr), but the two smaller peaks of Sgurr Beag and Sgurr na h-Uamha beyond Sgurr nan Gillean at the end of the main ridge are worth a closer look.

Sgurr Beag★ (765m/2,511ft, Skoor Bake, Little Peak)
Sgurr na h-Uamha (736m/2,416ft, Skoor na *Hoo*-aha, Peak of the Cave)

These two peaks complete the north end of the Cuillin horseshoe. They are unjustly ignored by Sgurr nan Gillean Tourist Routers, despite lying only a short distance away and offering good views of Sgurr nan Gillean. Sgurr na h-Uamha in particular is a fine little mountain whose exciting ascent is of a similar standard to the final section of the Tourist Route.

From the foot of the south-east ridge of Sgurr nan Gillean the stony summit of Sgurr Beag is only a short walk away, and then slopes of grass and stones descend to the Bealach a' Ghlas-choire between Sgurr Beag and Sgurr na h-Uamha. From the bealach a straight-forward descent eastwards into An Glas-choire (An Glass Choira, The Grey Corrie) leads to Glen Sligachan, but note that the River Sligachan would have to be forded to gain the path along the glen back to Sligachan. A descent westwards leads to either Lota Corrie or Harta Corrie and eventually to the path along Glen Sligachan, and this return route is recommended to those who wish to extend the day by exploring some of the wilder parts of the Cuillin (9hr complete round). (See page 73 for description of Harta and Lota corries.)

Beyond the Bealach a' Ghlas-choire the beautiful conical peak of Sgurr na h-Uamha forms a fitting 'last nail' in the Cuillin horseshoe. From all other approaches its ascent involves rock climbing, and even from Sgurr Beag the two-tiered north ridge that rises from the bealach looks extremely sharp. On closer inspection, however, the first tier provides lovely simple scrambling on satisfying gabbro blocks, with little exposure. The second tier is hard but handholds are

Sgurr Beag and Sgurr na h-Uamha from the Sgurr nan Gillean Tourist Route, with Sgurr na Stri in the distance

excellent; the route goes initially left then back right and straight up the centre of the face towering overhead. This second tier should be attempted by experienced scramblers only, who should remain aware that they will have to reverse it.

2.3 SGURR NAN GILLEAN TO BRUACH NA FRITHE

West of Sgurr nan Gillean the main ridge and its satellites enclose secluded Coire a' Bhasteir to form one of the most symmetrical, majestic and photographed skylines on Skye. The left-hand rim of the corrie is formed by Pinnacle Ridge of Sgurr nan Gillean. At the back of the corrie the main ridge dips steeply to the Bealach a' Bhasteir, rises steeply again to Am Basteir and then falls away vertically to the Basteir Tooth — the prominent rock tower well seen from Sligachan. Beyond the Tooth lies the Bealach nan Lice, and from there a subsidiary ridge runs out to Sgurr a' Bhasteir to form the right-hand rim of the corrie.

Hidden behind Sgurr a' Bhasteir lies Fionn Choire and its peaks. From the Bealach nan Lice the main ridge continues around the back of this corrie over Sgurr a' Fionn Choire to Bruach na Frithe, whose north-west ridge forms the far rim of the corrie. The Bealach nan Lice lies almost at the junction of Coire a' Bhasteir and Fionn Choire, enabling easy access to the main ridge from either corrie, and the peaks around the corrie rims can be considered as a single group.

Coire a' Bhasteir (Coira *Vash*-tyir, Corrie of the Executioner)
Bealach a' Bhasteir (833m/2,733ft, *By*aloch a *Vash*-tyir, Pass of the Executioner)

Coire a' Bhasteir is the most northerly and secluded of the Cuillin corries. The lochan at its heart is given an air of secrecy by the difficulty of the approach route and the towering peaks that surround it and block out the sun for most of the year. The Bealach a' Bhasteir perches on the ridge at the back of the corrie in a fine situation between the steeply rising west ridge of Sgurr nan Gillean and the equally steep east ridge of Am Basteir. The former ridge is not recommended to non-climbers (see page 39); the latter ridge is a hard scramble but it is the only route to the summit of Am Basteir for non-climbers, and hence the route up to the corrie and bealach is well used.

From Sligachan follow the Sgurr nan Gillean Tourist Route (see previous section) as far as the fork at the bridge over the Allt Dearg

Am Basteir, Sgurr nan Gillean and Sgurr a' Fionn Choire from the east ridge of Bruach na Frithe

Beag, then instead of going left across the bridge continue up the left bank (right side) of the river towards Coire a' Bhasteir. On approaching the corrie the stream flows through a gorge whose high rock walls merge on the right into slabs at the foot of the north-east ridge of Sgurr a' Bhasteir. The cairned route through the slabs climbs high above the gorge, cutting across the shoulder of the ridge. There are one or two places where simple, slightly exposed scrambling is required, and it is important not to lose the line of cairns in mist. On exit from the gorge two cairned lines lead into the bowl of the corrie, one beside the river and one higher up (600m/2,000ft, 2¹/₂hr).

Note that the corrie can also be reached via the left side of the gorge, along the fine broad ridge, dotted with outcrops and erratic boulders, that leads to the foot of Pinnacle Ridge. This side of the gorge is barely more than a walk and is easily gained by crossing the Allt Dearg Beag below the gorge. Once above the gorge bear immediately right into the corrie, or continue up to the Bealach a' Bhasteir on a path that traverses beneath the crags of Pinnacle Ridge.

Towering over the back of the corrie are the summit cliffs of Am Basteir, with scree and boulder ruckles leading up each side to the main ridge: left to the Bealach a' Bhasteir, right to the Bealach nan Lice. The path to the foot of the cliffs crosses the stream at the outflow of the lochan and outflanks the band of crags at the back of the corrie on the left. On reaching the foot of the summit cliffs climb left beneath them to reach the Bealach a' Bhasteir (3hr from Sligachan).

Am Basteir (935m/3,069ft, Am *Bash*-tyir, The Executioner)

From Coire a' Bhasteir the summit cliffs of Am Basteir and the Basteir Tooth tower overhead with a menacing air that is well captured in the mountain's name. From the Bealach a' Bhasteir the east ridge rises steeply and impressively to provide the only access route to the summit for the non-climber. With one exception, its ascent involves mostly walking and simple scrambling along a narrow exposed crest, with any harder sections easily bypassed on ledges on the Lota Corrie side (beware loose rubble on ledges).

The one exception is an unavoidable obstacle that has turned back many a hopeful scrambler — a 3m (10ft) vertical rib directly on the crest about two-thirds of the way up. On ascent this rib must be descended by facing inwards, lowering yourself from step to step; it is hard, but there are good jug-handles, and these make it easier to haul yourself up on the return. Once the rib has been negotiated the small summit platform is soon reached without further ado (1/2hr from bealach, 31/2hr from Sligachan).

Beyond the summit it is possible to continue a short distance along the ridge to the top of the western cliffs, to view the top of the Basteir Tooth. This involves a hard scramble down a wall and across a slab, easier on the way back.

The only descent route from Am Basteir, unless you can abseil, is the way you came up. From the Bealach a' Bhasteir the main ridge can be regained beyond the Tooth by traversing stony slopes on the Coire a' Bhasteir side beneath the summit cliffs of Am Basteir. The ridge is reached again at a large outcrop of rock at the junction of the main ridge and the south ridge of Sgurr a' Bhasteir. This traverse enables an ascent of Am Basteir to be combined with ascents of Sgurr a' Bhasteir and Bruach na Frithe. The junction of ridges can also be reached directly from Coire a' Bhasteir by climbing right beneath the summit cliffs of Am Basteir rather than left to the Bealach a' Bhasteir.

Sgurr a' Bhasteir★ (899m/2,951ft, Skoor a *Vash*-tyir, Peak of the
  Executioner)

The south ridge of Sgurr a' Bhasteir forms the western rim of Coire a'
Bhasteir, and its narrow shattered crest makes a fine walk with
matchless views of Pinnacle Ridge and the Basteir Tooth. The
shapely summit lies a few hundred metres along at the apex of the
south ridge, the north-east ridge and the north-west ridge. These
latter two ridges rise from the moor and make pleasant approaches to
the main ridge from Sligachan.

On approaching the gorge of the Allt Dearg Beag below Coire a'
Bhasteir, the north-west ridge is on the right and the north-east ridge
is on the left. To gain the north-west ridge leave the path below the
gorge and make for the bealach between Sgurr a' Bhasteir and
Meallan Odhar (Mellan *Oa*-ar, Dun-coloured Hill); avoid an initial
steepening of the ridge on broken slopes to the left. To gain the north-
east ridge strike right once the path has negotiated the slabby section
above the gorge. Both ridges are similar in nature to the south ridge
and provide enjoyable routes to the summit, with simple scrambling
in places.

Fionn Choire (Fyoon Choira, Fair Corrie)
Bealach nan Lice (c855m/2,900ft, *Byal*och nan *Leech*-kya, Pass of the
  Flat Stones)

Immediately west of the rock outcrop at the junction of the main
ridge and the south ridge of Sgurr a' Bhasteir is one of the easiest
passes in the Cuillin — the Bealach nan Lice, linking Sligachan to Lota
and Harta corries (but not Coruisk). On its south-east side a stone
shoot descends towards Lota Corrie (see page 74 for description),
while on its north-west side slopes of boulders and scree descend to
Fionn Choire; in mist the bealach can be recognised by the paths that
go down each side.

Fionn Choire is perhaps the least spectacular but most charming of
all Cuillin corries, untypically broad and grassy and well-deserving
its Gaelic name, if only for the attractive shelf of small lochans that
huddle beneath the north-west ridge of Bruach na Frithe. On ascent
the corrie is reached from Sligachan or Glen Brittle via the Bealach a'
Mhaim path (see page 32). Look for a large cairn where the Fionn
Choire path branches off to follow the banks of the Allt an Fhionn-
choire (Owlt an Ee-*yoon* Choira, Stream of the Fair Corrie) up into
the corrie.

There are cairned paths on each side of the Allt an Fhionn-choire; it is best to keep to the right bank (left side on ascent) as the left bank path eventually climbs onto the north-west ridge of Bruach na Frithe. If you lose the path on descent in mist keep close to the stream, as the moor below the corrie is featureless and difficult to navigate. Higher up, the path climbs slopes of boulders and scree in the south-east corner of the corrie to reach the main ridge at the Bealach nan Lice (2½hr from Sligachan or Glen Brittle roadside).

Sgurr a' Fionn Choire★ (935m/3,068ft, Skoor a Fyoon Choira, Peak of the Fair Corrie)

Immediately west of the Bealach nan Lice stands the rock bastion of Sgurr a' Fionn Choire, whose summit yields easily to a simple 50m (160ft) scramble if you keep well right of the vertiginous cliff face overlooking Lota Corrie. The descent westwards towards Bruach na Frithe is more awkward as the crest of the west ridge consists of a series of large blocks, like giant steps, that involve rock climbing if taken direct. Attempts to outflank the steps on ledges on the Fionn Choire side usually lead to frustrating impasses. The easiest route westwards from the summit is to redescend towards the Bealach nan Lice and take the traverse path that bypasses the peak completely to regain the ridge at the saddle between Sgurr a' Fionn Choire and Bruach na Frithe.

Bruach na Frithe★ (958m/3,143ft, *Broo*ach na *Free*-a, Slope of the Forest)

Bruach na Frithe is one of the most ascended mountains in the Cuillin. It is one of the easiest of the Cuillin Munros, with several routes to the top, and the view from the summit is one of the finest, with the savage rock peaks around Coire a' Bhasteir cleaving the sky in Dolomitic splendour to the north and peak upon peak crowding the skyline to the south. The easiest route to the summit is via Fionn Choire and the Bealach nan Lice. From the bealach take the traverse path around Sgurr a' Fionn Choire and climb the stony east ridge — an easy ascent of some 60m (200ft) that is no more than a walk, with a spot of simple scrambling on the crest near the summit should you wish (½hr from bealach).

The narrow shattered north-west ridge, rising in a fine situation between Fionn Choire and Coire na Creiche, offers a more exhilarating ascent, with some simple though reasonably exposed scrambling higher up. There are no real difficulties, but the rock is basalt and is best avoided when wet and slippery. In its lower reaches the ridge divides into two spurs, and the shallow basin between them, drained by the Allt Mor an Fhinn Choire, contains the most featureless terrain in the Cuillin; in mist it seems more like an enormous beach than a mountainside, and compass bearings may be required.

The ridge can be approached from either Sligachan or Glen Brittle. The Glen Brittle approach takes the Bealach a' Mhaim path and climbs the western spur, which rises above the bealach. The Sligachan approach climbs the eastern spur, reached by the path along the left bank of the Allt an Fhionn-choire (see page 44). The two spurs join and ascend to a level section where the scrambling starts, and then the upper ridge rears up more steeply to the summit (3hr from Sligachan or Glen Brittle roadside).

Yet another route takes a path that traverses right beneath the crest of the north-west ridge across the stony slopes falling to Coire na Creiche. This path leaves the ridge some distance along the level section, just before the first rock scramble; a second branch joins it from higher up the ridge. Look for cairns to avoid being led out along sheep paths. The path reaches the south ridge at a gully and then climbs the ridge to the summit (3½hr).

Although there are no real difficulties on this route, walkers wishing to avoid all scrambling should note that the south ridge gully is steep and bare at the top, while the south ridge itself is quite narrow and exposed, with one or two short scrambles. On exit from the gully a slab requires a couple of steps that can be awkward when wet. On descent, note that the south ridge offers a route with no more than moderate scrambling to the head of the easy gully between Sgurr na Bhairnich and An Caisteal, which can be descended into Coir' a' Tairneilear (see page 48).

The relative ease and variety of approaches to Bruach na Frithe make it one of the most popular peaks in the Cuillin, especially for first-timers, but its ascent should not be treated with disdain. The atmosphere is serious, the terrain is complex and in mist route-finding is extremely difficult. Note that the easiest descent in mist is down the east ridge (despite the magnetic rock, approximate compass bearings are possible here), following the path around Sgurr a' Fionn Choire to the Bealach nan Lice and down into Fionn Choire.

2.4 BRUACH NA FRITHE TO SGURR A' MHADAIDH

Between Bruach na Frithe and Sgurr a' Mhadaidh the main ridge curves around the vast open spaces of Coire na Creiche, which is so low-lying that the path into it from the Glen Brittle road begins with a descent. The corrie is bounded on the north by the north-west ridge of Bruach na Frithe (see previous section) and on the south by the ridge linking Sgurr a' Mhadaidh to the outlier of Sgurr Thuilm (see next section).

At the back of the corrie the main ridge undulates over the lower peaks of Sgurr na Bhairnich, An Caisteal and Bidein Druim nan Ramh, from where a short spur leading out to Sgurr an Fheadain divides the upper corrie into two: Coir' a' Tairneilear to the north and Coir' a' Mhadaidh to the south. *Note:* do not be misled by some old maps and guidebooks which named these corries the other way round.

The complete traverse of the main ridge at the back of the corrie involves unavoidable rock climbing in places, but there is still much to interest the non-climber here, including spectacular scrambles on An Caisteal and Sgurr an Fheadain, a relatively easy descent from Bruach na Frithe over Sgurr na Bhairnich, and a pass to Coruisk (the Bealach na Glaic Moire between Bidein and Sgurr a' Mhadaidh).

Coire na Creiche (Coira na *Craich*-ya, Corrie of the Spoils)

The flat moorland floor of Coire na Creiche seems unappealing from the roadside, yet it contains arguably the finest stretch of waterfalls and rock pools in the Cuillin (GR 434257). Here the crystal clear waters of the Allt Coir' a' Mhadaidh cascade from cauldron to cauldron between walls of sculptured rock. At one point a half-submerged arch of rock forms a bridge across a pool.

The Coire na Creiche path begins at the start of the Bealach a' Mhaim path in Glen Brittle (see page 32), descends to the River Brittle and follows its right bank up into the corrie. At the first bend in the river are to be seen a number of grassy mounds formerly topped by cairns that commemorate those who fell in the Battle of Coire na Creiche in 1601. This place used to be called Tom nan Tighearnan (Towm nan *Tchie*-ernan, Knoll of the Lords). The battle has a place in history as the last battle ever fought between the MacLeods and the MacDonalds, and the corrie is named after the division of the spoils following the defeat of the MacLeods.

The pools are reached within half an hour (Grade 1, 1+hr return). The path continues beyond the pools past more fine waterfalls into the upper corrie, giving access to the main ridge.

Sgurr na Bhairnich★ (861m/2,826ft, Skoor na Varnich, Limpet Peak)

The northern section of the corrie headwall makes a reasonably straightforward route of descent from Bruach na Frithe into Coir' a' Tairneilear. Although narrow and exposed in places, it is mainly a walk with occasional short simple-to-moderate scrambles. The route descends the south ridge of Bruach na Frithe, traverses Sgurr na Bhairnich, where some moderate moves on the crest can be easily avoided on the right (Coire na Creiche side) if necessary, and descends steeply to the defile between Sgurr na Bhairnich and An Caisteal.

Much of the descent from Sgurr na Bhairnich to the defile is on rubble-strewn ledges that will be appreciated most by masochists. A short distance down, a 5m (16ft) vertical descent to the head of a gully is easily avoided on the left (Harta Corrie side). Immediately beyond here keep left and hold to the steeply descending crest; ledges on the right look more tempting initially but become awkward lower down. From the defile a stony gully provides a straightforward descent to Coir' a' Tairneilear (not recommended for ascent).

Coir' a' Tairneilear
Bealach Coir' a' Tairneilear (760m/2,494ft, Byaloch Coira Tarnyela, Pass of the Corrie of the Thunderer)

Coir' a' Tairneilear on the north side of Sgurr an Fheadain is a long narrow corrie enclosed by featureless broken slopes but made interesting by the two pointed peaks at its head: An Caisteal and Bidein Druim nan Ramh. As an approach to the main ridge it offers routes up to the defile between Sgurr na Bhairnich and An Caisteal and to the Bealach Coir' a' Tairneilear between An Caisteal and Bidein Druim nan Ramh. It also provides an approach to Sgurr an Fheadain via the saddle at the end of the south–east ridge beneath the cliffs of Bidein.

To reach the corrie, take the Coire na Creiche path to the foot of Sgurr an Fheadain, crossing the traverse path from the Bealach a' Mhaim (which enables an approach from Sligachan — see page 32). Paths continue up both banks of the river into Coir' a' Tairneilear; if anything the going is better on the right bank (left side). At the head of the corrie the broad stone shoot from the defile between Sgurr na

Bhairnich and An Caisteal comes down from the left (easier to descend than ascend).

The route to the Bealach Coir' a' Tairneilear goes straight up the screes at the back of the corrie, bears right to avoid broken ground and then continues straight up to the skyline beneath the crags of Bidein; cairns indicate the best line if you can find them (3hr from Glen Brittle roadside). To reach the saddle at the end of the south-east ridge of Sgurr an Fheadain aim further right. All routes up to the skyline cross scree and featureless terrain and should be avoided in mist.

An Caisteal (830m/2,724ft, An *Cash*-tyal, The Castle)

An Caisteal is not named on either the 1:50,000 or Outdoor Leisure map, yet from Coir' a' Tairneilear it appears as a fine pointed peak and its traverse involves some sensational moves. Approached from Sgurr na Bhairnich to the north, it rears up in such an improbable fashion that most scramblers will rightly think twice before tackling it. Its ascent from the defile at its foot begins with a polished vertical wall whose holds force you off-balance. Most mortals will regard this as more than a hard scramble and only those who are sure of their ability should attempt it. Above the wall there are no comparable difficulties, so you should at least be able to tackle it in the knowledge that a retreat (which would be even harder) should not be necessary.

Above the wall the route veers left until beneath the imposing summit buttress, then regains the crest of the ridge by a gully on the right. The final section to the summit, which looks impossibly sharp and exposed from Sgurr na Bhairnich, turns out to be a short stroll along a sensational path.

Most scramblers will find this ascent outside their capabilities and should content themselves with an ascent of An Caisteal from the Bealach Coir' a' Tairneilear to the south. This is mostly a moderate scramble, but it too has its moments, with one or two spectacularly exposed hard moves that are not for the squeamish.

From the Bealach Coir' a' Tairneilear a vertical knob of rock on the ridge presents an immediate obstacle. Bypass it by an exposed but easy traverse along a ledge on the right (Harta Corrie side), or descend to easier slopes on the left (Coire na Creiche side) and traverse around. The ridge beyond continues narrow but easy, barely more than a walk until it rises to the sharp summit crest and becomes harder and more exposed. At one point a notch in the ridge requires a step across the void a few metres down on the left (look for a path), while further along a second notch can be avoided on rubble-strewn ledges on the right (care required). There are few sharper summits in the Cuillin (½hr from bealach).

Bidein Druim nan Ramh (869m/2,850ft, Beejan Dreem nan Rahv, Pinnacle of the Ridge of Oars)

To the south of the Bealach Coir' a' Tairneilear the trio of tops that form the attractive summit of Bidein Druim nan Ramh is a no-go area for non-climbers; the traverse of the three tops, of which the central is the highest, is a rock climb of Moderate to Difficult standard. The walker traversing along the main ridge between the Bealach Coir' a' Tairneilear and the Bealach na Glaic Moire must be content to bypass the peak by contouring beneath the summit crags on stony slopes on the Coire na Creiche side.

From the summit of Bidein a satellite ridge (the Druim nan Ramh) runs south-eastwards down to Coruisk. Although its upper section involves rock climbing, its lower section makes a fine excursion from Coruisk, with magnificent views all around the horseshoe of the main ridge.

Coir' a' Mhadaidh (Coira Vatty, Corrie of the Fox)
Bealach na Glaic Moire (759m/2,492ft, Byaloch na Glachk Moara, Pass of the Big Defile)

Coir' a' Mhadaidh on the south side of Sgurr an Fheadain is a much more attractive corrie than Coir' a' Tairneilear, with a fine waterfall and pool and huge walls of rock all around. The route into the corrie is as for Coir' a' Tairneilear until the junction of the Coire na Creiche path and the Bealach a' Mhaim traverse path. Instead of continuing up into Coir' a' Tairneilear from here, follow the traverse path beneath Sgurr an Fheadain and branch left around the cliffs on another path that takes a diagonal line up into Coir' a' Mhadaidh.

The traverse path continues across the Allt Coir' a' Mhadaidh and eventually peters out on the slopes of Sgurr Thuilm. A second path into the corrie climbs up the right bank of the stream; it is marked on the Outdoor Leisure map but is longer and less straightforward than the first path mentioned. The two paths into the corrie merge beside the stream at a grassy section higher up.

At the back of the corrie is the broad saddle of the Bealach na Glaic Moire between Bidein Druim nan Ramh and Sgurr a' Mhadaidh.

This provides a route to Coruisk (see page 79) but as an objective for ridge walkers it has little to offer as progress along the main ridge in either direction soon involves rock climbing.

The route to the bealach avoids the craggy headwall by a stone shoot in the far left-hand corner of the corrie beneath the south-east ridge of Sgurr an Fheadain, but it is a purgatorial ascent route and cannot be recommended. It is described below as a descent route. The best ascent route is via Coir' a' Tairneilear: follow the Bealach Coir' a' Tairneilear route as far as the foot of the summit crags of Bidein Druim nan Ramh, then traverse right beneath the crags to gain the main ridge not far above the Bealach na Glaic Moire (3½hr from Glen Brittle roadside).

To descend into Coir' a' Mhadaidh from the bealach, trend diagonally right from the south (Sgurr a' Mhadaidh) end of the bealach down a broad grassy shelf beneath the crags of Bidein; from the north (Bidein) end this shelf can be reached by descending diagonally right until a short stone shoot gives access.

Keep descending diagonally until you reach the head of the stone shoot beneath the south-east ridge of Sgurr an Fheadain (cairn; difficult to find in mist), then descend into the bowl of the corrie. Pick up a path on the right bank of the stream and continue down beside a short gorge to reach the grassy section mentioned above, then bear right (cairns) to gain the traverse path at the foot of Sgurr an Fheadain.

Sgurr an Fheadain★ (687m/2,253ft, Skoor an *Aite*nn, Peak of the Waterpipe)

Sgurr an Fheadain is an imposing pyramid-shaped peak that soars above the flat floor of Coire na Creiche. Its face is split by the deep Waterpipe Gully (a classic Very Severe rock climb) that is the outstanding feature of the corrie when viewed from the Glen Brittle road and which gives the mountain its name. The scrambler has a choice of two fine routes to the summit: a simple scramble along the south-east ridge or a spectacular ascent of the north-west spur to the left of the Waterpipe. Note that the rock is mainly basalt and should be left well alone when wet.

The south-east ridge is most easily gained by an ascent from Coir' a' Tairneilear to the saddle at its Bidein Druim nan Ramh end (see page 49). From here a pleasant stroll along the shattered ridge is followed by a simple scramble in a fine situation (care on loose rock) down to the small bealach below the towering summit buttress. Outflank the buttress by a simple scramble on the left to gain the summit

(3¹/₂hr from Glen Brittle roadside). The easiest descent route goes down scree slopes from the bealach into Coir' a' Tairneilear (not re-commended for ascent).

An ascent via the north-west spur is an altogether more exciting affair, which has a serious mountaineering air about it. Although the standard of scrambling required is no more than moderate if the crest is adhered to, the route rises through some spectacular rock scenery and gives a fine sense of achievement. It should be undertaken by ex-perienced scramblers only as the rock is often loose and the exposure above Waterpipe Gully is considerable.

The foot of the peak is reached by the Coire na Creiche path from Glen Brittle or the Bealach a' Mhaim traverse path if approaching from Sligachan. On the left of the lowest point a broad grassy rake pushes up into the cliffs, and it is possible to pick a route up slabs to the left of this. Once above the slabs, aim right to gain the spur and then climb skywards. There are numerous choices of route and the excite-ment increases as height is gained (2¹/₂hr to the top from Glen Brittle roadside). From the summit descend to the small bealach beyond (see above), then either descend scree slopes into Coir' a' Tairneilear or continue along the south-east ridge to the saddle at its far end and descend into either Coir' a' Tairneilear or Coir' a' Mhadaidh (via the stone shoot from the Bealach na Glaic Moire).

2.5 SGURR A' MHADAIDH TO SGURR NA BANACHDICH

From Sgurr a' Mhadaidh to Sgurr na Banachdich the main ridge forms the headwall of Coire a' Ghreadaidh and offers some of the finest continuous scrambling in the Cuillin. When combined with the long subsidiary ridges that run out to Sgurr Thuilm and Sgurr nan Gobhar to form the north and south bounding ridges of the corrie, the round of the corrie skyline is aesthetically as well as technically pleasing, with some fine situations and a real mountaineering flavour (allow up to 9hr for the complete round). The skyline involves hard scrambling in parts (easier from north to south), but it is possible to climb some of the peaks individually by easier and more direct routes from the corrie.

Coire a' Ghreadaidh (Coira Graity, Corrie of the Clear Waters or Mighty Winds)

Coire a' Ghreadaidh is a beautiful corrie whose pools and waterslides can be irresistibly inviting when the rocks are baked by sunlight reflected from the surrounding corrie walls. The corrie headwall is formed by the three massive Munros of Sgurr a' Mhadaidh, Sgurr a' Ghreadaidh and Sgurr na Banachdich; between Sgurr a' Ghreadaidh and Sgurr na Banachdich is the smaller peak of Sgurr Thormaid. The defile of An Dorus between Sgurr a' Mhadaidh and Sgurr a' Ghreadaidh provides the only access to the main ridge from the bowl of the corrie, but note that progress along the ridge in either direction then involves at least moderate scrambling.

From Sgurr a' Ghreadaidh a short spur juts out to the minor peak of Sgurr Eadar Da Choire (Skoor *Ai*tar Dah Choira, Peak Between Two Corries) to divide upper Coire a' Ghreadaidh into two. The summit of Sgurr Eadar Da Choire can be reached easily from the north side beneath An Dorus, but its rubble-strewn slopes do not make for an enjoyable ascent and the route onwards to the summit of Sgurr a' Ghreadaidh involves rock climbing.

The north and south bounding ridges of the corrie are easily reached, but the routes along them to the main ridge are very different from each other: the north bounding ridge between Sgurr Thuilm and Sgurr a' Mhadaidh involves hard scrambling, while the south bounding ridge between Sgurr nan Gobbar and Sgurr na Banachdich is mostly a walk. From this latter ridge a spur descends over An Diallaid (An *Jee*-alitch, The Saddle) to enclose the small bowl of Coir' an Eich (Coiran Yich, Horse Corrie), and this provides a route to the summit of Sgurr na Banachdich that is one of the easiest ascents in the Cuillin.

The main path into Coire a' Ghreadaidh begins at Glen Brittle Youth Hostel and climbs along the left bank (right side) of the stream to the flat bowl of the corrie and the pools and waterslides at the back (1hr).

Sgurr a' Mhadaidh (918m/3,012ft, Skoor a Vatty, Peak of the Fox)
Sgurr Thuilm★ (879m/2,885ft, Skoor *Hool*im, Peak of the Knoll or Holm)
An Dorus (847m/2,779ft, An Dorrus, The Door)

The summit of Sgurr Thuilm is easily reached from the mouth of Coir' a' Ghreadaidh via its western shoulder, but this would mean missing the waterslides at the back of the corrie. From the waterslides a route can be made directly up steep slopes of grass and scree to the saddle seen above on the summit ridge. It is also possible to reach the western shoulder of Sgurr Thuilm directly from the Glen Brittle road, but the moorland crossing has little to recommend it in comparison with the corrie approach.

Sgurr a' Mhadaidh has four tops, the highest and most southerly of which lies at the junction of the main ridge and the ridge to Sgurr Thuilm. The traverse of the four tops involves Moderate and exposed rock climbing, and non-climbers must therefore content themselves with an ascent via Sgurr Thuilm from the west (hard scrambling) or An Dorus from the south (moderate scrambling).

From Sgurr Thuilm the round of the corrie skyline begins with a walk down the narrow south-east ridge to the saddle at the foot of the upper cliffs of Sgurr a' Mhadaidh. The climb up from here attacks the left of two ribs and should be attempted by experienced scramblers only; it is a hard, exposed scramble and the best line is difficult to find. An initial, very steep section is bypassed on the right, and then there is an adrenalin-pumping section on the crest before an easier line can again be taken on the right. Higher up, beneath the summit crags of Sgurr a' Mhadaidh, a cairn marks the start of a path that goes right beneath the crags to reach the south ridge just below the summit. From here a simple scramble soon leads to the narrow summit crest, which offers a stunning prospect of Loch Coruisk (3½hr from Glen Brittle).

If you do not wish to include Sgurr Thuilm in the ascent of Sgurr a' Mhadaidh it is possible to take a more direct route from the corrie to the saddle between Sgurr Thuilm and Sgurr a' Mhadaidh. From the waterslides continue up beside the stream into the upper corrie at the foot of An Dorus; there are traces of paths on each side of the stream. The left bank path takes a short cut across the flanks of Sgurr Eadar Da Choire and becomes a cairned route up the stony gully that leads to An Dorus. To reach the saddle keep left of this route, go straight up the scree towards Sgurr a' Mhadaidh, then cut back left and scramble up through breaks in the broken crags.

If the ascent of Sgurr a' Mhadaidh from the saddle proves too exciting, it is possible to traverse from the saddle across scree slopes beneath the cliffs of Sgurr a' Mhadaidh to reach the gully below An Dorus; a cairn on the saddle marks the start of this traverse. Note that the gully leading up to An Dorus forks halfway up; An Dorus is the left branch, the right branch leads to the Eag Dubh (see below). All routes to An Dorus are best avoided in mist.

An Dorus is reputed to be an historically important pass used in the days of clan warfare, but the actual location of the pass is open to debate and some old maps and guidebooks locate it elsewhere.

Certainly, a descent on the Coruisk side of An Dorus cannot be re-commended as chockstones in the gully force you out onto the loose and exposed left wall.

The route up Sgurr a' Mhadaidh from An Dorus begins with a short moderate scramble on solid clean rock, then bouldery slopes (which are loose and require care but involve no more than simple scrambling) lead up to the summit crest (½hr from An Dorus, 3hr from Glen Brittle). Note that this route can be very confusing on descent in mist.

Sgurr a' Ghreadaidh (973m/3,192ft, Skoor a Graity, Peak of the Clear Waters or Mighty Winds)

On the south side of An Dorus rises the fine mountain of Sgurr a' Ghreadaidh, whose summit ridge is the narrowest and most sensa-tional on the skyline of Coir' a' Ghreadaidh. After an initial moderate scramble out of An Dorus the ascent is mainly a walk as far as the Eag Dubh (Aik Doo, Black Cleft), a deep narrow cleft that descends into Coire a' Ghreadaidh (the descent is awkward and greasy and should be avoided; the descent on the Coruisk side is a rock climb). Above the Eag Dubh a hard slabby scramble leads up to the Wart, a large rock bastion that is bypassed by an unexpectedly simple walk on the Coire a' Ghreadaidh side to reach the summit of Sgurr a' Ghreadaidh im-mediately beyond (1hr from An Dorus, 3½hr from Glen Brittle).

The ridge now narrows in spectacular fashion over the south top to provide a long knife-edge scramble that is hard, dramatic and totally absorbing; the view of Coruisk beneath your feet will be forever in-grained in your memory. The continuous scrambling requires con-stant care and much physical and mental effort; it should be taken slowly and savoured. Beyond the south top the ridge descends more steeply to the Ghreadaidh–Thormaid bealach; all difficulties are avoid-able on the Coire a' Ghreadaidh side but it remains a hard scramble.

Sgurr Thormaid (927m/3,040ft, Skoor Hurramij, Norman's Peak)

The minor peak of Sgurr Thormaid looks impressively steep when approached from Sgurr a' Ghreadaidh, but it yields relatively easily to a frontal assault. En route you pass three rock 'teeth', the last of which overhangs; a path on the Coire a' Ghreadaidh side bypasses them all. The easiest line over Sgurr Thormaid keeps to the left on the way up and to the right on the descent of the far side; the scrambling is reasonably exposed but seems easy after the traverse of Sgurr a' Ghreadaidh.

The bealach beyond (ie south of) Sgurr Thormaid provides a descent to Coruisk but offers no easy route down into Coire a' Ghreadaidh. On the far side of the bealach rises Sgurr na Banachdich.

Sgurr na Banachdich★ (965m/3,166ft, Skoor na *Banach*-ich, Smallpox Peak)
Sgurr nan Gobhar★ (631m/2,069ft, Skoor nan *Goa*-ar, Goat Peak)

Sgurr na Banachdich ranks alongside Bruach na Frithe as one of the easiest of all Cuillin peaks for, despite its sharp summit crest, its rough western slopes are reasonably gentle by Cuillin standards. If approaching via Sgurr a' Ghreadaidh the ascent from the Ghreadaidh–Thormaid bealach via the north ridge is easy provided you keep to broken slopes on the Coire a' Ghreadaidh side of the crest. If descending this way, keep left of the summit buttress for a couple of hundred metres, in order to avoid crags overlooking Coruisk, before heading down towards the bealach. But remember, as noted above, that there is no easy route between this bealach and Glen Brittle.

There are three routes from Glen Brittle directly to the summit, however, that need involve no more than simple scrambling: the main (south-east) ridge from the Bealach Coire na Banachdich, the west ridge from Sgurr nan Gobhar and the Coir' an Eich route.

The Sgurr nan Gobhar ridge provides a fine approach to the mountain on ascent and a satisfying end to the round of Coire a' Ghreadaidh on descent, but note that on ascent the easiest line between Glen Brittle and the summit of Sgurr nan Gobhar involves the negotiation of purgatorial scree slopes on the south-west shoulder. If ascending this way reach the foot of Sgurr nan Gobhar from either the Coire a' Ghreadaidh or Coire na Banachdich path and then keep to the south of crags and a large gully. Once the top has been gained, the narrow ridge leading to Sgurr na Banachdich offers an enjoyable mixture of walking and simple scrambling. A small plateau is reached at the junction with the An Diallaid spur, and beyond here numerous cairned lines climb the stony slopes of the broad summit dome of Sgurr na Banachdich (3hr from Glen Brittle).

On descent from Sgurr na Banachdich to Sgurr nan Gobhar the many cairns confuse, rather than help, especially in mist when the small plateau can be a confusing place. The summit of Sgurr nan Gobhar itself is a fine eyrie at the end of the ridge that makes a wonderful sunset viewpoint within easy reach of Glen Brittle for scree runners.

The easiest ascent route to Sgurr na Banachdich, and the shortest descent route, is via Coir' an Eich between An Diallaid and Sgurr nan Gobhar. The route is barely more than a walk but should still be avoided in mist owing to route-finding problems. From Glen Brittle Youth Hostel follow the Coire a' Ghreadaidh path as far as the Allt Coir' an Eich, then climb the left bank (right side) of this stream. A path will soon be found that climbs into Coir' an Eich, crosses to the right bank of the stream and ascends stony slopes at the back of the corrie to join the Sgurr nan Gobhar route at the small plateau described above (3hr to the summit).

The final non-climber's approach to Sgurr na Banachdich is along the main ridge from the Bealach Coire na Banachdich to the southeast (see page 58 for description of ascent to the bealach). If taken direct the crest of the ridge is a hard and exhilarating scramble; a traverse path on the Coire na Banachdich side avoids the hardest sections, but is not always easy to follow, and unless you find the right line it is easy to get into difficulties on rubble-strewn ledges.

From the bealach the route begins as an easy walk along a narrow shattered ridge over a subsidiary top. The rock then improves over a second top to provide the most sensational scrambling. From the gap between the two tops the traverse path goes off to the left (Coire na Banachdich side) and omits the second top altogether. The ascent of the second top involves the negotiation of a hard section near the start (easily bypassed on the left) and, higher up, a narrow rib of large blocks that require dramatic step-ups.

On the descent of the far side of the second top the only hard section is a short wall near the foot, which is steep but has good holds; the going is probably easier from north to south, ie on descent from Sgurr na Banachdich, so that this wall can be tackled on ascent. From the gap beyond the second top the final section of ridge to the summit of Sgurr na Banachdich becomes a shattered crest once more and involves mostly simple scrambling, with any awkward bits easily avoided on the Coire na Banachdich side (1hr from bealach).

2.6 SGURR NA BANACHDICH TO SGURR DEARG

Coire na Banachdich (Coira na *Banach*-ich, Smallpox Corrie)

From Sgurr na Banachdich to Sgurr Dearg the main ridge encloses Coire na Banachdich, a large open corrie with a fine shape but whose bounding ridges, of Sgurr nan Gobhar to the north and the west ridge of Sgurr Dearg to the south, surround the corrie with mainly featureless slopes of broken crag and scree. On the plus side Coire na Banachdich boasts the longest waterfall in the Cuillin and, at the low point on the corrie headwall between Sgurr na Banachdich and Sgurr Dearg, a bealach that provides a route to Coruisk and an approach to the main ridge for ascents of the peaks on either side of it. The route to the bealach is barely a scramble if the correct line is adhered to, but it is not obvious, especially in mist.

The main path into the corrie begins at Glen Brittle Hut and climbs diagonally right around some sheep pens to the Allt Coire na Banachdich, which it crosses (to the left bank) at a pipeline. This point can also be reached by a path directly up the left bank from the road-side near Glenbrittle House; go through the gate beside the cattle grid and keep left through the trees. Continuing up the left bank, the path soon reaches an enormous gorge into which plunges the 24m (80ft) Eas Mor (Aiss Moar, Big Waterfall), a marvellous sight when in spate. The waterfall must have been particularly spectacular on a certain day in 1855, when a waterspout broke at the head of the corrie and flooded Glenbrittle House to a depth of over 3m (10ft).

At the head of the gorge the path forks; the right branch crosses the moor to Coire Lagan (see page 60). Follow the left branch, which hugs the river bank initially and then crosses the broad floor of the corrie well away from the river. This path eventually rounds the foot of Window Buttress (the spur on the right that rises to the west ridge of Sgurr Dearg) to reach a fine deep-cut gorge on the right at the foot of the corrie headwall. Note that this point can also be reached by a path along the right bank of the river (as marked on the Outdoor Leisure map).

Coire na Banachdich can also be reached from Glen Brittle camp-site by a path that begins behind the toilet block and makes a rising traverse left across the moor to the Allt a' Mhuilinn (Owlt a Voolin, Mill Stream). The path follows the right bank of this stream, crosses the path from Glen Brittle Hut to Coire Lagan and climbs to a conspicuous cairn-shaped boulder at the foot of the south-west ridge of Sgurr Dearg. From here cut left into the corrie to join the main path.

Bealach Coire na Banachdich (851m/2,791ft, *Byaloch* Coira na
   Banach-ich, Pass of the Smallpox Corrie)

From the foot of the headwall of Coire na Banachdich the route to the bealach avoids the crags at the back of the corrie by veering right towards Sgurr Dearg and following the main stream that flows

Eas Mor and Coire na Banachdich, with Sgurr nan Gobhar (left) and Sgurr na Banachdich (right) behind

through the deep-cut gorge noted above; a cairned line climbs the slabs on the right bank (left side) of the stream. The going is rocky but straightforward, with no scree to hinder the ascent. Looking back, note the hole on the crest of Window Buttress that gives the buttress its name; the negotiation of the window is a classic rock climb graded Difficult.

The route cuts back left above the crags at the back of the corrie, traversing to the bealach across a broad bouldery shelf (2½hr from Glen Brittle Hut). On descent from the bealach in mist this shelf will be found by descending a boulder ruckle until the crags on the left give way to bouldery slopes; at this point traverse left across the shelf to pick up the line of cairns down into the corrie. Note that this traverse may be hard to find in mist, and missing it will lead to difficulties on the cliffs of the corrie headwall.

From the bealach it is possible to descend to Coruisk (see page 79) or ascend Sgurr na Banachdich (see page 57) or Sgurr Dearg (following a path [cairns] up the stony summit dome; ½hr from bealach). For a full description of Sgurr Dearg see next section.

2.7 SGURR DEARG TO SGURR ALASDAIR

South of Sgurr Dearg the main Cuillin ridge rims the rock climber's paradise of Coire Lagan. The round of the corrie skyline is a classic climber's test piece, with situations worthy of an Alpine route. Here, among others, are to be found the highest peak in the Cuillin (Sgurr Alasdair) and the most spectacular peak (The Inaccessible Pinnacle). Here also is the greatest rock face in the Cuillin — the ½ mile (1km) long 300m (1,000ft) high wall of Sron na Ciche, which abounds in spectacular rock climbs of all grades.

Coire Lagan (Coira Lakken, Corrie of the Little Hollow)

Coire Lagan is a beautifully glaciated corrie, wonderfully wild and rocky, in whose upper bowl a lovely lochan nestles among boiler-plate slabs at the foot of the cliffs. On the left (north) the corrie is bounded by the west ridge of Sgurr Dearg. At the back the main ridge erupts into a succession of dramatic peaks: The Inaccessible Pinnacle, Sgurr Mhic Choinnich and Sgurr Thearlaich. From Sgurr Thearlaich an important satellite ridge runs south-west over Sgurr Alasdair, Sgurr Sgumain and Sron na Ciche to form the right-hand rim of the corrie. Non-climbers must pick and choose their routes with care on these precipitous peaks, and those who find exposure less than exhilarating would do well to go elsewhere.

The path up to the corrie has been so well worn by generations of climbers that it is now more a set of parallel paths, which cut a wide swathe across the moor. In an attempt to combat erosion the Countryside Commission for Scotland instigated a footpath management project here in 1986. The path has two starting points: Glen Brittle campsite and Glen Brittle Hut.

The campsite path begins behind the toilet block and climbs onto the moor. It veers right to reach a stream at a small gorge, then veers back left to climb past Loch an Fhir-bhallaich (Eer *Vall*ich, Spotted Man) and around the south-west shoulder of Sgurr Dearg into the corrie (560m/1,850ft, 2hr). The path from Glen Brittle Hut climbs to the Eas Mor (see page 58) then cuts diagonally right across the moor above Loch an Fhir-bhallaich. At a fork alongside the loch keep left to join the campsite path (the right branch crosses the campsite path lower down and makes for Sron na Ciche; see page 64).

From the lochan in the bowl of the corrie there are two scree routes up to the skyline, neither of which makes a good ascent route. On the left are An Stac screes, which lead to the Bealach Coire Lagan between Sgurr Dearg and Sgurr Mhic Choinnich and which are a useful descent route from Sgurr Dearg. On the right, between Sgurr Thearlaich and Sgurr Alasdair, is the Great Stone Shoot, the easiest way up Alasdair but a purgatorial ascent route (see page 63). Note that the Bealach Mhic Choinnich between Sgurr Mhic Choinnich and Sgurr Thearlaich provides no way along the ridge in either direction without rock climbing, and the slopes of scree and rock that lead up to it are best avoided.

Sgurr Dearg★ (978m/3,209ft, Skoor Jerrak, Red Peak)
The Inaccessible Pinnacle (986m/3,234ft)

Sgurr Dearg is the easiest of the Coire Lagan peaks, sporting no less than three routes to the top that involve no more than simple-to-moderate scrambling: via the Bealach Coire na Banachdich, via the west ridge and via An Stac screes. The Bealach Coire na Banachdich route is barely more than a walk (see page 59); the west ridge route is more exhilarating if you enjoy moderate scrambling in occasionally exposed situations; An Stac screes are recommended for descent only.

The west ridge is reached by the south-west shoulder, which is in turn reached by paths from either Glen Brittle Hut or the campsite. From the campsite follow the Coire na Banachdich path to the cairn-shaped boulder at the foot of the shoulder (see page 58). From Glen Brittle Hut follow the Coire Lagan path until about 200m past the Eas Mor and then branch left on the path to the cairn-shaped boulder.

The stony, well-trodden route up the shoulder is very steep at first and then eases off to reach a narrow section of ridge just below the summit. The scramble along this final section is no more than simple-to-moderate (a path of sorts on the Coire Lagan side takes the easiest line) but does have a sense of exposure (3½hr).

The summit is a short sharp arête that is one of the most awesome spots on the Cuillin ridge, for looming even higher is the vertiginous blade of rock known as The Inaccessible Pinnacle (In Pin to its friends). This mighty monolith teeters some 24m (80ft) above the south-east slopes of Sgurr Dearg, overtopping the summit by about 8m (25ft) to form the most difficult Munro in all Scotland. Its sensational situation above abysmal drops on each side has been known to cause more than one normally rock-steady ridge wanderer to hug the ground for confirmation of its solidity.

Climbers undertaking the round of the Coire Lagan skyline will ascend the facing (west) ridge of The In Pin (Difficult) and descend its far (east) ridge (Moderate) but, fortunately for others, a broad ramp at its base on the Coire Lagan side provides a fairly straightforward bypass route to An Stac screes. The going hardly constitutes a scramble, yet the situation and the occasional rubble on the ramp will cause most walkers to negotiate this section in a less than upright posture.

From the foot of the east ridge of The In Pin a worthwhile simple scramble leads back up to the crest and along to the lump of An Stac (An Stachk, The Stack), from where there is a tremendous view of the pinnacle. The descent of An Stac is a Difficult rock climb, so retrace your steps to the ramp and follow it beneath An Stac to the Bealach Coire Lagan; at one point the ramp rounds a corner to the left (cairn), and it is important here not to continue down inviting screes towards Coire Lagan, as these lead onto crags.

Continue towards the Bealach Coire Lagan until An Stac screes can be seen descending to the corrie; in mist it is probably best to continue to the bealach before descending. Note that the gully on the Coruisk side of the Bealach Coire Lagan is not called Rotten Gully for nothing and should be left well alone.

Sgurr Mhic Choinnich (948m/3,111ft, Skoor Veechk Choan-yich, MacKenzie's Peak)

Sgurr Mhic Choinnich is a great wedge-shaped peak whose traverse is one of the most difficult on the ridge. From the Bealach Coire Lagan its north-west ridge rises steeply to perhaps the narrowest crest in the Cuillin, providing a scramble that is no more than moderate but which is sensationally exposed and which must be reversed as there is no way onwards beyond the summit without rock climbing. The most difficult section is near the top and, as it is no harder on the way back, the ascent can be tackled as far as you think fit.

The first part of the ascent is on good solid gabbro blocks that provide delightful simple scrambling. Then the angle eases to become little more than a walk until the dramatic final section — a thin scramble along the top of exposed slabs; the scrambling is no more than moderate but should be avoided by those who suffer from even a suspicion of vertigo. Note that the rock here is basalt and is best avoided when wet.

Beyond the summit the main ridge soon reaches the top of King's Chimney, a Difficult rock climb that on descent requires an abseil to reach the Bealach Mhic Choinnich below. King's Chimney can be avoided only by an exposed traverse along a ledge on the Coire Lagan side, reached by a steep descent from the north-west ridge a short distance below the summit. This is Collie's Ledge, a Moderate and exposed rock climb, which should be attempted only by those with rock climbing experience. Others must return to the Bealach Coire Lagan.

Sgurr Thearlaich (978m/3,208ft, Skoor Hairlich, Charles's Peak)

Sgurr Thearlaich lies on the south side of the Bealach Mhic Choinnich and is yet another hard and airy Coire Lagan peak whose ascent involves rock climbing of at least Moderate standard on all sides. Climbers can reach the summit via either the north ridge from the Bealach Mhic Choinnich or from the head of the Great Stone Shoot (aiming right to find easier rock). Those without rock climbing experience should avoid the mountain altogether.

Sgurr Alasdair★ (993m/3,257ft, Skoor Alastir, Alexander's Peak)
Sgurr Sgumain★ (947m/3,108ft, Skoor Skoomen, Stack Peak)
Sron na Ciche★ (859m/2,817ft, Strawn na *Keech*-ya, Nose of the Cioch)

From Sgurr Thearlaich a side ridge runs over Sgurr Alasdair, Sgurr Sgumain and Sron na Ciche to form the southern rim of Coire Lagan. Sgurr Alasdair is a beautiful pointed peak that makes a fitting highest Cuillin, even though its summit is composed of basalt rather than gabbro (and should therefore be avoided when wet and slippery). For non-climbers there are only two routes to the top: via the south-west ridge from Sgurr Sgumain and via the Great Stone Shoot.

The Great Stone Shoot is the normal route of descent for climbers completing the round of Coire Lagan. At one time its 400m (1,300ft) of scree provided the fastest descent in the Cuillin, and although its lower section still provides a good run its upper section is now very steep and bare and requires care. As an ascent route it is not to be recommended to friends, but it does provide the only way to the highest summit in the Cuillin that involves no more than simple scrambling.

The scree begins at the back of Coire Lagan beyond the lochan and ascends to the gap between Sgurr Thearlaich and Sgurr Alasdair. The ascent should be avoided in mist, when it is possible to lose one's bearings on the featureless terrain of the lower scree slopes and veer too far right towards Sgurr Sgumain. From the top of the stone shoot a short, simple but somewhat exposed scramble leads to the airy summit (4hr from Glen Brittle). *Note:* the scree on the Coir' a'

Ghrunnda side of the stone shoot leads onto crags and is a dead-end for walkers.

The ascent of Sgurr Alasdair's south-west ridge from Sgurr Sgumain is a far more interesting route, but it involves hard scrambling and is not without its route-finding problems. There are two routes up Sgurr Sgumain: one via the cliff top of Sron na Ciche and one via the cliff foot. The cliff-top route takes the Coir' a' Ghrunnda path (see page 66) as far as the foot of the south-west slopes of Sron na Ciche, then climbs up uniform slopes of grass and outcrops to reach the flat stony summit plateau of Sron na Ciche and the Bealach Coir' a' Ghrunnda beyond (between Sron na Ciche and Sgurr Sgumain) (2¹/₂hr from Glen Brittle).

The view from the plateau, both over the cliff edge and out to sea, is stunning, but the cliff-foot approach is even more spectacular, giving a glimpse of a world of rock rarely seen by the walker.

Paths lead to the foot of the cliffs from both Glen Brittle Hut and the campsite. From the Hut follow the Coire Lagan path until the fork alongside Loch an Fhir-bhallaich, then take the right branch across the moor to the cliffs. This path crosses the track from the campsite to Coire Lagan and makes access from the campsite equally easy; follow the Coire Lagan path from the campsite until above Loch an Fhir-bhallaich then branch right on the Sron na Ciche path. Note that this path heads towards the Sgumain Stone Shoot, which runs up beneath the cliffs of Sron na Ciche to the Bealach Coir' a' Ghrunnda, and should not be confused with a traverse path that contours around the south-west shoulder of Sron na Ciche (see page 66).

Note also that a traverse from the lochan in upper Coire Lagan to the Sron na Ciche cliffs is not straightforward owing to the slabby lower flanks of the west buttress of Sgurr Sgumain that bar the way. The only straightforward connecting route is to descend from the lochan on the Coire Lagan path until below the boiler plates that guard the upper corrie, then cross level ground beneath all slabs.

From the cliff foot the route to Sgurr Sgumain ascends the Sgumain Stone Shoot beneath the Sron na Ciche cliffs to the Bealach Coir' a' Ghrunnda (2¹/₂hr from Glen Brittle). As you climb, crane your neck skywards to view the remarkable wall of clean contorted gabbro that towers 300m (1,000ft) overhead; there is nothing like it anywhere else in Britain. Note the markings on the rock that indicate the start of famous climbs.

About two-thirds of the way up the stone shoot are some enormous boulders that form a cave, and on the cliff face to the right of here is the most extraordinary piece of rock in the Cuillin — The Cioch (*Kee*-och, Breast), a wodge of rock that seems to have been affixed to the cliff face as an afterthought.

Note that from the Bealach Coir' a' Ghrunnda at the top of the stone shoot the sandy shores of Loch Coir' a' Ghrunnda are only 140m (450ft) below. The route down to the lochan is easy and can be linked with the Coir' a' Ghrunnda approach route to make a fine round (see page 66).

The ascent of Sgurr Sgumain from the bealach follows a path up the bouldery summit dome (1/2hr from bealach). The route onwards to Sgurr Alasdair, up the impressive south-west ridge that towers overhead, is not so easy; it involves hard scrambling and route-finding on loose rock and should be attempted by experienced scramblers only.

Even reaching the Sgumain–Alasdair bealach can be a problem if the correct line is not found. An immediate short sharp scramble up an exposed rib of rock leads to a narrow ridge that ends in a steep drop to the bealach. This drop can be turned by a simple scramble on either side; the right (Coir' a' Ghrunnda) side looks more obvious but lower down involves a move across a slab that can be awkward when greasy. All difficulties between Sgurr Sgumain and the Sgumain–Alasdair bealach can be avoided, if necessary, by quitting the crest of the ridge at the foot of the initial rib and descending ledges on the Coire Lagan side to reach a path that traverses to the bealach.

A gendarme on the bealach is easily passed on the right by a path that leads away from the crest of the ridge to a chimney at the foot of the Sgurr Alasdair cliffs. On the crest itself the scrambling becomes increasingly difficult and soon reaches a *mauvais pas* — a 4m (12ft) wall graded a Very Difficult rock climb. The only way onwards for scramblers is via the well-worn chimney further right; it is a hard scramble but the holds are good. Above the chimney pick a route up the steep and shattered summit slopes (care), trending back left to the crest to reach the summit (1hr from Sgurr Sgumain).

2.8 THE SOUTH END

Coir' a' Ghrunnda (Coira Ghrunnda, Floored Corrie)

Coir' a' Ghrunnda is at the same time the wildest and most beautiful of all Cuillin corries. Its large sandy-shored lochan, hemmed in by high peaks, the barrier of vast boiler-plate slabs that guard its entrance and the incredibly rough rocks at the back of the corrie are all without equal. Two interesting approach routes enable the corrie to be included in a fine round trip that involves no more than a bit of simple scrambling, while from the upper corrie the delightful south end of the main Cuillin ridge is within easy reach.

The main route into the corrie begins at Glen Brittle campsite. Follow the Coire Lagan path as far as the small gorge, then cross to the far side of the stream where another large path heads straight on across the moor (this is the coast path to Coruisk — see page 78). By ignoring this path and turning immediately left along the far side of the stream, a smaller path will be found that climbs above the Coruisk path to the foot of the south-west shoulder of Sron na Ciche. Here it joins a traverse path that contours right beneath the shoulder then cuts steeply left around a corner into the trough of lower Coir' a' Ghrunnda.

Note that the traverse path can also be reached easily from the Coruisk path by taking the left (upper) branch at each fork. Note also that the traverse path begins on the far side of Coire Lagan (see page 64) and can be used as a direct route to Coir' a' Ghrunnda from Glen Brittle Hut.

Once into the corrie the rock scenery is outstanding. The lower section consists of a rising trough floored by wave upon wave of boiler-plate slabs, which seem to flow down the corrie in the manner of the glacier that formed them. Walls of clean rock rear skywards all around. The skyline ahead is the lip of the upper corrie, behind which hides the lochan.

The path keeps high on the left at the foot of the walls of gabbro that form the south-east face of Sron na Ciche. You may wish to leave the path to explore the central boiler-plates in order to better appreciate their immensity, but avoid trying to scramble up the centre of the corrie as tempting lines may lead to difficulties. Enjoyable scrambling can be sought on the left of the corrie or bypassed on the path above according to choice.

As you gain height a wonderful view opens up back through the jaws of the corrie across Soay to Eigg and Rum. The path climbs to the nick in the skyline from which the stream tumbles; towards the top there are one or two passages of simple scrambling that may be awkward when wet. The route is difficult to follow in mist and on descent; when leaving the lochan on descent keep well to the right of the stream initially (look for cairns) in order to avoid crags.

In Coire Lagan.·The peak is Sgurr Mhic Choinnich, and the scree run is the **Great Stone Shoot**

Over the skyline you emerge into the secret bowl of the upper corrie, cupped high beneath the Cuillin ridge. The craggy slopes of the surrounding peaks make a savage setting for the highest and largest of all Cuillin lochans, whose clear waters and shores of clean rock and sand make it irresistible on a hot day (700m/2,300ft, 2¹/₂hr from Glen Brittle).

Owing to the height of the corrie and the broken terrain there are several routes up to the skyline. The left-hand rim of the corrie is formed by the ridge that runs over Sron na Ciche, Sgurr Sgumain and Sgurr Alasdair to Sgurr Thearlaich. The Bealach Coir' a' Ghrunnda, 140m (460ft) above the lochan between Sron na Ciche and Sgurr Sgumain, provides a second route into Coir' a' Ghrunnda from Coire Lagan (see page 64) and can be linked with the above approach to make a fine round. At the back of the corrie the main Cuillin ridge runs from Sgurr Thearlaich across Sgurr Dubh na Da Bheinn and Caisteal a' Garbh-choire (the rock bastion that towers over the lochan) to Sgurr nan Eag. The south-west shoulder of Sgurr nan Eag forms the right-hand rim of the corrie.

Between Sgurr Thearlaich and Sgurr Dubh na Da Bheinn the Bealach Coir' an Lochain provides a route to Coruisk (see page 80). Note that if heading for Glen Brittle via this bealach, either from Coruisk or on return from a trip to the south end of the main ridge, it is possible to traverse beneath the Alasdair–Thearlaich crags to the Bealach Coir' a' Ghrunnda or the Sgumain–Alasdair bealach without much loss of height.

The most interesting route up to the main ridge is to the gap between Sgurr Dubh na Da Bheinn and Caisteal a' Garbh-choire; this involves some delightful simple scrambling on large boulders that are the roughest in the Cuillin. The rock is peridotite, described by an early guidebook writer as 'absurdly and painfully adhesive'; watch out for your fingers and clothes. The exit onto the skyline goes through a window formed by a leaning slab.

The most common route up to the main ridge lies further right, to the Bealach a' Garbh-choire between Sgurr Dubh na Da Bheinn and Sgurr nan Eag. At the far right-hand corner of the lochan a cairn marks the start of the ascent; the scrambling required is minimal and there are traces of a path. The bealach is linked to the gap on the Sgurr Dubh na Da Bheinn side of Caisteal a' Garbh-choire by a path that

The south ridge of Bla Bheinn from near Am Mam

traverses the base of Caisteal a' Garbh-choire on the far (An Garbh-choire) side, and from either end there is an easy descent to Coruisk via An Garbh-choire (see page 80).

Further right still it is possible to take an easy and more direct route from the lochan up onto the north ridge of Sgurr nan Eag (look for traces of a path).

Sgurr Dubh na Da Bheinn★ (938m/3,078ft, *Skoor Doo* na *Dah Vain*, Black Peak of the Two Mountains; spelt Sgurr Dubh an Da Bheinn on OS map)
Sgurr Dubh Mor (944m/3,096ft, Skoor Doo Moar, Big Black Peak)

Sgurr Dubh na Da Bheinn's broken but shapely summit is easily reached from the gap between it and Caisteal a' Garbh-choire to the right (south) or from the Bealach Coir' an Lochain to the left (north); a frontal assault from the corrie should be avoided owing to craggy ground. The ascent is usually combined with that of Sgurr Dubh Mor, the Munro on the Coruisk side of the main ridge that is hidden from sight from the corrie.

The main ridge north of the Bealach Coir' an Lochain, rising to Sgurr Thearlaich, is a no-go area for walkers as it contains the famous Thearlaich–Dubh Gap — a great cleft in the ridge that is a polished Very Difficult rock climb on each side. Even reaching the south side of the gap involves an exposed Moderate rock climb that should be left well alone by walkers.

The ascent of Sgurr Dubh na Da Bheinn from the Bealach Coir' an Lochain is no more than a rough walk on peridotite blocks, with any difficulties easily avoided on the Coir' a' Ghrunnda side (1hr from lochan). From the gap between Sgurr Dubh na Da Bheinn and Caisteal a' Garbh-choire the ascent is of a similar nature; the actual crest gives harder scrambling, but any difficulties are again easily bypassed on the Coir' a' Ghrunnda side.

From the summit of Sgurr Dubh na Da Bheinn the traverse eastwards along the connecting ridge to Sgurr Dubh Mor makes an exciting scramble. A short easy descent leads to the saddle between the two peaks, and then it is necessary to keep right (An Garbh-choire side) to find a practicable line up Sgurr Dubh Mor. Keep right until you can climb a gully, and from the top of this climb right, left and right again, following cairns and scratch marks, to reach the summit. The scrambling is mostly moderate with one or two moves that some may find hard (1hr return from Sgurr Dubh na Da Bheinn).

The summit of Sgurr Dubh Mor is a narrow crest with a cairn at one end and a mossy tuft of grass perched precariously at the other, beyond which the ridge (the Dubhs Ridge) continues level for some distance before descending towards Sgurr Dubh Beag and Coruisk. The ascent of the Dubhs Ridge from Coruisk ('doing the Dubhs') is a classic rock climb graded only Moderate but with some tremendous situations. For a taste of Dubhs Ridge climbing, wander out along the level section of ridge on beautiful clean slabs of gabbro; they give exhilarating scrambling that is never more than moderate. You can reach the end of the level section, from where the ridge drops away steeply to Sgurr Dubh Beag, before returning to the summit of Sgurr Dubh Mor (1hr return).

Sgurr nan Eag★ (924m/3,031ft, Skoor nan Aik, Notched Peak)
Caisteal a' Garbh-choire (829m/2,719ft, *Cash*-tyal a Garrav Choira, Castle of the Rough Corrie)

The 400m (1,300ft) level summit ridge of Sgurr nan Eag, the most southerly Munro in the Cuillin, is easily reached via the north ridge from the Bealach a' Garbh-choire or more directly from the lochan in Coir' a' Ghrunnda. From Sgurr Dubh na Da Bheinn the route to the Bealach a' Garbh-choire is blocked by Caisteal a' Garbh-choire, but this is easily bypassed on the An Garbh-choire side as noted above. The traverse of Caisteal a' Garbh-choire is a Very Difficult rock climb whose forbidding appearance will tempt not even the most experienced of scramblers.

The true crest of the north ridge of Sgurr nan Eag involves more than scrambling on occasion, but all difficulties are avoidable on the right (Ghrunnda side) to give exciting scrambling of all grades on firm blocks of gabbro. A path further right makes the ascent barely more than a walk. The summit is the third of three tors and lies at the far end of the long summit ridge (1hr from lochan or Sgurr Dubh na Da Bheinn). The south-west shoulder of Sgurr nan Eag, which rises above the coast path to Coruisk, should be avoided. It is a long and tedious route (both on ascent and on descent) owing to long slopes of scree and boulders and route-finding problems among outcrops.

Sgurr a' Choire Bhig★ (875m/2,872ft, Skoor a Choira Veek, Peak of the Little Corrie)
Gars-bheinn★ (875m/2,935ft, Garss-vain, Echoing Mountain; wrongly marked as 910m on Outdoor Leisure map)

Gars-bheinn from Sgurr a' Choire Bhig

These two peaks at the southern end of the main Cuillin ridge make a delightful high-level stroll from Sgurr nan Eag, with wonderful views over Loch Coruisk on one side and Soay Sound on the other (allow 3hr return from Sgurr nan Eag). The walk begins with a 150m (500ft) descent of Sgurr nan Eag's south-east shoulder. By keeping to the cliff top overlooking An Garbh-choire scrambling of all grades can be sought (more enjoyable on the return journey than on descent); one deep chimney on the crest (after which the mountain is named) can be crossed by a dramatic rock bridge.

The 100m (330ft) rise to Sgurr a' Choire Bhig begins gently then narrows towards the summit. The crest of the ridge is barely more than an exposed walk, but a path below the crest on the right takes an even easier line. A short descent of 35m (120ft) follows, where it is necessary to put hand to rock on occasion, and then the main ridge ends with an extremely pleasant walk out to Gars-bheinn. Just before the short final rise to the summit two stone shoots on the left are passed, the second of which contains a pinnacle. Beyond the summit there are no more Cuillin, only the boundless sea.

Between Sgurr nan Eag and Gars-bheinn the main ridge rims the shallow hollow of Coire nan Laogh (Looh, Calf), which is of little interest to either climbers or walkers and allows no easy access to the ridge. A way up the featureless southern flank of Gars-bheinn can be made from Glen Brittle campsite by following the Coruisk coast path as far as the Allt Coire nan Laogh then striking uphill on some of the most tedious scree in the Cuillin (about 4hr from Glen Brittle). This route can be used to vary the approach to Gars-bheinn, but on both ascent and descent it is terminally frustrating and involves a long walk across the moor.

On the north-east side of the main ridge Coire Beag (Bake, Little) and Coire a' Chruidh (*Chroo*-y, Horseshoe) enable ascents of Gars-bheinn to be made from Coruisk (the former by either of the two stone shoots mentioned above, the latter by an ascent to the east ridge just below the summit), but they have little to recommend them. If staying at Coruisk the most interesting ascent of Gars-bheinn is via the east ridge. Reaching the foot of the ridge can be problematical owing to rocky ground above the shore, but higher up the ridge narrows pleasantly and towards the summit passes some fine crags overlooking Coire a' Chruidh.

2.9 HARTA AND LOTA CORRIES

The remote eastern reaches of the Cuillin, enclosed within the horse-shoe of the main ridge, are divided into two massive basins by the long ridge of Druim nan Ramh. To the south of this ridge lies Coruisk and its satellite corries (see next section), while to the north lies the deep U-shaped trench of Harta Corrie (Corrie of the Hart), whose flat desolate confines are among the least trodden in the whole Cuillin. The walk from Sligachan to the Bloody Stone at the mouth of the corrie makes a fine excursion, which follows a good, flat path all the way. Beyond the Bloody Stone the route to the upper corrie is long and mostly trackless; there is a fine water chute to be seen higher up, but if you are going that far the walk is best combined with an ascent to or descent from the main ridge.

Most walkers prefer to use the corrie as a descent route as the peaks to which it gives access are more quickly and pleasurably reached directly from Sligachan. As a descent route it provides an opportunity to extend the day with an interesting and unusual Cuillin walk through a remote mountain fastness.

The direct route into Harta Corrie from Sligachan follows the Coruisk path along Glen Sligachan (see page 77) as far as the point where the River Sligachan turns sharp right into the corrie (1¹/₂hr). From here the prospect along Harta Corrie, as it curves out of sight around the flanks of Sgurr na h–Uamha, is one of the most desolate on Skye, having an air of wildness and remoteness unequalled even by Coruisk. Two cairns on the Glen Sligachan path mark the start of the Harta Corrie path, which cuts down to the river and follows its right bank. In the mouth of the corrie stands a curious, isolated boulder, some 10m (30ft) high, crowned by bushes that seem oddly out of place in the surrounding desolation (4¹/₂ miles/7 km, 2hr from Sligachan). This is the Bloody Stone, around which were piled the bodies of MacLeods and MacDonalds after yet another bloody battle between those feuding clans on yet another godforsaken patch of remote moorland.

Beyond the Bloody Stone the path continues a short distance along the right bank of the river but gradually peters out as the corrie narrows and curves to the right around the rocky flanks of Sgurr na h–Uamha. Here the flat going ends with a short rise into the upper corrie, a fine spot beneath the eastern buttresses of An Caisteal, whose huge walls of rock, over 300m (1,000ft) high, hang above the corrie like curtains. At the head of the corrie is a tremendous water chute, the longest in the Cuillin and quite a sight in wet weather. Above the chute lies Lota Corrie (High Corrie), a small crag-girt bowl hemmed in by the peaks of the northern Cuillin. The route to Lota Corrie is cairned and follows the left (east) bank of the stream.

There are several routes between Harta/Lota corries and the main ridge but most of them cross awkward terrain and involve difficult route-finding. Note especially that the route to the Bealach a' Bhasteir between Am Basteir and Sgurr nan Gillean should be avoided as it is steep, bare and loose on the Lota Corrie side. The only recommended access points on the main ridge are the Bealach a' Ghlas-choire and the Bealach nan Lice, from which rough and long descents into the remote inner recesses of Harta and Lota corries can be combined with ascents of Bruach na Frithe and Sgurr nan Gillean respectively.

The Bealach a' Ghlas-choire lies between Sgurr Beag and Sgurr na h-Uamha. Steep, broken slopes lead down into Lota Corrie and upper Harta Corrie; the going is rough, with numerous small crags to be bypassed, but the route is without technical difficulty. Once beneath the crags of Sgurr na h-Uamha, it is also possible to take a short-cut left down Coire nan Clach (Stony Corrie) into lower Harta Coire.

The Bealach nan Lice lies between Sgurr a' Fionn Choire and the Basteir Tooth, linking Fionn Choire (or Coire a' Bhasteir) and Lota Corrie (see page 44 for a description of Fionn Choire side). On the ridge the top of the bealach is recognisable by a knob of rock. The direct descent into Lota Corrie is not technically difficult if the correct line is taken, but route-finding is not straightforward; after a stone shoot a slabby section is reached where an easy line may be awkward to find. On ascent, follow the main stream to the back of the corrie then make a direct ascent north-westwards to reach the bealach.

2.10 CORUISK

Loch Coruisk is the jewel in the crown of the Cuillin. Cradled in the long narrow basin of Coir' Uisge (Corooshka, Water Corrie) at the heart of the remote eastern side of the range, it is justly famed for its rugged yet picturesque scenery. Unlike the desolate wildness of the neighbouring basin of Harta Corrie, the appeal of Coruisk lies in a happy juxtaposition of all that is best in the Cuillin mountain environment. The loch itself is studded with islands and fringed with sandy bays. Around its rocky shores tower the vertiginous parapets of the Cuillin, from where streams tumble into wild corries. Beyond the isthmus at the mouth of the loch lap the emerald waters of Loch Scavaig, itself fringed by attractively craggy shores. There is such a profusion of forms and colours, on both land and water, that the senses are overpowered. At Coruisk the forces of nature have run wild.

Coruisk is at its most colourful when slanting sunlight highlights its intricate forms, but it is at its most glorious and dramatic on a stormy day, when the crashing waters of loch and sea and the foaming mountainsides are a truly awesome sight. The difficulty of reaching Coruisk when rivers are in spate, however, should not be underestimated.

The Coruisk river and its tributaries at the head of the loch, the Abhainn Camas Fhionnairigh at Camasunary, the Allt a' Chaoich at the foot of An Garbh-choire and the River Scavaig, which crosses the short isthmus between Loch Coruisk and Loch Scavaig (and is normally crossed on stepping stones) are all impassable in spate. Coir' Uisge did not receive its Gaelic name for nothing; the waters of Loch Coruisk have been known to rise 2.5m (8ft) in one day. Climbers camping at Coruisk or staying at the JMCS hut on the west side of the River Scavaig may well find themselves trapped in adverse weather.

Tourists came to Coruisk to stand and stare long before the Cuillin were climbed. Sir Walter Scott came in 1814 while on a yachting tour of the west coast of Scotland. At his exhortation the painters William Danielson and J.M.W. Turner followed, and their paintings encouraged others. Early tourists came by boat across Loch Scavaig, and today it is still possible to take a boat from Elgol during the summer months. The short sea journey is a magnificent way into the heart of the Cuillin and can be combined with any of the routes described below to make an unforgettable day.

The best lochside view is obtained from the south-east shore, from where the prospect up the loch to the splintered Cuillin skyline is exquisite. Provided that the Rivers Scavaig and Coruisk are not in spate and can be forded, it is possible to walk all the way around the loch in about two hours. There is a boggy path all the way; the south side provides slightly easier going, as the north side is narrow and rutted.

At the head of the loch is a rugged amphitheatre of rock whose scale and complexity is such that the peaks on the main ridge above are indistinguishable to the inexperienced eye. The floor of the corrie is a combination of boulders and tussocky heather that makes heavy going, but indistinct paths wend their way through the wilderness, providing access to the skyline (see below).

Sgurr na Stri★ (497m/1,630ft, Skoor na Stree, Peak of Strife)

At the mouth of Loch Coruisk stands Sgurr na Stri, a minor hill by Cuillin standards but of such rugged grandeur and in such a perfect situation that its ascent is highly recommended. The capable scrambler should be able to find a route to the summit directly from the lochside; a steep route involving less route-finding and scrambling can be found by starting at the foot of Coire Riabhach, and further round there are easier routes up from Loch a' Choire Riabhaich and Druim Hain (see below). A direct ascent from Camasunary also makes a good scramble. The summit itself is an extremely complex series of rocky knolls, of which the two most southerly are the highest — one an eyrie above Camasunary, the other an eyrie above Coruisk; the views are stunning.

Historical note: Sgurr na Stri's name is said to derive from an eighteenth-century boundary dispute between the MacLeods and MacKinnons, each of whom laid claim to the land on which the mountain stands. A compromise was agreed, but the dispute was soon forgotten as the land was of no use to either clan.

Routes to Coruisk
There are a number of routes to Coruisk both around the Cuillin
(routes 1 to 3 below) and over passes between peaks (routes 4 to 7
below). Routes around the Cuillin are described ending at Coruisk,
whereas routes over passes are described beginning at Coruisk (route-
finding being generally more difficult in this direction). In addition,
there are a number of routes from Coruisk to the main ridge that have
no direct connections with Sligachan or Glen Brittle; these have been
described in preceding sections of this chapter where appropriate.

1 From Sligachan via Glen Sligachan and Druim Hain (Grade 4,
    7½ miles/11km, 350m/1,150ft, 4hr).
This is a magnificent walk along probably the best path in the Cuillin,
but its length should not be underestimated. In the past it was possible
to hire a pony at Sligachan, but today the journey must be done under
your own steam.

From Sligachan cross the old bridge and follow the path signposted
'Footpath to Loch Coruisk' along Glen Sligachan. At the Allt na
Measarroch (Mess-arroch, Temperance) at the foot of Marsco the
map shows an upstream diversion to cross the river, but under
normal water conditions it is better to take a shortcut straight across,
following cairns and a developing path. A short distance beyond the
river Clach na Craoibhe Chaoruinn (Clach na *Cræ*-ya *Chæ*ran, Stone
of the Rowan Tree) can be seen beside the path on the right.

The path continues along the broad glen and forks at the foot of Am
Fraoch-choire (Am *Fræch Choira*, The Heather Corrie). The left
branch goes past Loch an Athain (*A*-hin, Little Ford) into the jaws of
Srath na Creitheach below Bla Bheinn and leads to Camasunary and
beyond (see 4.1 and 5.1). Take the right branch, crossing the broad
flats of upper Srath na Creitheach, a remote basin that has an air of
spaciousness unequalled in the Cuillin. The conjunction of the flat
floor of the strath and the steep western wall of Bla Bheinn gives the
place the appearance and scale of an Alpine cirque.

The path climbs to a large cairn on the crest of Druim Hain (310m/
1,000ft, Dreem *Hah*-in, Ridge of Hinds), from where the sparkling
waters of Loch Coruisk and Loch Scavaig can be seen for the first time
(3hr from Sligachan). The main path appears to go straight on into
Coire Riabhach but leads only to a viewpoint over Loch a' Choire
Riabhaich (worth the short detour). The true path goes left (south) for
a short distance to another large cairn, then forks. The main route
again appears to go straight on, but the Coruisk path branches right,

taking a diagonal line down through Coire Riabhach (*Ree*-avach, Brindled) to reach the lochside.

The left branch is worth exploring by those who do not wish to descend to Coruisk, as it affords fine views of Coruisk without loss of height. It continues across the hillside below Sgurr Hain and after about 20min passes Captain Maryon's Cairn (marked on Outdoor Leisure map as 'Monument'), which can be seen 100m below on the right. This 2m (7ft) stone pyramid was erected by a friend to the memory of Captain Maryon, whose body was found on this spot two years after his disappearance in 1946. Five minutes further along, a stream drains a shallow grassy depression on the left that offers an easy ascent of Sgurr na Stri.

About 10min beyond Captain Maryon's Cairn the path to all intents and purposes ends at a cliff top, but easy-angled slabs on the right can be descended without difficulty to join the Coire Riabhach path. *Warning:* ten metres down these slabs, cairns can be seen marking a continuation of the path left along a shelf. This path eventually becomes eroded and impassable, and should be avoided.

2 The coast route from Glen Brittle (Grade 5, 7 miles/11km, 300+m/1,000+ft, 4+hr)

This route should not be undertaken lightly as it involves difficult route-finding and a spot of slabby scrambling that some people may find awkward. The Coruisk coast path begins at Glen Brittle campsite and crosses the moor high above Soay Sound (see page 66). Approaching Gars-bheinn the path peters out, and as precise directions beyond here are difficult to follow it is perhaps best to round Gars-bheinn at about the 300m (1,000ft) mark and then choose your own route through the frustrating three-dimensional maze of crags that fall to Loch Scavaig.

Stay high until you can descend to the shore at the stream before the Allt a' Chaoich (Owlt a *Chœ*-ich, the Mad Burn, named after its appearance in spate). If travelling from Coruisk to Glen Brittle a good route is even harder to find, and it is perhaps best to stick to the equally frustrating shoreline until beyond Gars-bheinn. An equable temperament is a useful virtue on the Brittle–Coruisk coast route.

Beyond the Mad Burn a slabby section by the shoreline involves a short moderate scramble that may be awkward when wet. Once past here Coruisk is only a few minutes' walk away.

3 The coast route from Elgol or Kilmarie via Camasunary (Grade 5,

6 miles/10km, 4 hr from Elgol; 5 miles/8km, 3½hr from Kilmarie). This magnificent coast walk follows a path all the way but involves the fording of the Abhainn Camas Fhionnairigh and the negotiation of the Bad Step (see page 132 for description).

4 Via the Bealach na Glaic Moire at the head of Coir' a' Mhadaidh
   (Grade 5, 9½ miles/15km, 900m/2,950ft, 6½hr from Sligachan).
This 760m (2,492ft) bealach between Bidein Druim nan Ramh and Sgurr a' Mhadaidh is the lowest pass to Coruisk on the main ridge and the shortest way between Sligachan and upper Coir' Uisg. The route is marked on the Outdoor Leisure map. See page 50 for description of Coir' a' Mhadaidh side.
   On ascent from Coruisk take either of the lochside paths to the head of the loch and the end of the level floor of Coir' Uisg, then follow the stream that bears right beneath the crags of Druim nan Ramh into the broad gully of the Glac Mhor; a cairned path will be found on the left bank (right side) of the stream. The gully rises past the crags that guard the high corrie of Coir' an Uaigneis (Oo-*aig*-nis, Solitude) and splits into two branches. The left (south) branch deposits you at the Sgurr a' Mhadaidh end of the bealach and is easier on ascent, with grass and rocks to ease the stony going. The right (north) branch deposits you at the Bidein Druim nan Ramh end of the bealach and its loose stones are perhaps easier on descent.

5 Via the Bealach Coire na Banachdich at the head of Coire na
   Banachdich (Grade 5, 6 miles/10km, 850m/2,800ft, 5hr from Glen
   Brittle Hut).
This 851m (2,791ft) bealach between Sgurr na Banachdich and Sgurr Dearg provides technically the easiest way to Coruisk from Glen Brittle (coast route included). The route is marked on the Outdoor Leisure map. See page 58 for description of Coire na Banachdich side.
   On ascent from Coruisk take either of the two lochside paths to the head of the loch and the end of the level floor of Coir' Uisg, then follow the stream that bears left around the leaning tower of Sgurr Coir' an Lochain into the large hollow of Coireachan Ruadha (*Coira*chan *Roo*-aha, Red Corries); a cairned path will be found on the right bank (left side) of the stream. Higher up, keep well to the left of the stream to outflank waterfalls then cut back right into the upper corrie and pick a route up steep slopes of boulders and scree at the back to reach the bealach.

Note that this route also provides the most straightforward approach to the rarely visited summit of Sgurr Coir' an Lochain, the last Cuillin (and British) peak to be climbed. From Coireachan Ruadha bear left under the cliffs of the Sgurr to gain the south ridge, then continue without difficulty to the summit, avoiding any problems on the right.

6 Via the Bealach Coir' an Lochain at the head of Coir' a' Ghrunnda (Grade 5, 7 miles/11km, 850m/2,800ft, 5¹/₂hr from Glen Brittle campsite).

This 855m (2,806ft) bealach between Sgurr Thearlaich and Sgurr Dubh na Da Bheinn connects Coir' a' Ghrunnda and Coir' an Lochain, two of the wildest corries in the Cuillin, and it is perhaps the most picturesque of all the passes over the main ridge. See page 66 for description of Coir' a' Ghrunnda side.

Coir' an Lochain is a high (580m/1,900ft), remote and magnificently untamed corrie that is approached from neighbouring Coir' a' Chaoruinn (*Chœran*, Rowan) by a hidden terrace. Coir' a' Chaoruinn is a shallow corrie from which several streams descend over slabs to the head of Loch Coruisk. From the path along the south shore of the loch climb left beside the first (southernmost) stream. The slabs cannot be avoided altogether and require care, but the line of least resistance has little difficulty.

At about 360m (1,200ft) a cairned terrace will be found on the right (look for a large leaning slab), which makes a curious rising traverse around the slabby north-eastern slopes of Sgurr Dubh Mor to emerge in Coir' an Lochain a few hundred metres below the lochan (on descent follow cairns down to the right). There are no more secret places in the whole Cuillin. The route to the Bealach Coir' an Lochain goes up grass and rocks at the back of the corrie to finish in a stone shoot.

7 Via the Bealach a' Gharbh-choire at the head of Coir' a' Ghrunnda (6 miles/10km, 800m/2,600ft, 5hr from Glen Brittle campsite).

This 797m (2,614ft) bealach between Caisteal a' Garbh-choire and Sgurr nan Eag is the only Cuillin pass that leads almost directly to the mouth of Loch Coruisk. See page 65 for description of Coir' a' Ghrunnda side.

On ascent from Coruisk there are two routes into An Garbh-choire. One route follows the shore of Loch Scavaig as far as the stream beyond the Allt a' Chaoich and then climbs beside the left bank of this stream into the lower corrie (traces of path). The going is good, but note that a short moderate scramble is required before the Allt a' Chaoich is reached (see route 2). A second route avoids all difficulties; from halfway along the south side of Loch Coruisk climb the shallow corrie of tussocky grass and heather on the south side of the Dubh slabs. At the head of this corrie is a low ridge and beyond that the broad basin of lower An Garbh-choire.

Once into An Garbh-choire follow the path up the left bank (right side) of the stream towards Caisteal a' Garbh-choire, the unmistakable rock fortress seen ahead on the main ridge. The upper corrie becomes a narrow V-shaped defile choked with Herculean boulders whose negotiation requires nimbleness and humour. The place has a savage charm that may not be fully appreciated until you reach the skyline. Aim either left or right of the Caisteal to gain the main ridge. On descent upper An Garbh-choire makes a classic boulder hop.

2.11 SHORT WALKS FROM GLEN BRITTLE AND SLIGACHAN

The walks in this section are intended as suggestions for whiling away a few hours at Sligachan or in Glen Brittle, perhaps when the high peaks are in cloud, or in the evening following a long journey from the mainland, or simply as enjoyable excursions for those who do not wish to climb the Cuillin. Most of the walks cover parts of routes already described in preceding sections and are therefore given in outline form only; further details can be found by referring to the appropriate section. Where this is not the case, more detailed route information is given.

Short walks from Glen Brittle
1 The beautiful pools and waterfalls of the Allt Coir' a' Mhadaidh in Coire na Creiche (Grade 1, 1+hr return; see page 47). The walk can be extended into Coire na Creiche and a return made the same way or via the Bealach a' Mhaim traverse path.
2 Coire a' Ghreadaidh: fine waterfalls lower down and irresistible waterslides higher up, with a riverside path all the way (Grade 3, 2+hr return, see page 53).
3 Eas Mor: a 24m (80ft) waterfall at the foot of Coire na Banachdich (Grade 1, 1hr return; see page 58). The walk can be extended into Coire na Banachdich.
4 Loch an Fhir-bhallaich: an attractive moorland loch in a hollow at the foot of the south-west ridge of Sgurr Dearg, offering good views

of Glen Brittle and the remarkable rock face of Sron na Ciche. Paths from both Glen Brittle Hut and campsite pass the loch en route to Coire Lagan (Grade 3, 2hr return; see page 58). The walk can be extended into Coire Lagan.

5 Loch Brittle: from the campsite a path follows the eastern shore of Loch Brittle out to Rubh' an Dunain, offering fine views both across the loch and into the southern Cuillin corries (see page 136 for description). The basalt crags of Creag Mhor lie about 1hr along this path. By following the shoreline rather than the path some deep and craggy creeks not far from the campsite can be explored, with opportunities for scrambling. The western shore of the loch is less interesting but provides magnificent and less foreshortened views of the Cuillin.

6 West Glen Brittle: the unremarkable hills on the west side of Glen Brittle are overshadowed by the Cuillin and surrounded by forestry plantations, but they are magnificent viewpoints and are easily reached with the aid of forest roads. The key to these hills is the Bealach Brittle (GR 395231), reached by a forest road that leaves the Glen Brittle road 400m north of the bridge over the River Brittle (GR 419249). Without transport along the glen the bealach can be reached from the campsite by crossing the river (suspension bridge, GR 408209) and climbing around the forest edge.

From the bealach An Cruachan (435m/1,428ft, An *Croo*-achan, The Little Mound), Truagh Mheall (413m/1,354ft, *Troo*-a Vell, Wretched Hill) and Beinn Staic (411m/1,350ft, Bain *Sty*-chk, Stack Mountain) are all within reach. They are all pathless, boggy hills that should be tackled in boots and not without respect (Truagh Mheall via forest road: Grade 4, 6 miles/10km, 380m/1,250ft, 4hr return).

Short walks from Sligachan

1 Allt Dearg Beag: just below the bridge over this river (GR 475279) are some exquisite pools and waterfalls (Grade 2, 2hr return; see page 38). The walk can be extended into Coire Riabhach, Coire a' Bhasteir or across the moor to Nead na h-Iolaire, the outlying crag prominent in the view from Sligachan.

2 Allt Dearg Mor: not as attractive as sections of the Allt Dearg Beag, but with some fine waterfalls easily reached on the Bealach a' Mhaim path (Grade 2, 2hr return; see page 32). The walk can be extended to the bealach or into Fionn Choire.

3 Allt Daraich: a fine gorge close to Sligachan which, unusually for the Cuillin, is wooded with birch and rowan. At the head of the gorge is a two-tiered waterfall and above here smaller cascades and limpid

green pools lead up onto the moor at the foot of Glamaig (Grade 2, 1+hr return). To reach the gorge cross the old bridge at Sligachan and follow the left bank (right side) of the Allt Daraich, first along the Coruisk path and then along a muddy path that branches left along the edge of the gorge. Traces of a path continue above the head of the gorge, and the stream can be followed all the way up into secluded Coire na Sgairde (see page 107).

4 Glen Sligachan and the Bloody Stone: the path along Glen Sligachan cuts a dramatic route between the Cuillin and the Red Hills, and the infamous Bloody Stone in Harta Corrie makes an interesting objective for a walk along the glen (Grade 2, 9 miles/14km, 4hr return; see page 74).

5 Loch Sligachan: the peaceful northern shore of Loch Sligachan carries a good path that makes a pleasant coastal stroll. The path begins at the far right-hand corner of the campsite and goes all the way to Peinchorran at Braes road-end (Grade 2, 2+hr return). The walk can be extended to include an exploration of the Braes (see page 196).

6 Loch Mor an Caiplaich (Loch Moar an *Kep*lich, Big Loch of the Horse): an attractive moorland loch hidden above the Portree road, with wooded islands and fine views of the Cuillin. A good but occasionally boggy path to it begins on the west side of the road 600m from Sligachan road junction (GR 483304; look for cairns opposite a gap in the wall on the east side of the road). (Grade 1, 1hr return from roadside.) A less distinct path continues from the loch to the Dunvegan road, but it is overgrown and goes through new forestry plantations; you will need to be able to read a map well to follow it. From the Dunvegan road it can be gained by starting at a rusty iron gate (GR 466314) and then heading diagonally right along the edge of the plantations, but the Portree road approach is much easier.

7 One of the shortest and most enjoyable walks at Sligachan is from the campsite to the hotel, where the merits or otherwise of guidebook writers can be discussed at leisure.

3 sleat

On an island where every major peninsula has its own character the landscape of Sleat is still surprisingly distinctive. While the rest of Skye is mountainous, Sleat is relatively flat, with no point reaching the 300m (1,000ft mark); hence its name (pronounced Slate, meaning Moorland). Although it is north of Moscow its climate is comparable to that of Cornwall. Although it is composed of the oldest rocks on Skye its landscape is the most vibrant.

Apart from the moors that form its backbone, Sleat gives an overriding impression of lushness and luxuriance. Here are gardens, hedgerows and trees; there are even palm trees at Ord, while in the gardens of Armadale Castle there were once more than 1,000 species of exotic trees. Green wooded knolls, winding roads and near horizons give an air of intimacy a world away from the spacious landscapes of northern Skye. The creeks, islets and rocky bays that line the coast have an almost Greek ambience.

From the walker's point of view the one major omission in Sleat's landscape is mountains, and hence the peninsula is visited often only on wet days when the Cuillin are in cloud. On such days the moorland approach and rain-swept coast can seem dismal indeed, and one can imagine the restlessness felt by Dr Johnson when he was stormbound at Ostaig for five days waiting to get off the island.

In sunshine, however, Sleat is transformed into the most colourful place on Skye. In spring cherry blossom and bluebells line the roadside, in summer the sea and sand glisten, in autumn the birch and alder give eye-catching displays of colour. At any time of year there is plenty to see and explore: sea cliffs and caves, sandy bays, romantic castles and a green landscape that is balm to the eyes. Do not dismiss the 'garden of Skye' for its lack of height, for many a Cuillin lover has been captivated by it.

Drumfearn

Unless you arrive by ferry at Armadale there is only one road into Sleat: the Broadford–Armadale road, which in its first few miles crosses a heathery tangle of moor that is more like Rannoch Moor than Skye. After 5 miles (8km) the neck of the peninsula is reached, less than 1¹/2 miles (2¹/2km) wide, and on the right a minor road goes to Drumfearn at the head of Loch Eishort (*Ishort*, Ice Fjord).

(right) *The route to Spar Cave*
(pp86-7) *The Cuillin from picturesque Tarskavaig Bay*

From Drumfearn road-end the shore is only a few minutes' walk away along a cart track (Grade 1), but the seaweed-encrusted upper reaches of Loch Eishort do not make for attractive walking. Nearer the head of the loch two further paths reach the shoreline, one from Drumfearn (GR 682160) and one from the main road (GR 692171), but neither has much to recommend it either as a path or an objective.

Kinloch

Just beyond the Drumfearn turn-off a minor road branches left to Kinloch Lodge Hotel, from where there is a fine walk through natural woodland to Ardnameacan Cottage at the mouth of Loch na Dal (Grade 1, 1+hr return). The path begins on the far side of the hotel; keep left at an immediate fork (the right branch goes down to the shore), then at a fork further into the woods keep right. There are fine views across Loch na Dal to Isleornsay.

The left branch at the second fork is the path to Kylerhea (see page 116); this leads up onto a higher forestry road that also provides a pleasant walk with fine views. *Note:* the forest has been much extended by conifer plantations since the OS map was published, and it is best to stick to the paths.

Isleornsay

Beyond Kinloch the main road reaches Isleornsay, a lush oasis on the east coast where a small community huddles around a sheltered bay. The offshore island of Ornsay, as its Norse name implies (Ebb-tide Island), can be reached AT LOW TIDE ONLY from the eastern end of the bay.

Beyond Isleornsay the road turns inland again past Loch nan Dubhrachan (*Doorachan*, Water-cress). Like many Skye lochs this is reputed to house a legendary water horse, but unlike many it was officially searched for the beast in 1870 (unsuccessfully). If the water horse still lives there today it seems to do little to impede modern fish farming methods.

Castle Camus

The coast is reached again at Knock Bay, where a crag-girt headland is crowned by the gaunt ruins of Castle Camus (Caisteal Chamuis (*Cash*-tyal *Chamm*ish, Bay Castle) in Gaelic and on OS map; also known as Knock Castle). Held at one time by the MacLeods, the

Preshal More from Talisker

stronghold was later captured by the MacDonalds and inhabited by them until they moved to Dunscaith (see below). One MacDonald tale tells of a fifteenth-century siege by the MacLeods, during which one Mary of the castle inspired her MacDonald clansmen to hold out and defeat the enemy. Another tradition says that the castle is haunted by a *glaistig* (a female spirit). Among the eerie ivy-clad ruins of the castle today, where remnants of wall perch at the cliff edge, such things are not beyond belief.

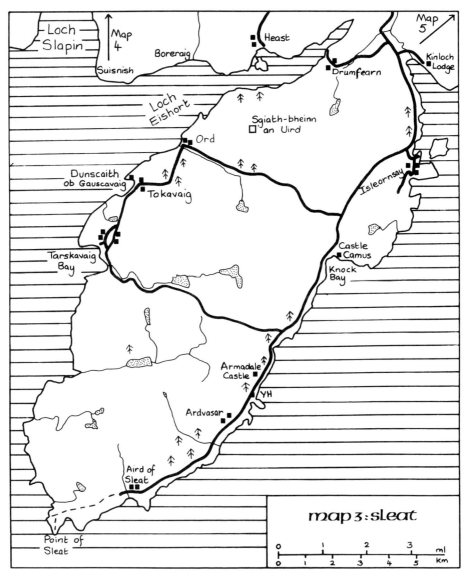

map 3: sleat

To reach the castle take the rough but drivable road (100m south of Toravaig House Hotel) that goes down past a farm to a cottage on the north side of the bay. Walk over the bridge just before the cottage and go right through a gate to pick up a path to the castle, which is only a few minutes' walk away (Grade 1).

Beyond Knock Bay the road continues down the east coast of Sleat to the ferry terminal at Armadale pier and the main Sleat village of Ardvasar. There are wonderful views across the Sound of Sleat to Loch Hourn, Knoydart and Loch Nevis, with the houses of Mallaig and the sands of Morar and Arisaig glinting in the sun.

Armadale Castle

By the roadside at Armadale stand the ruins of Armadale Castle. The present building, more of a stately home than a castle, was begun around 1820 and inhabited until 1925, when it became unsafe. In 1971 the Clan Donald Lands Trust turned what parts remained safe into a 'sculptured ruin' and opened a visitor centre. The museum and exhibition are recommended to anyone interested in Skye history, while the exotic garden shows what can be achieved at this latitude, proving, in the perceptive words of Dr Johnson, that 'the present nakedness of the Hebrides is not wholly the fault of Nature'.

Point of Sleat

The main road ends at Ardvasar, but a minor road continues above the rocky coastline to Aird of Sleat. Many of the bays and headlands along this stretch of coast are well worth exploring, notably the cliffs of Tormore and the stack on the west side of Port na Long. The road ends at Aird Old Church (GR 589008) just beyond Aird of Sleat, and from here there is a fine walk to Point of Sleat at the lonely southern tip of Skye.

From the road-end take the cart track that continues straight on across the moor, becoming an excellently constructed path that winds its way around craggy knolls to a creek on the west coast. Here brambles line the path, remote cottages stand at the waterside and coastal crags merit closer investigation; the amount of unclimbed rock in the area is a climber's dream.

The path crosses the stream that drains into the creek and ends. The path to Point of Sleat, initially indistinct, goes left, following the line of a fence. When the fence turns left continue straight on (the path is temporarily lost at this point), leaving some peat cuttings to your left and making for the defile at the foot of the south-east ridge of the hill marked as spot height 74m on the OS map. At the far end of the defile the path reappears and descends concrete steps to a rocky bay.

Once onto the shore the path goes left along the beach, crosses a narrow isthmus and climbs more steps to reach Point of Sleat lighthouse, perched on a rocky headland at this most southerly point on Skye. Note the contorted folding of the rock and the honeycombed overhangs below the lighthouse on the right (west). Much time could be spent exploring the coastline around the Point before returning to Aird of Sleat (Grade 3, 6 miles/10km, 3+hr return).

West coast
The wild west coast of Sleat is mostly remote and untracked country, relatively flat but indented by numerous rocky bays that are a delight to explore. The most southerly section from Point of Sleat to Tarskavaig Bay is rarely visited on foot; as the eagle flies it is a distance of about 7 miles (11km), but for the coast walker it is much further, and any exploration here would require a commitment beyond the bounds of most people. Between Tarskavaig and Ord is perhaps the finest stretch of coastline in all Sleat (see below), easily reached by a loop road from the main Broadford–Armadale road. North of Ord tamer scenery lines the inner reaches of upper Loch Eishort.

Tarskavaig to Tokavaig
The road to Tarskavaig leaves the Broadford–Armadale road at Ostaig House and crosses the desolate moors that form the backbone of Sleat. Soon a stunning view of the Cuillin opens up across Loch Dhughaill, but if anything the prospect is even more magnificent from Tarskavaig Bay, whose sands and rocky islets provide a perfect foreground.

The shoreline from Tarskavaig Bay to Ob Gauscavaig (Ob Go-ascavaig, East Bay) near Tokavaig makes a fine ramble, with the Cuillin dominating the western horizon beyond the wave-lapped shore. The route follows the foot of shoreline cliffs past a variety of interesting coastal scenery, here seen on a more intimate scale than in the north of Skye. The going is relatively rough and tiring on rounded sea-worn boulders. Without transport at both ends the walk can be curtailed once the best scenery is passed at Uamh Tarskavaig for a short return trip across country to your starting point.

Begin at the car park on the north shore of Tarskavaig Bay (GR 583097); the road to here is surfaced (although unmarked as such on OS map). Continue along a cart track to an old church hidden

further round the bay, then keep walking to reach Tarskavaig Point
— a fascinating rock playground of labyrinthine creeks, canyons,
beaches, rock shelves and other formations.

Beyond Tarskavaig Point take to the beach and boulder-hop up the
coast. The only coastal feature marked on the map is Uamh
Tarskavaig (Oo-a Tarskavaig, Tarskavaig Cave); it is only one of
many caves but it is the largest and is unmistakable when it comes into
view. The covered portion of the cave is some 20m (65ft) deep by 5m
(16ft) high, not large by Skye standards but nevertheless impressive
enough and made something out of the ordinary by its entrance
canyon, in whose southern wall (facing on approach) is a natural arch.
Not far beyond the cave Dunscaith Castle on the north shore of Ob
Gauscavaig comes into view, and soon afterwards the cliffs begin to
peter out and the shoreline rocks become sharper. At this point it is
easier to take to the grass above the beach in order to reach the roadside at Ob Gauscavaig (Grade 3, 3 miles/5km, 2+hr).

Dunscaith Castle
The ruined castle of Dunscaith crowns a rocky headland on the north
side of Ob Gauscavaig bay, in a commanding position at the entrance
to Loch Eishort. To reach it, leave the road at the north end of the bay
and walk out along the shore (Grade 1, 1+hr return).

Few castles can have such a dramatic situation. The rock on which
it stands rises 13m (40ft) from the sea and is surrounded by water on
three sides. On the landward side it is separated from the mainland of
Sleat by a ravine bridged by two arched walls whose intervening
bridge has long since collapsed, making access to the castle awkward.
This may be a blessing in disguise for the modern visitor, however,
for Ossianic tradition tells that the old bridge 'narrowed until it became as narrow as the hair of one's head, and the second time it
shortened until it became as short as an inch, and the third time it grew
slippery as an eel of the river, and the fourth time it rose up on high
against you until it was as tall as the mast of a ship'.

The bridge must have shrunk considerably in recent times for the
gap across the ravine is now only 2m (6ft) long. Nevertheless, the
crossing should not be attempted by those of a nervous disposition as
it requires edging along a narrow ledge beside either arched wall.
Once across, a winding staircase leads to the now grassy summit of
the rock. An alternative route to the top goes via a simple scramble
from the beach to the left of the bridge.

Dunscaith is one of the oldest fortified headlands in the Hebrides, its origins lost in the mists of time and steeped in legend. The castle itself was inhabited by the MacDonalds until they abandoned it in the early seventeenth century for Duntulm at the more prosperous northern end of Skye. One dark episode from this period was the murder of Donald Galloch, third chief of the MacDonalds, by his half-brother Black Archibald on the shore nearby in 1508.

It is with Cuchullin, the legendary Irish warrior-hero, however, that Dunscaith will forever be associated. Before the MacDonalds took up residence it was the legendary home of Sgathach, an Amazon queen famed for her skill in battle training. It was here that Cuchullin came to complete his education, and with the help of Sgathach and her attendants, 'thrice fifty handsome marriageable girls', completed it was. Many were the deeds of Cuchullin at Dunscaith. The grass-topped rock on the shore beneath Dunscaith is Clach Luath (Clach Loo-a, Luath's Stone), where Cuchullin tied his hound Luath on return from the hunt.

Dunscaith is listed as an Ancient Monument but it is not maintained and disintegrates a little more each year in its battle against Skye storms. In places the wall still reaches a height of 5m (16ft) but, like the bridge, it cannot last forever. Long may it remain standing as a haunting reminder of times long past.

Ord

North of Ob Gauscavaig the road winds through Tokavaig village and climbs through its famous ashwood, formerly a sacred grove and now designated a Site of Special Scientific Interest by the Nature Conservancy Council. The shore is reached again at the sands of Ord, where the view across Loch Eishort to the coast of Suisnish and Boreraig, with Bla Bheinn and the Cuillin beyond, has been described as the most magnificent in Scotland. It was here that Alexander Smith stayed when he wrote his classic book *A Summer in Skye* in 1865. Of Loch Eishort he wrote: 'On a fine morning there is not in the whole world a prettier sheet of water.'

One of the offshore islands north of Ord has a fine 'coral' strand that can sometimes be reached dryshod as follows. Beside the shore, at the corner where the road turns eastwards to cross back to the east coast, stands the house named An Acarsaid (An *A*kershut, The Anchorage). Follow the road eastwards up the hill and take the road on the left behind An Acarsaid to a right-hand bend where stands Ord House. Park here and walk straight on past Ord House to pick up a well-built stone path along the coast. The path reaches some holiday chalets and continues left of the last chalet to a bay. A few hundred metres beyond the bay a spit of sand leads out to the coral strand, and AT VERY LOW TIDE ONLY it may be possible to cross dryshod. (Grade 2, 1½+hr return.) It is possible to continue along the coast to Drumfearn, but shoreline crags, seaweed and trees make for frustrating going.

In the gardens of An Acarsaid, accessible to the public by a gate at the corner of the shoreline road, are some interesting artefacts, including the skeleton of a water horse! On a knoll behind the houses above An Acarsaid stands a memorial cairn to St Congan, who preached here in about 720. The ruins of his chapel no longer exist, although marked on the map as Teampuill Chaon.

There is much bare white quartzite in the Ord district, including a conspicuous outcrop on the beach at Ord and an old quarry on the road across the peninsula. The summit plateaus of the Sgiath-bheinns, between which the road runs, carry extensive quartzite pavements that glisten from afar in the sunlight.

The Sgiath-bheinns (*Skee*-a Vain, Wing Mountain) are not high hills and their ascent is boggy, but once on top, their long summit plateaus provide fine views and good going on exposed rock. Sgiath bheinn an Uird (of Ord) to the north of the road is the highest of the Sgiath-bheinns (295m/968ft) and provides the easiest ascent and best views. To reach the summit begin anywhere west of the woods of Coill a' Ghasgain (*Cull*-ya Ghasgin, Wood of the Green). The watery summit panorama includes Loch Eishort to the west, the Inner Sound to the north and the Sound of Sleat to the east. Note also the beautiful hill lochan of Loch na Starsaich (*Stars*ich, Barrier), cupped in a hollow to the north of the summit (Grade 3, 2hr return).

Sgiath-bheinn Tokavaig and Sgiath-bheinn Chrossavaig to the south of the road are of similar character to Sgiath-bheinn an Uird, but their ascent is steeper and involves the fording of the Ord river.

Note that Ord appears on the south-east corner of the Outdoor Leisure Map.

4 strath

The old parish of Strath contains the most diverse scenery on Skye. Its mountainous areas contain soaring gabbro and basalt peaks (4.1 Bla Bheinn, 4.2 The Garbh-bheinn Group), eroded granite domes (4.3 The Red Hills) and rough sandstone hills (4.4 The Kylerhea Group). The moors and coastline are no less fascinating, with ruined villages such as those of Suisnish and Boreraig (4.5), limestone caves (4.6) and deep coast-to-coast glens (4.7). South of the mountains lies the peninsula of Strathaird, whose coastline is entirely different again, with sea caves and sandstone cliffs and fine paths by which to explore them (4.8).

4.1 Bla Bheinn

Bla Bheinn (928m/3,044ft, Blah Vain, often anglicised to Blaven, possible meanings: Blue Mountain, Warm Mountain, Mountain of Bloom)
Clach Glas (787m/2,582ft, Clach Glass, Grey Stone)

When viewed across Loch Slapin from near Torrin the bold gabbro peak of Bla Bheinn presents one of the most compelling mountain sights in Britain. That great pioneer of Cuillin exploration, Alexander Nicolson, considered it to be the shapeliest mountain on Skye. Several poets have been moved by it to put pen to paper, notably Alexander Smith, whose lengthy Victorian eulogy, beginning with the line 'O wonderful mountain of Blaavin', is worth keeping in mind as you toil up the stony summit slopes.

Bla Bheinn has a dramatic appearance from all angles, with the fearsome north face of the east ridge and the soaring rock tower of Clach Glas providing some classic rock climbs. Energetic rock climbers can combine the traverse of Bla Bheinn and Clach Glas with the traverse of the main Cuillin ridge to form the Greater Cuillin Traverse, a major test of mountaineering competence and stamina that involves nearly 4,300m (14,000ft) of ascent.

For ordinary mortals there are two routes to the summit in fine weather: via the south ridge and via Coire Uaigneich (Ooaignich, Remote). The south ridge rises attractively in one clean sweep from beautiful Camasunary; it gives superb views of the main Cuillin ridge across Srath na Creitheach (Stra na Cree-ach, Valley of the Brushwood) and provides a surprisingly dry ascent even after rain. The Coire Uaigneich route is less scenic but is shorter and affords close-up views of the cliffs of the east ridge. Neither route need involve more than elementary handwork, although both give ample scope for scrambling of all grades.

The south ridge route approaches Camasunary by the Land-Rover track from Kilmarie (see page 134 for description). In the superb view from Am Mam across Camasunary to the Cuillin, the sharp crest and purity of line of the south ridge do much to enhance the grandeur of the scene. Twenty metres before the hairpin bend on the descent from Am Mam to Camasunary, branch right (look for cairn) on a path that cuts across the hillside to the Abhainn nan Leac (*A*-win nan Lyachk, River of Flat Stones) at the foot of the south ridge, where there are some picturesque waterfalls.

The path continues beyond the river to join the Camasunary–Sligachan path and should be followed for another couple of hundred metres to a large cairn on a boulder on the right. Turn right here on another path from Camasunary that climbs the south ridge.

The lower section of the ridge consists of steep grass slopes that lead to the craggy brow seen above. The path bypasses the crags on the right to reach the increasingly rocky upper ridge whose solid gabbro is a pleasure to negotiate. Scrambling of all grades can be sought, or avoided almost altogether by keeping to the path, which takes the line of least resistance. The ridge eventually merges with the south-east slopes of the mountain to culminate at the stony dome of the south top.

The higher north top lies 200m away across a short dip whose negotiation involves some simple scrambling. The easiest route descends a steep earthy gully to just below the dip. A more direct and interesting route involves a simple if slightly exposed scramble along a ledge on the left near the top of this gully. From the dip the north top, perched at the edge of the northern cliffs above Clach Glas, is reached without difficulty. The view from the two tops across Srath na Creitheach to the Cuillin is superb (Grade 5, 4 miles/6km, 1,010m/ 3,300ft; 4½hr; 7hr return).

In adverse weather return via the route of ascent; if in doubt the easiest line is unfailingly to the left (east). In fine weather a return via the lochan-studded plateau of Slat Bheinn (Slat Vain, Wand or Stately Mountain) makes a delightful contrast to the ascent route. From the south top descend the steep stony south-east slopes that rim Coire Uaigneich; in places there is an indistinct path, partly cairned. At the foot of the slope is a small lochan, and beyond that a dip and a short rise to a point marked on the Outdoor Leisure map as 625m.

From this point stroll across the flat grassy plateau of Slat Bheinn to pick up the Camasunary–Kilmarie Land-Rover track at Am Mam. The many moorland lochans, clear and full of aquatic plants, add charm to the scene, and the going is surprisingly dry, despite the marsh marked on the Outdoor Leisure map (7hr round trip).

The Coire Uaigneich route begins at the foot of the Allt na Dunaiche (Owlt na *Doonich*-ya, Burn of Sorrow) near the head of Loch Slapin (GR 561217). Cars can be parked beside a bridge 150m south of here. Take the path on the right side of the river up into Choire a' Caise (*Kasha*, Steepness). There are some fine pools and

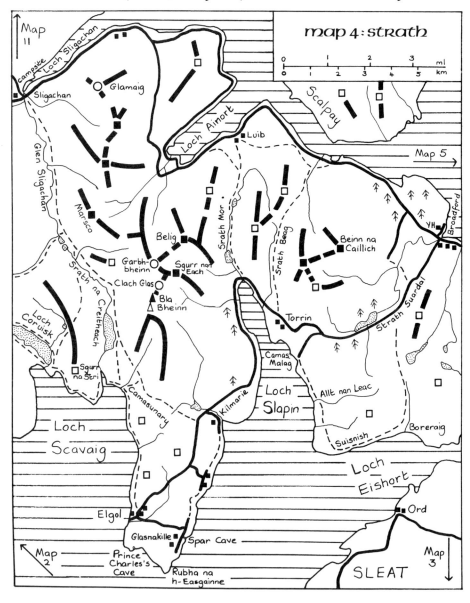

waterfalls along the way, and the cheerful character of the tumbling river is in direct contrast to its name, which according to tradition derives from a shieling where seven girls were killed by supernatural forces.

The path bears left across the Allt na Dunaiche and climbs steeply beneath the towering east face of Bla Bheinn into the bowl of Coire Uaigneich, which is unusually rich in Alpine flora owing to a small outcrop of Jurassic limestone. The path curves right into the heart of the corrie and then turns sharp right to climb towards the skyline of the east ridge; it is indistinct in places but well cairned.

Once onto the east ridge the path meanders up stony slopes (with optional scrambling) to the summit, with occasional glimpses of Clach Glas seen across the yawning gullies of the north face (Grade 5, 3 miles/5km, 920m/3,000ft, 3½hr; 6hr return). If crossing to the south top, the obvious line from the dip between the two tops is along the ledge described above; the earthy gully a few metres down to the left provides an easier route.

In fine weather a descent from the south top to Coire Uaigneich can be made via the south-east slope, as described above. At the foot of the slope cairns bear left in front of the lochan to mark a further stony descent into the corrie; alternatively, continue to the dip a short distance beyond the lochan and descend grass slopes.

The complex north face of the east ridge, which faces Clach Glas, is a no-go area for non-climbers except for two stony gullies with large cairns at their heads. The higher gully descends into Coire Dubh (Doo, Black) on the Srath na Creitheach side of the mountain. The lower gully opens onto the stone shoot below the Bla Bheinn– Clach Glas bealach and eventually descends to Choire a' Caise. It is not an attractive descent route until the lower scree is reached, but it does provide close-up views of the fantastic architecture of the north face. The rib of rock on the right (east) of the gully is The Great Prow, which looks very impressive from below.

The bealach between Bla Bheinn and Clach Glas is accessible by stone shoots on either side, but cannot be recommended as an objective for the non-climber. Although it affords magnificent views of the north face cliffs, the ascent to it is purgatorial and little progress in the direction of either Bla Bheinn or Clach Glas is possible without rock climbing and complex route-finding.

Ascents from the Srath na Creitheach side of Bla Bheinn are also hard going and cannot be recommended unless you happen to be in the vicinity. The only straightforward route to the summit is via the

Coire Dubh gully noted above. The long gully that descends all the way to the strath from the dip between the two tops looks tempting from above but should be avoided owing to complications lower down.

4.2 THE GARBH-BHEINN GROUP

To the north of Bla Bheinn and Clach Glas stand three craggy peaks whose narrow ridges provide pleasant scrambling: Garbh-bheinn, Sgurr nan Each and Belig. The proximity of the three summits, clustered around the head of the Allt Aigeann (*Aiken*, Abyss), would make the traverse of their connecting ridges a fine round were it not for a frustrating rock tower on the west ridge of Sgurr nan Each, which demands ropework. The walker is thus faced with a logistical problem in deciding how best to tackle the peaks.

Sgurr nan Each (716m/2,350ft, Skoor nan Yech, Peak of the Horses)

Sgurr nan Each must be climbed on its own as a separate expedition as there is only one route to the top that does not involve rock climbing — the south-east ridge. The foot of this ridge is reached from the head of Loch Slapin by the path along the Allt na Dunaiche (see page 98). The route up the ridge begins gently on grass and heather, steepens over broken ground to the east top and then veers west to the summit. The craggy basalt slopes leading up to the east top are very broken, and although scrambling can be sought there is much awkward stony ground to be negotiated (craggier on the right, stonier on the left).

Beyond the east top the going improves as solid gabbro is encountered, and a short simple scramble soon leads to the summit (Grade 5, 2 miles/3km, 730m/2,400ft, 2½hr; 5hr return). From here it is a further ten-minute scramble (occasionally hard on the crest, easier below on the left) to the top of the rock tower on the west ridge. It is unfortunate that this one frustrating obstacle bars a connection to the main spine of the Garbh-bheinn group.

Returning to the dip between the main top and the east top, a grassy slope on the right (south) makes a tempting descent route, but it soon leads onto steep broken ground that is no improvement on the route of ascent. A stony gully on the left (north) of this dip, however, makes a straightforward descent to the glen of the Allt Aigeann (see below) should you wish a different way down.

Belig (686m/2,250ft, Birch Tree Bark)
Glas Bheinn Mhor (570m/1,870ft. Glass Vain Voar, Big Grey
  Mountain)

Belig can be climbed from either Loch Slapin or Loch Ainort. In good
weather a round from Loch Slapin that climbs the fine south-east
ridge and descends via the south-west ridge and the beautiful streamway of the Allt Aigeann is recommended. Begin at the head of Loch
Slapin and cross the grassy flats above the road to reach the Allt
Aigeann at the point where curiously (except after heavy rain) it disappears into its stony bed. Sheep paths lead up either bank of the
stream to the foot of the south-east ridge where the good going continues on short, sheep-cropped grass.

At about 250m (800ft) the ridge steepens appreciably among small
crags (look for sheep paths) and then becomes rockier and more interesting. A prominent rock tower goes direct (easier on the right,
harder and more exposed on the left) or can be avoided altogether on
the right. Above here the crest of the ridge develops into a delightfully
simple scramble, quite narrow and exposed in parts, but with no unavoidable problems. Note that the rock is basalt and hence less adhesive than Cuillin gabbro. A flat grassy section is reached before the
final rise to the summit, from where there are fine views northwards
across Loch Ainort and the Red Hills to the east coast of Trotternish
(Grade 5, 2 miles/3km, 690m/2,250ft, 2½hr; 4hr return).

For a different return route descend the south-west ridge to the
Bealach na Beiste (*Baish*-tcha, Beast) between Belig and Garbh-
bheinn. This bealach is named after the legendary water horse of Loch
na Sguabaidh in Srath Mor (see page 124), which was killed here by a
MacKinnon. The upper part of the ridge would provide an interesting
scramble were it not for a loose drystone wall that takes the crestline
and makes it necessary to resort to an indistinct path below on the
right. Lower down towards the bealach the ridge broadens onto loose
stony slopes that provide rough going.

From the bealach it is possible to continue to Garbh-bheinn (see
below) or descend steep broken slopes to the corrie of the Allt
Aigeann and then use sheep paths on the left bank of that stream to
descend to your starting point (5hr round trip). The Allt Aigeann is
one of the most beautiful streams on Skye. Just before it turns to
descend into the lower glen, at a tiered waterfall, are a series of
breathtakingly beautiful pools and cascades, and all the way down the
glen are pools and waterfalls that make the descent a constant delight.

From Loch Ainort the ascent of Belig is less interesting but easier, and is recommended in wet weather when the grass and rocks of the south-east ridge are slippery. A round that includes Garbh-bheinn and Glas Bheinn Mhor is also possible. Like Beinn na Cro (its neighbour across Srath Mor), Glas Bheinn Mhor appears as an unprepossessing heap of scree from most angles, but it is a wonderful viewpoint above Loch Ainort, and from the bealach between it and Belig it is easily ascended by its south ridge, following the line of an old wall. The gentle north ridge rising above Luib also makes a pleasant ascent route from the lochside.

From Loch Ainort Belig is climbed by its north ridge, the foot of which is gained by heading directly across the moor from the roadside. About halfway up there is a steeper, craggier section, and above here the ridge rises more uniformly to the summit (Grade 5, 2 miles/ 3km, 670m/2,200ft, 2½hr). Unless continuing to Garbh-bheinn the best route is to reverse the north ridge as far as the steep section, then descend scree slopes either left (west) to regain the moor or right (east) to the bealach leading to Glas Bheinn Mhor (4hr round trip).

Garbh-bheinn (806m/2,644ft, *Garrav* Vain, Rough Mountain)

Like Belig, Garbh-bheinn is readily climbed from Loch Ainort via its north ridge. From the roadside cross the moor and climb Druim Eadar Da Choire (*Dreem Aitar Dah Choira*, Ridge Between Two Corries) to the grassy hump (Point 489m on the Outdoor Leisure map) between Marsco and Garbh-bheinn. Beyond here there is a short dip and then the north ridge of Garbh-bheinn rises steeply ahead. The final section narrows interestingly to provide a fine simple scramble to the summit (Grade 5, 2½ miles/4km, 840m/2,750ft, 2½hr).

The best descent is by the same route (4 hr). The north-east ridge descending to the Bealach na Beiste offers scrambling opportunities at first but soon develops into a uniformly steep, stony slope that is penitentially loose and awkward.

If you wish to include Belig in the round, whether from Loch Ainort or Loch Slapin, it is better to climb Belig first in order to tackle Garbh-bheinn's north-east ridge on ascent. The Loch Slapin round is recommended as it includes Belig's south-east ridge and also Garbh-bheinn's south-east ridge, which leads onwards towards Sgurr nan Each and Clach Glas, the imposing rock tower that bars a continuation to Bla Bheinn. The south-east ridge of Garbh-bheinn requires

The Garbh-bheinn group and Bla Bheinn from the Beinn Deargs

care at the top, where it is steep, broken and loose, but it develops into another pleasant scramble as it approaches the bealach below Sgurr nan Each. From this bealach scree slopes on the left can be descended to the gorge of the Allt Aigeann and the beautiful lower glen noted above (7hr complete round).

Before descending from the bealach it is worth exploring the west ridge of Sgurr nan Each. Halfway up, a level ridge branches right towards Clach Glas, and above this junction the ridge narrows suddenly across gabbro slabs to the impassable rock tower described above. Do not be tempted into the gullies on either side of the tower as these lead onto difficult ground with no way back up to the ridge.

Retrace your steps and wander out along the level ridge to the bealach at the foot of Clach Glas. From here it is possible to descend a stone shoot into Choire a' Caise to reach the path along the Allt na Dunaiche (see page 98). The tempting stone shoot on the Srath na Creitheach side of the bealach, which can be seen descending through a rock window, develops into a rock climb and should be avoided.

Beyond the bealach the summit of Clach Glas rears up improbably 162m (532ft) overhead. The ascent is not possible for non-climbers; it begins as a hard scramble but becomes a rock climb higher up.

4.3 THE RED HILLS

Across the trench of Glen Sligachan the rounded granite peaks of the Red Hills line up incongruously against the bold gabbro peaks of the Black Cuillin. In such exalted company their featureless appearance does not immediately spur one to action, yet their purity of line and sheer physical presence are such that they eventually become impossible to ignore. Ascents are tough (the geologist John MacCulloch named the hills Red after their long fans of granite scree), but once up, Red Hill walking has much to recommend it, with easy ridges to wander along and superb views.

Glamaig (775m/2,542ft, *Glah*-mak, Deep Gorge)

Glamaig is the epitome of Red Hill architecture. From Sligachan it appears as an enormous cone-shaped mountain that dominates the moor, but its true shape is more that of a sphinx, whose long backbone runs out towards Sconser at the mouth of Loch Sligachan. The view from the summit is exceptional even by Skye standards.

The only ascent route not bedevilled by scree is the north ridge from near Sconser. Begin 400m south of the Moll turn-off (GR 536314), at the point where a roadside fence does a right-angled turn to head up the ridge. Climb to the north top (An Coileach, An *Cul-lach*, The Cockerel), then continue across a shallow dip up to the short grassy ridge that forms the main summit (Sgurr Mhairi, Skoor Varry, Mary's Peak) (Grade 4, 2 miles/3km, 800m/2,600ft, 2½hr; 4hr return).

The view from the summit demands superlatives. Westwards is beautiful Loch Bracadale on the far side of the island, northwards is the coast of Trotternish and the whole of Raasay, eastwards are Scalpay and the islands of the Inner Sound, while southwards lie the inimitable Cuillin, with Bla Bheinn looking especially magnificent.

The ascent from Sligachan is unrelentingly tedious and requires more than the usual amount of motivation, yet a directissima line to the summit does have a certain appeal. The slopes are very steep, are riddled with scree and should be approached with care; you are unlikely to remain upright for the whole of the ascent. Grass rakes can be used to ease the going lower down, but these should be avoided in wet weather, when a slip could be disastrous. Also to be avoided are the

The cliffs of Oronsay, with the Talisker-Fiskavaig coastline behind

broken crags on the left as viewed from Sligachan, where the going is very steep and dangerous.

If motivation falters during the ascent it may be helpful to meditate on the view that awaits you at the summit. It may also be useful to recall the exploits of a certain Havildar Harkabir Thapa, a Gurkha soldier who in 1899 reached the summit from the old bridge at Sligachan in 37 minutes, followed by a descent of 18 minutes. And this in bare feet. The higher you climb the more Havildar Harkabir Thapa will rise in your estimation (Grade 5, 2 miles/3km, 770m/ 500ft, 2½hr).

The easiest descent route to Sligachan goes down the south-east slopes of the mountain to the Bealach na Sgairde (*Skarr*-stcha, Scree) between Glamaig and the Beinn Deargs. Care is required in mist as the natural trend of the summit ridge of Sgurr Mhairi is out towards cliffs; the broken slope leading to the bealach is further right and is very steep; it would make a tough ascent route but scree runs make it easy to descend.

Scree runs continue from the bealach into Coire na Sgairde, where the Allt Daraich (*Darrich*, Oak Timber) is as inviting as any Cuillin burn and where in summer dragonflies of many colours add to the picturesqueness of the scene. Lower down is a path on the left bank of the Allt Daraich above a wooded gorge, which has some fine water-falls and pools, and this path eventually meets the Glen Sligachan path near Sligachan (4hr round trip).

The Beinn Deargs:
Beinn Dearg Mhor (732m/2,402ft, Ben *Jerrak* Voar, Big Red Mountain)
Beinn Dearg Mheadhonach (652m/2,139ft, *Vee*-onach, Middle)

On the far side of the Bealach na Sgairde from Glamaig the main spine of the Red Hills continues over the Beinn Deargs to form an increas-ingly interesting traverse that makes a fine extension to the ascent of Glamaig. From the bealach the steep stony ascent of more than 300m (1,000ft) to Beinn Dearg Mhor looks monstrous, but secure good-sized rocks enable you to bound up in true Gurkha style and soon reach the north ridge and the summit.

Beyond the summit the going becomes increasingly pleasant and interesting. The stony ridge leads on across the Bealach Mosgaraidh (*Mosk*-arry, Dry-rot shieling) to the summit of Beinn Dearg

The wild Greshornish coastline

Mheadhonach, which has a fine narrow summit ridge a few hundred metres long, with a cairn at each end. From here the descent back to the moor follows a cairned path down the summit boulder field and along the level ridge of Druim na Ruaige (Dreem na *Roo*- ig-ya, Ridge of the Hunt), where there are welcome patches of turf to add some spring to the step.

From the end of Druim na Ruaige it is possible to descend either to the path along Glen Sligachan or, more interestingly, into Coire na Sgairde (see above). Note also that upper Coire na Sgairde can be reached from the summit of Beinn Dearg Mheadhonach by a descent of the Teanga Bheag (*Tchen*ga Vake, Little Tongue) to the north of Druim na Ruaige (Round trip of Glamaig and the Beinn Deargs from Sligachan 7 miles/11km, 1,230m/4,050ft, 6¹/₂hr).

The traverse of the two Beinn Deargs without the ascent of Glamaig is best done in the reverse direction to that described above, enabling an ascent by path along Druim na Ruaige and a descent by scree slopes from the Bealach na Sgairde. This route is the easiest route in the Red Hills, with a stroll along their finest ridges and a descent via the lovely Allt Daraich, but it misses the view from Glamaig (Grade 4, 6 miles/10km, 770m/2,250ft, 5hr).

Marsco (736m/2,414ft, Sea-gull Rock)

Marsco is the most isolated and attractive of the Red Hills. Separated from Beinn Dearg Mheadhonach to the north by a 280m (920ft) bealach and from Garbh-bheinn to the south by a 320m (1,050ft) bealach, it provides an attractive backdrop to the view along Glen Sligachan. It is a much more sturdy mountain than Glamaig and the Beinn Deargs and can be climbed without resort to scree.

The mountain can be approached from either Sligachan or Loch Ainort. From Sligachan follow the Coruisk path along Glen Sligachan (see page 77) as far as the Allt na Measarroch, then leave it to follow a less distinct path up the near (right) bank of that stream. Note that this was also the route taken by Prince Charlie on his journey across Skye (see page 17). The path continues as far as the bealach of the Mam a' Phobuill (Mahm a Foe-pill, People's Moor), where it becomes lost among sheep paths, but leave it before here and climb steep grass slopes to the north-west ridge and narrow summit of Marsco (Grade 4, 4 miles/6km, 730m/2,400ft, 3hr; 5 hr return).

Glamaig from the old bridge, Sligachan

The excellent all-round view from the summit encompasses Harta Corrie and the main Cuillin ridge, Loch Ainort and the isles of the Inner Sound, and Bla Bheinn towering over the lump of Ruadh Stac (*Roo*-a Stachk, Red Stack). Note especially the distinctive colourings of Am Fraoch-choire (Frœch, Heather), where the grass slopes of Marsco meet the red rocks of Ruadh Stac.

For an alternative return route, continue over the top of Marsco and down the south-east ridge to a dip, then follow an old fence down around the eastern rim of Coire nan Laogh (Looh, Calf) to the Mam a' Phobuill to regain the path along the Allt na Measarroch (5¹/₂hr round trip). It is also possible to extend the day by a descent southwards into Am Fraoch-choire and Glen Sligachan. The extremely rough direct descent from the dip into the corrie is not recommended, but the south-east ridge makes an interesting way down, with the waters of Am Fraoch-choire's beautifully clear stream beckoning below.

From Loch Ainort the ascent of Marsco is shorter but mostly pathless, and the Cuillin remain hidden from view until the summit is reached. Begin at the Eas a' Bhradain (GR 533265; Aiss a *Vratt*in, Salmon Waterfall) and follow the left bank of the stream past the waterfall into Coire nam Bruadaran (traces of path). Hold to the tributary that climbs past more waterfalls into Coire nan Laogh and follow the fence up the eastern rim of this corrie onto the summit ridge. Descend by the same route or by the south-east ridge (Grade 4, 2¹/₂ miles/4km, 720m/2,350ft, 2¹/₂hr; 4¹/₂hr return).

Beinn na Caillich (732m/2,403ft, Bain na *Kyle*-yich, Mountain of the Old Woman)
Beinn Dearg Mhor (709m/2,326ft, Bain *Jerr*ak Voar, Big Red Mountain)
Beinn Dearg Bheag (584m/1,916ft, Bain *Jerr*ak Vake, Little Red Mountain)

Of Skye's two Beinn na Caillichs, that to the immediate west of Broadford is the higher and more imposing. It is one of the most prominent hills on Skye, its bald grey dome towering over the moorland and capped by a huge cairn that is visible for miles around. The shortest and time-honoured ascent begins from near Coire-chatachan at the end of the minor road which leaves the Broadford–Portree road just north-west of Broadford (GR 619227) — note the limestone outcrops on the east side of this road. The road-end can also be reached by a path from the Broadford–Elgol road that begins 150m

Beinn na Caillich towers over Broadford

south of the right-angled bend at the head of Strath Suardal (GR 626218); there is a footbridge across the Broadford river.

Coire-chat-achan means Corrie of the Place of the Wildcats, this being the last stronghold of wildcats on Skye before their extermination. It was from Coire-chat-achan House, now ruined, that Pennant climbed Beinn na Caillich in 1772 to make the first recorded ascent of any mountain on Skye. It was here also that Johnson and Boswell spent two nights in 1773 during their tour of Skye, and it was of Beinn na Caillich that Johnson made his one and only famous throwaway remark on the mountains of Skye: 'The hill behind the house we did not climb. The weather was rough and the height and steepness discouraged us.' That Johnson could travel the length and breadth of Skye and fail to find at least the Cuillin worthy of note is astonishing, but no more so than the thought of him attempting Beinn na Caillich in any weather.

The foreshortened view from Coire-chat-achan of the steep stony slopes of the Caillich is enough to give anyone pause for thought, and one may well feel the 'lethargy of indolence' that Boswell noted in his journal here. The ascent, however, is not as steep and formidable as it seems, and once up there is a fine horseshoe ridge walk around Coire Gorm (*Gorram*, Blue) to Beinn Dearg Mhor and Beinn Dearg Bheag, with stunning views across the islands of the Inner Sound.

From the road-end the best going across the moor will be found by aiming for the right-hand skyline. Once onto the bouldery hillside any way up is as good as any other, so choose whichever boulder ruckle appeals and go for it. The rock on Beinn na Caillich has weathered into larger blocks than on the other Red Hills, and boulder-hopping enables height to be gained fast. Be patient with the convex slope and the unexpectedly grassy summit will be reached without excessive effort (2hr).

Walk to the edge of the short summit plateau for the superb northern view. It may not include the Inner and Outer Hebridean islands that are such a feature of west coast views, but the islands of the Inner Sound (Raasay, Scalpay, Pabay etc) make a glorious alternative, with the peaks of the mainland forming a fine backdrop. Beneath the huge summit cairn is said to lie a Norse princess, entombed here at her own wish so that she could forever face the land of her birth.

From the west end of the plateau (care in mist) a ridge leads off around the tight horseshoe of Coire Gorm. It descends pleasantly on grass and boulders, then narrows attractively above steep corrie head-walls on each side to the summit of Beinn Dearg Mhor (3hr). There is a path most of the way.

Another large cairn adorns the stony summit of Beinn Dearg Mhor, from where there is a magnificent unimpeded view of Bla Bheinn. The route onward to Beinn Dearg Bheag goes down the steep and featureless scree slopes of the south-west face to the Bealach Coire Sgreamhach (*Scree*-avach, Loathsome). In mist great care is required if the correct line to the bealach is to be found. The scree precludes doing the route in the reverse direction, which would otherwise have the advantage of ending the day on the viewpoint of Beinn na Caillich.

A short rocky ascent from the bealach leads to the summit of Beinn Dearg Bheag, which sports yet another large cairn (4hr). Each of the three peaks on the horseshoe has an attractively different view; that from Beinn Dearg Bheag includes a fine vista down Loch Slapin across the Cuillin Sound to Rum, and also across Strath Suardal to the fascinating country between Loch Slapin and Loch Eishort (see 4.5).

To complete the horseshoe descend the gentle ridge curving down around Coire Odhar (*Oa*-ar, Dun-coloured), picking up a path among the heather and boulders. Go straight off the end of the ridge down steep heathery slopes across the mouth of Coire Gorm and make a beeline across the moor back to your starting point. The going underfoot is not the best of the day, but the sweeping panorama more than compensates, for before you lies the glorious Inner Sound, fringed with the white cottages of Broadford and Breakish like a string of pearls, and in the midst of all, the island of Pabay, set like a jewel in the sea (Grade 4, 5 miles/8km, 980m/3,200ft, 5hr).

4.4 THE KYLERHEA GROUP

At the eastern tip of Skye, dominating the straits of Kyle Akin (*Akin*) and Kyle Rhea (Ray), stand the two commanding viewpoints of Sgurr na Coinnich and Beinn na Caillich. From Kylerhea ferry their steep slopes rise directly from the sea to give an impression of great height, yet they are easily climbed from the Bealach Udal (279m/ 915ft) at the high point of the Kylerhea–Broadford road. On the opposite side of the bealach the lower Ben Aslak completes a trio of hills above Kylerhea which are characterised by rough terrain, numerous lochan-filled hollows and fine views.

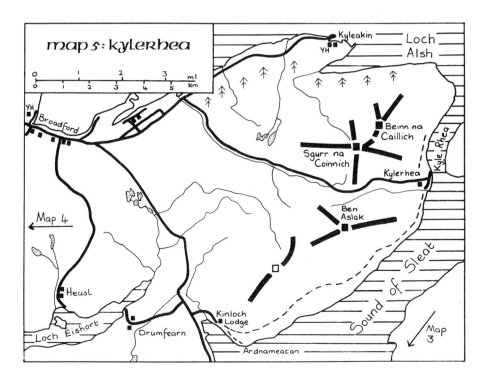

Sgurr na Coinnich (739m/2,424ft, *Coan*-yich, Moss)

The direct ascent of Sgurr na Coinnich from the Bealach Udal involves very rough going on tussocky grass and heather liberally strewn with boulders; easier going will be found further east, on the south ridge. Begin a few hundred metres east of the bealach, at the top of the steep descent to Kylerhea. Aim to the left of a prominent buttress to gain the south ridge. The going gets easier as height is gained and eventually becomes very pleasant on short turf. Keep a lookout for a beautiful lochan hidden in a hollow. Higher up, another lochan marks the start of the broad summit ridge, at the far end of which lies the highest point (Grade 4, 1½ miles/2km, 460m/1,500ft, 1½+hr; 2½hr return).

From the summit there are tremendous panoramic views: southwards is the Sleat peninsula, westwards over Broadford the Cuillin and the mountains of Strath crowd upon each other, northwards lies the Inner Sound, with Kyleakin at your feet, and eastwards are Kylerhea, Loch Alsh and the mainland peaks. The two kyles are traditionally named after Acunn and Readh, two brothers of the legendary Fiennes, a race of powerful hunters and fighters. Readh was drowned during an unsuccessful attempt to leap the strait; both brothers were buried at Glenelg.

Beinn na Caillich (733m/2,405ft, *Kyle*-yich, Old Woman)

Beinn na Caillich is separated from Sgurr na Coinnich by the deep Bealach nam Mulachag, whose negotiation involves a 170m (560ft) descent and reascent, repeated in reverse on the return journey to the Bealach Udal. From Sgurr na Coinnich the Caillich appears as a steep stony dome, but a route can be picked out on grassy rakes to ease the going; the ascent is worthwhile for the unrivalled summit views of the kyles and Loch Alsh. The mountain is traditionally named after Grainnhe (wife of Fionn, chief of the Fiennes), who is said to be buried at the summit (Grade 4, 2 miles/3km, 330m/1,100ft, 1½hr return from Sgurr na Coinnich).

Beinn na Caillich can also be climbed from Kyleakin, but the ascent involves a long moorland approach, guarded by forestry plantations, that can hardly be recommended. If nevertheless approaching from this side, the best route onto the open moor takes the forestry road 1½ miles (2km) west of Kyleakin (GR 733258).

Ben Aslak (610m/2,001ft, Mountain of the Ridge or Hollow)

Ben Aslak is a less imposing hill than its two neighbours across the Bealach Udal, but its fine complex summit makes a good short tramp. From the bealach climb heathery slopes towards the summit of Beinn Bheag (Vake, Little), then cut left across the Kylerhea river onto the north-west ridge of Ben Aslak. Short turf and rock ease the ascent to the broad and knobbly summit ridge, which has a top at each end and a fine lochan in the middle.

The west top is the higher of the two tops and has the better views southwards over Sleat and westwards over Broadford to the Cuillin. The east top has better views of Kyle Rhea, Loch Alsh and the magnificent mountains of Knoydart across the mouth of Loch Hourn (Grade 4, 1½ miles/2km, 340m/1,100ft, 1½hr; 2½hr return).

South-west of Ben Aslak are two similar but slightly lower hills — Beinn na Seamraig (Bain na *Shem*raik, Shamrock Mountain) and Beinn Dubh a' Bhealaich (Bain Doo a *Vyal*ich, Black Mountain of the Pass), which are rarely visited owing to the length of their moorland approaches.

Circular walk
A circular route over Beinn na Caillich, Sgurr na Coinnich and Ben Aslak, which involves no retracing of steps, is possible by beginning at sea level at Kylerhea. From Kylerhea climb directly up Beinn Bhuidhe (*Voo*-ya, Yellow) and cut right beneath Sgurr na Coinnich to the Bealach nam Mulachag. From here climb Beinn na Caillich, then return to the bealach and follow the routes described above across Sgurr na Coinnich and the Bealach Udal to Ben Aslak. Descend Ben Aslak's north-east ridge (a lovely gentle descent, with fine views all the way) to reach the coastal path from Kylerhea to Kinloch Lodge Hotel, and so return to your starting point (Grade 4, 8½ miles/14km, 1,230m/4,050ft, 7hr).

Coastal paths
Until recently it was possible to climb Beinn na Caillich from the coastal path that ran along the narrows from Kylerhea to the lighthouse at GR 789223, but afforestation in Coire Buidhe now prevents this. The new forestry road that crosses the hillside above the lighthouse (follow signs to Otter Haven) offers good views along the kyle (at least until the trees grow). Kylerhea Otter Haven is a conservation

project whose aim is to maintain the coastal strip as an otter habitat. An observation hide, equipped with displays, was opened near the lighthouse in 1988 (Grade 1, 1½ miles/2km, 1hr return).

The fine coastal path from Kylerhea to Kinloch Lodge Hotel is a considerable undertaking but a magnificent walk if transport can be arranged at both ends. The path begins in Kylerhea village, reached by an unsurfaced road that leaves the Kylerhea–Broadford road at the point where it turns away from the shore. Beyond a house the unsurfaced road bears right as a grassy cart track alongside the Kylerhea river. The path leaves this track at the first house on the left (GR 785205) and goes left beside a fence to cross the river at a bridge.

The path continues south-westwards along the Sound of Sleat and climbs high above the shore to give extensive views. On the approach to Kinloch Lodge Hotel, the fine natural woodland has been much extended by conifer plantations; the path is overgrown in parts, but this adds to its mysteriousness as it plunges through the undergrowth. Upon arrival at the forestry road above the hotel (marked by a cairn and post), the continuation to the hotel is difficult to locate. Look for a cairn on the left half-hidden by bracken, just before a right-hand bend on the forestry road; the path is initially indistinct but a shallow diagonal line should pick it up, and in any case the trees are sparse here. For other routes in the vicinity of Kinloch Lodge Hotel see page 89 (Grade 3, 7 miles/11km, 280m/900ft, 4hr).

Caisteal Maol (Cash-tyal Mœl, Hill Castle)

If you are in the vicinity of Kyleakin, the ruins of Caisteal Maol, so conspicuous from the ferry, are worth a look. From the ferry take the first road on the left (signposted South Obbe) to an old pier. An exceptionally boggy path continues around a small bay to the mound on which the castle stands; at a boathouse halfway round it is best to take to the beach. There are good views of Kyleakin (Grade 1, ½hr return).

Only two tall, dramatic fragments of wall now remain of what was once the stronghold of the MacKinnons of Strath, a clan whose survival depended on perfect judgement during the long feud between the MacLeods and the MacDonalds. According to tradition the castle was built by 'Saucy Mary', a Norwegian princess who stretched a chain across to the mainland in order to extract a toll from passing ships.

4.5 SUISNISH AND BORERAIG

The stub of land that juts out into the Cuillin Sound between Loch Slapin and Loch Eishort displays few features of interest on the map. Yet, as is so often the case on Skye, the map tells only a small part of the story, for here are to be found exciting limestone scenery, sea cliffs, stacks and caves, disused marble quarries, deserted villages razed during the Clearances, ancient Celtic sites, beautifully sited duns and many other features of historical interest. Two ancient moorland paths and a fine coastal path link the cleared villages and enable a circular walk which is as fascinating as any on Skye. The whole route is marked on the Outdoor Leisure map.

Begin at the ruined church of Kilchrist in Strath Suardal (Green-sward Dale) on the Broadford–Elgol road (GR 617207). Walk down the road to the corner of Loch Cill Chriosd and pick up a path on the left that runs alongside a fence, crosses the shoulder of the grassy knoll in front of you and doubles back left to the ruined village of Kilchrist.

This old village lies in a tremendous situation, with bulky Beinn na Caillich brooding across Strath Suardal and spectacular Bla Bheinn etching the skyline beyond Loch Cill Chriosd. The site is unmistakably limestone — a beautiful oasis of green turf and rock outcrops in the midst of the dull granite moor. Today only the walls of the old Manse remain to testify to the village's former importance in the strath.

From Kilchrist aim south-westwards across the boggy moor, slightly downhill, to reach more ruins at another green limestone oasis. At the near edge of these ruins pick up an indistinct path that climbs left (southwards) onto the moor, initially heading slightly away from the Allt an Inbhire (Owlt an *In*yirra, Stream of the River-mouth) but then doubling back to cross the stream. If you cannot find the path follow the riverbank.

The path recrosses the stream (back to the true right bank) and emerges onto the skyline at the head of the valley of the Allt nan Leac. The Allt nan Leac is crossed 10m above the point where it sinks underground to form the Uamh Cinn Ghlinn (Valley Head Cave), the longest limestone cave on Skye. The limestone country around here is extremely interesting and is well worth exploring in its own right (see next section).

Continuing south-westwards, the path crosses a fence and rises across the far side of the valley onto open moor once again, becoming increasingly difficult to follow. If you are lucky you will pass some small circular ruins, the function of which is still debated. They may have been cells used for some ancient religious purpose or they may even have been hides once used by bear hunters. Fortunately bears are no longer a danger to the walker on Skye.

The path heads directly southwards now, keeping well above Glen Boreraig, but it is more interesting to leave it and head down the glen to the prominent grassy knoll formerly crowned by Dun Kearstach (*Kyar*stach, Justice). Climb to the flat summit of the knoll to survey the land, for few places are more conducive to contemplation than this lonely moorland outpost. It would make a wonderful pitch for a tent were it not for the fact that sheep use it for more commonplace functions.

From Dun Kearstach continue down to the Land-Rover track that runs along the coastline from Camas Malag to Suisnish. Near the track is a ruined hut circle that further testifies to the area's ancient importance. Turn left along the track to reach the deserted village of Suisnish (*Soosh*nish, Seething Headland).

It is difficult to remain unmoved by the desolate ruins of Suisnish, where once potato, herring and kelp were in such abundance that one traveller complained that life here was too easy. From Suisnish and Boreraig hundreds of people were evicted during the Clearances, turned out homeless and penniless to find shelter and sustenance as best they could, their dwellings razed to the ground to prevent their return. Details are preserved in the records of a trial of some Suisnish crofters who resisted the constables. In October 1853, with snow on the ground, some old folk in their eighties and nineties died after being evicted. One man returned to his ruined home at night and was found dead from exposure on his doorstep the following morning.

Such evictions were no different from thousands of others all over the Highlands and Islands, but were no less tragic for all that, and they have been given a special poignancy by the evocative eye-witness account of Sir Archibald Geikie, the distinguished geologist. Returning from a ramble, Geikie heard the cries of the evicted crofters: 'the long plaintive wail like a funeral coronach . . . (which) seemed to re-echo through the whole wide valley of Strath in one prolonged note of desolation.'

The Clearances are now long past, but the memory lingers and it is impossible to walk through the ruins of Suisnish today without feelings of sadness and anger and the same sense of loss as Geikie later felt: 'I have often wandered since then over the solitary ground of Suisnish. Not a soul is to be seen there now, but the green patches of field and the crumbling walls mark where an active and happy community once lived.'

The Land-Rover track continues through Suisnish but misses an exciting stretch of coastline that is well worth a diversion. Cut down the fields below the village to Stac Suisnish, whose two tops, although only about 5m (16ft) high, will provide great sport for boulderers. The lower seaward top can be attained by a short scramble up the steep wall between the two tops (care if wet). The higher landward top can be gained via a prominent chimney on the landward side, whose negotiation, requiring more caving than scrambling technique, is difficult to achieve with any semblance of dignity.

Southwards from the stack a rock pavement at the foot of overhanging 30m (100ft) cliffs leads beside the lapping waters of Loch Slapin around the point of Rubha Suisnish. The walk along the (occasionally greasy) pavement makes a thrilling shoreline trip, but it can be undertaken AT LOW TIDE ONLY and there is no escape for the next ½ mile (1km), until the point has been rounded. The undercutting of the cliffs should leave you in no doubt as to the effect of wave power at high tide. A small cave up on the left is passed, and then the more impressive Calaman Cave (Pigeon Cave) is reached. Further along,

Stac Suisnish

around the point, is a collapsed cave, and beyond that a bay from where you may regain higher ground.

Return to the Land-Rover track and follow it to its end at a sheepshed, then continue straight on across a field to pick up the path to Boreraig (*Borr*eraik, Castle Bay). This splendid path, evolved by generation upon generation of travellers commuting between the rich pastures of Suisnish and Boreraig, holds initially to high ground and then wends down to the shores of a beautifully curving bay beneath the cliffs of Beinn Bhuidhe (*Voo*-ya, Yellow). The dramatic Cuillin skyline is now left behind for the less severe horizons of Sleat, with the whitewashed cottages of Ord prominent across the upper reaches of Loch Eishort.

You will pass one or two waterfalls before reaching verdant Boreraig, where streams meander across green meadows to a lovely bay. As at Suisnish, so at Boreraig, one cannot help but be moved by the sheer number of ruined buildings, eternal memorials to man's inhumanity to man. He who loves wild places such as this can only survey such dereliction, now softened by the passage of time, with mixed feelings, for before the Clearances this was well-populated country.

If time permits explore Boreraig. Using the Outdoor Leisure map as a guide, seek out the dun, the site of the ancient temple and the solitary standing stone. What tales these ruins could tell.

The path out of the village is difficult to distinguish among many others; to find it from the standing stone, head up to the right of some higher ruins. The path goes northwards in front of these ruins, becoming more distinct as it climbs steadily above the gorge of the Allt na Pairte (*Parsh*-tya, Part). At the top of the climb the path descends slightly around a corner, and on the far side of the river from here can be seen a large tree-filled hollow. This is the entrance to Allt na Pairte Cave (see page 123).

Continuing along the right bank (left side) of the Allt na Pairte, the path climbs gently onto the moor. Towards Loch Lonochan (Marshy) it becomes quite boggy, but improves again as it reaches the pleasurable dry turf of limestone country on the descent towards Strath Suardal. The hillside at this point is dotted with spoil heaps from old marble quarries, remnants of a thriving nineteenth-century marble industry that closed in 1912 (although marble is still quarried near Torrin). Marble from here was used for the main altar in Iona Abbey, as well as at Armadale Castle and, if tradition is to be believed, in the building of the Vatican and the Palace of Versailles.

The path continues northwards along the line of the old marble railway to Broadford, although the map marks it as descending by an old bothy to reach the roadside 500m beyond Kilchrist church, midway between the first two houses north of the church. Once the first spoil heap is encountered, however, it is better to cut down to Kilchrist village to rejoin the outward route. This short cut will take you past an old quarry, which is worth exploring if you have time. Take care not to be overtaken by darkness, for Strath Suardal is haunted by the malevolent goblin Ludag who, according to tradition, hops about on his one leg dealing 'heavy blows on the cheeks of benighted travellers!' (Grade 3, 10 miles/16km, 420m/1,400ft, at least 5hr).
Note: the Land-Rover track from Camas Malag provides a short, easy approach route to Suisnish and Boreraig for those who do not wish to undertake the whole of the above walk. Camas Malag is reached by a minor road from Kilbride just east of Torrin (GR 593201).

4.6 LIMESTONE CAVES OF STRATH

The limestone areas of Strath are a delight to explore. The porous rock is carved into all sorts of fantastic shapes, the going is usually dry, often on lush green grass, hollows (known as shakeholes) dot the moor and streams disappear underground (at sinks) and reappear (at resurgences). Yet Strath limestone country remains virtually unknown except to a select band of troglodytes — strange humanoid creatures who can be seen at intervals wandering erratically across the moors as though searching for holes in the ground. And that is precisely what they are doing, for the real thrills of limestone exploration lie underground, where water-scoured caves tunnel through the earth.

The delights of caving are mixed; it is a wet, dirty and strenuous activity (so is hillwalking on occasion), yet it can also be tremendously exciting, offering the only remaining opportunity for real exploration in the British Isles. The caves of Strath are particularly rough and strenuous (cavers refer to them euphemistically as 'sporting'); their interiors are normally constricted, convoluted and best left to masochists. No one without caving experience should venture inside. Many caves carry icy streams that flood after heavy rain. Even in dry weather there may be only a thin layer of air space. Suitable clothing (wet suit, helmet etc), torch, fitness and experience are essential to the Skye caver.

Those not bitten by the caving bug will be properly deterred from entering into the 'realm of darkness' by the sight of most cave entrances, which are usually narrow, dirty, vegetated and infested with spiders and midges. There is much fun and excitement to be had, however, in searching for caves, and this is particularly true in the vicinity of the Allt nan Leac, where there are four 'through' caves (ie caves in which a caver can enter at one place and exit at another) whose underground meanderings can be followed on the surface from stream sink to resurgence.

The route to the Allt nan Leac (Owlt nan Lyachk, Stream of the Flat Stones) begins at the bay of Camas Malag, reached by the minor road from Kilbride just east of Torrin (GR 593201). Beyond the bay the road continues as a rough Land-Rover track to Suisnish. Around the first corner it reaches the Allt na Garbhlain (Garravlin), which sinks into a large hole on the right. This is the upper entrance of Camas Malag Cave, the first of the four through caves. Lower down the hillside the water reappears and sinks again into a 6m (20ft) pothole, and immediately below is the 'tip entrance', full of household rubbish from a time when it was used for dumping. The stream exits from the system at a fissure in a shoreline cliff, which can be reached by a short scramble. The total length of the cave is about 250m (830ft).

Along the track beyond Camas Malag Cave, the next stream reached is the Allt nan Leac itself, whose glen is the caving centre of Skye. The second through cave (Uamh Sgeinne, Oo-a Skain-ya, Cave of the Knives) is only a couple of minutes' walk upstream from here on the right (near) bank. Make for the small waterfall that can be seen less than 100m upstream; to its left a small stream emerges from the hillside, disappears underground and reappears again. The upper resurgence is the lower entrance to the cave — a low arch of rock behind which a tube tunnels into the hillside.

Finding the exit burrow will task your powers of observation, although it lies less than 100m further upstream. It is hidden among limestone outcrops about 10m up the hillside from a point where trees stand on each side of the Allt nan Leac just below a small waterfall and pool. The total length of the cave is about 105m (350ft).

Above the Uamh Sgeinne the glen levels off. Keep to the path along the right bank of the river. Fifty metres beyond the point where a fence crosses to the near (right) bank, the path crosses a small stream that exits from a nearby resurgence on the left. This is the rising for the third through cave — Beinn an Dubhaich Cave, whose main entrance, a 3m (10ft) tree-covered hole, can be found about 30m (100ft) diagonally uphill further right. Further right still is the upper entrance, where the stream sinks underground. The total length of the cave is about 175m (570ft).

Beyond the level section of glen containing Beinn an Dubhaich Cave there is a slight rise to another long flat section and then the glen narrows and climbs to yet another short flat section. Cross an old wall on reaching this upper section and 100m further along look for the tree that marks the spot where the young Allt nan Leac emerges from a hole at the foot of a line of crags. This is the lower entrance of the fourth through cave — the Uamh Cinn Ghlinn (Oo-a Keen Ghleen, Valley Head Cave), the longest (about 365m/1,200ft), finest and most sporting cave on Skye.

The streamway of the Uamh Cinn Ghlinn leads the caver through a series of exciting cascades, pools and chambers, where in many places there is very little air space. The walker must settle for seeking out the upper entrances, which can be found by following the dry valley up onto the moor. There is a sink entrance, where the stream enters the system, and 10m downstream is a dug-out dry hole, which drops 3m (10ft) to the underground streamway.

There are many other smaller known caves in the area, and no doubt many others yet to be discovered. It may well be worth your while to explore further before returning to Camas Malag by the outward route (allow at least 3 to 4hr round trip).

All of the caves in the Allt nan Leac area lie on the south side of Beinn an Dubhaich (Doo-ich, Darkness); the north side of the hill above Strath Suardal is also a major caving area, with so many holes in the ground that they almost defy classification. However, with the one exception of the Uamh an Ard Achadh (Oo-a an Ard Acha, High Pasture Cave), all are minor caves.

Moreover, the hillside is covered with thick natural woodland (Coille Gaireallach, Cullya Gar-yalloch, Wood of the Rough Countryside) that makes searching for cave entrances a frustrating task. Cavers at the end of their tether are warned by roadside notices that tree cutting is prohibited.

The Uamh an Ard Achadh is the second longest cave on Skye (about 320m/1,050ft), but its insignificant entrance hole is hardly worth the journey for the non-caver. Another long (about 190m/630ft) cave is to be found on the east bank of the Allt na Pairte (GR 626173) near Boreraig, but the long tramp to view its entrance hole is again hardly worthwhile.

There are also some minor limestone caves near Broadford (see page 126).

4.7 SRATH MOR AND SRATH BEAG

Sandwiched between the higher peaks of Belig and Beinn na Caillich, the scree-girt lump of Beinn na Cro (574m/1,883ft, Craw, Fold) will attract only the enthusiast, who will find the north and south ridges to be the easiest approaches. The deep glens of Srath Mor (Stra Moar, Big Strath) and Srath Beag (Stra Bake, Little Strath) that separate Beinn na Cro from its higher neighbours, however, both carry paths that link the east and west coasts of Skye at its narrowest point, and a coast-to-coast round that amounts to the girdle traverse of Beinn na Cro has a certain eccentric appeal.

The triangular route touches roads at three points and can be begun at any; it is described here beginning at Loch Slapin on the Broadford–Elgol road. Note that Srath Mor is particularly boggy after heavy rain and the path through it from Loch Slapin to Luib may be impracticable, but the paths from Luib to Strollamus, and through Srath Beag from Strollamus to Loch Slapin remain in excellent condition.

Begin 50m east of the bridge at the head of Loch Slapin (GR 565224) and take the cart track that heads up Srath Mor between Belig and Beinn na Cro. Further along, a large boulder will be found beside the path; this is Clach Oscar (Oscar's Stone), flung here from a nearby hilltop by the legendary Fienne giant in a burst of high spirits.

The cart track soon becomes a path along the shores of Loch na Sguabaidh (*Skoo*-aby, Sweeping), whose waters inundate it after much rain. According to tradition, this loch was inhabited for some years by a water horse who had a penchant for attractive girls; to be chased by him was good for a girl's reputation. The Bealach na Beiste between Belig and Garbh-bheinn was named after the beast (see page 101).

Beyond the loch the broad, flat corridor of Srath Mor cuts a fine swathe through the mountains, but such is the state of the path that one is not immediately overcome with admiration for one's surroundings. Prince Charlie came this way on his journey across Skye (see page 17) and one wonders if it was here that he was pulled waist-deep out of a bog. Halfway along the strath, at the mouth of Lochain Stratha Mhoir, the path crosses the Abhainn an t-Srath Mhoir (*A*–win a Tra Voar, River of the Big Strath) to the west side of the glen. This crossing is impossible after heavy rain and may necessitate a long detour; an indistinct cairned path has developed some way along the east bank, but it eventually peters out.

Approaching Luib, the path forks; the right branch is boggy but provides the most direct route to the village. On reaching the road at

Luib, bear immediately right across the fine old stone bridge that carries the old Broadford–Portree road onto the shoulder of Am Meall (Am Mell, The Hill) above Loch nam Madadh Uisge (*Matta Oosh*-ka, Dog Water). It is tempting to avoid Luib by taking a short cut from the Srath Mor path along the south side of this loch, but the boggy terrain does not allow any saving of time or effort.

From Luib onwards the going is much improved. As far as the Allt Strollamus the old road provides fine walking and grand views along the coast. At the Allt Strollamus leave the road for a good path that climbs along the left bank of the river into the narrow defile of An Slugan (An *Slookan*, The Gullet), which is a complete contrast to the boggy flats of Srath Mor. If starting the round from Strollamus, the start of this path is most easily reached from the gate in the fence at GR 600266, where the old road rejoins the new road.

The path climbs onto the broad grassy bealach between Beinn na Caillich and Beinn na Cro, whose summit can easily be reached from here via the north ridge. The path continues across the bealach and down Srath Beag to Loch Slapin, keeping high above the left bank of the Allt an t-Sratha Bhig (Owlt an *Tra*-ha Veek, Stream of the Little Strath). It reaches the roadside beside the cattle grid at the west end of Torrin (GR 576211); to avoid the road walk from here back to your starting point, cross the Allt an t-Sratha Bhig higher up and take a short cut across the saddle north of Cnoc Slapin (Crochk Slapin, Slapin Hill) (Grade 3, 10 miles/16km, 270m/900ft, 4¹/₂hr).

4.8 STRATH SHORT WALKS

South of Bla Bheinn the spine of the Strathaird peninsula degenerates into dull moorland, but the coastline is the most interesting in the whole of Strath. The west coast is traversed by an exciting path from Elgol to Camasunary, which is described elsewhere (see page 132). The east and south coasts are less frequented but provide several attractive objectives for short walks, including some unusual sandstone coastal features culminating in the breathtaking splendour of Spar Cave. Places of interest are described below in north to south order, beginning with some short walks around Broadford in northern Strath.

Broadford

The township of Broadford is second only in size to Portree, and with its campsite, youth hostel, restaurants and shops, it makes a good base for exploring southern Skye. There are also a number of interesting short walks in the immediate vicinity to while away a few hours.

On the west side of Broadford Bay a road runs along the shore to the pier. About 200m along is a tree-clad mound on the left. This is the Liveras Cairn, a chambered cairn whose discovery and excavation in the nineteenth century had a curious history, from the initial abandoning of excavation work owing to fear of ghosts to the accidental discovery of the chamber by a nine-year-old girl and the eventual finding of a number of artefacts, including some skulls, a metal buckle and an urn.

The shore road ends at the pier, but an unsurfaced road continues past Corry Lodge and becomes a path (keep right at all forks) to Rubh' an Eireannaich (Roo an *Ai*ranich, Irishman's Point), from where there are good views of Scalpay and Pabay. You can make a round trip by continuing along the shoreline round the edge of forestry plantations to Camas na Sgianadin on the Broadford–Sligachan road (Grade 2, 2+hr).

On the east side of Broadford Bay a twisting road runs along the coast to Waterloo (named after the Napoleonic battle at which 1,600 Skyemen fought). From the road-end a usually boggy path leads out along the Ardnish peninsula to Rubha Ardnish, from where there are fine close-up views of Pabay and where at low tide can be found 'coral' sands similar to those at Claigan. Take care not to get stranded on offshore rocks by the incoming tide (Grade 2, 2+hr return).

An unusual walk south of Broadford follows the line of the old railway by which marble was transported from the quarries of Kilchrist to the coast (see page 120). The line can be gained 50m beyond the first cattle grid on the Elgol road. A line of electricity pylons crosses the road; the first wooden pylon on the left, just beside the road, stands on the now overgrown and indistinct track. You can find a way along the track by walking parallel to the road past three trees; the track becomes more distinct as it progresses and can be followed all the way to the quarries (Grade 2, 2hr return).

East of Broadford the banks of the Allt Lochain Cruinn (*Croo*-in, Round) harbour a number of limestone caves. Only those with caving experience and equipment should enter the caves, but an exploration of the river banks provides an adventurous excursion for those not averse to wading in water. Begin at the bridge over the stream on the Broadford–Kyleakin road (GR 671229); cars can be parked 200m east of here at the junction with the Lower Breakish road. The largest cave entrance is that of Breakish Bridge Cave, 30m downstream on the left bank beneath an overhanging cliff. There are other smaller holes in the vicinity.

To reach the upper part of the stream wade upstream beneath the bridge. Here is a fine small limestone gorge with plenty of holes to poke your nose in, including one 130m from the bridge that leads cavers into the 140m (500ft) Breakish Cave (1+hr return).

The road crosses another stream 200m west of the bridge, and 30m downstream from here on the left bank, at the foot of a small water-fall, is a little cave with a large rectangular entrance. Access is via the right bank but at the time of writing is barred by a fence.

Those with transport at Broadford can explore the moorland road to Heast on the upper shores of Loch Eishort, where the bay of Loch an Eilean and its tidal island of Eilean Heast make a picturesque objec-tive for a short drive.

Torrin

The township of Torrin is beautifully sited close to the shores of Loch Slapin beneath the towering east face of Bla Bheinn. Below the houses are the sites of two duns (Dun More and Dun Beag), now completely dismantled. South of Dun Beag are two fine bays, the second of which (Camas Malag) can be reached by car along the minor road from Kilbride east of Torrin (GR 593201). On the west side of this road, in a field behind two ruined buildings, is the standing stone of Clach na h-Annait. From Camas Malag a Land-Rover track continues past the limestone caves of the glen of the Allt nan Leac (see page 122) to the cleared village of Suisnish (see page 118).

Dun Ringill

Dun Ringill (GR 562171) stands atop some curious sandstone cliffs on the east coast of Strathaird near Kilmarie, and the path to it makes a pleasant excursion. The path begins at Kilmarie House (GR 553173), reached by a minor road that leaves the Broadford–Elgol road on the south side of the bridge over the Abhainn Cille Mhaire. The gardens of Kilmarie House are notable for their fine trees, which can be seen from the roadside at the river mouth. Go through a gate in the fence on the opposite side of the road just before the house and cross the river (bridge, not marked on OS map). The path runs through fine woodlands to the river mouth and then follows the coastline round to the dun.

Dun Ringill was the stronghold of the MacKinnons before they moved to Caisteal Maol. It is typical of many duns on Skye in that it crowns a rocky headland surrounded by sea cliffs on three sides, but it is untypical in its landward entrance, an 8m (25ft) passageway that is partly covered. Little else but the passageway remains, the top of the dun now being deep in nettles. On the moor above the dun are numerous remains of later habitations.

The shoreline beyond the dun is worth exploring for a few hundred metres, where brittle sandstone cliffs teeter precariously. There is a cave, and an arch whose supporting walls have been holed as if by giant punches. Beware of falling rocks. The shoreline between the dun and the river mouth has some similar sandstone formations on a smaller scale (Grade 1, 1+hr return).

Further north, towards the head of Loch Slapin, are more shoreline cliffs, but the walk along the bouldery beach beneath forested slopes can be done AT LOW TIDE ONLY and is not particularly pleasant.

East coast walk
From Kilmarie a fine walk goes southwards along the east coast of Strathaird to Rubha na h-Easgainne (*Roo*-a na *Haiss*-kin-ya, Eel Point) at the south end of the peninsula. The route follows minor roads and cart tracks high above the shoreline, past small villages and isolated cottages, with good views across Loch Slapin to Sleat. Note that some of the tracks marked on the OS map are now surfaced.

The road to Kilmarie House described above continues along the shoreline to some cottages at GR 553165. From here it is possible to walk along the shoreline for some distance to explore sandstone sea cliffs, but eventually the route onward becomes barred. The east coast walk leaves the shore at the cottages and follows the old cart track that links the road-end with Drinan, climbing high above the thickly wooden cliff tops to meet another road at GR 549155 (this is the road that leaves the Broadford–Elgol road at GR 543156).

At the end of this road (GR 544144) the cart track continues past the ruins of Dun Liath, descends to a stream and climbs again to reach Glasnakille road-end at GR 540137. The Glasnakille road continues along the coast past Spar Cave (see below) and Dun Grugaig to end at GR 533121. The point of Rubha na h'Easgainne is only 800m distant from here, but it is a disappointing end to the peninsula; the cliffs peter out and the boggy tangle of moor is unattractive. The route to it continues straight on past the last houses, but most people will find the walk there insufficiently rewarding to make it worthwhile (1hr return).

The complete east coast walk requires transport at both ends; individual sections can be explored by car and on foot according to inclination.

Spar Cave

Spar Cave (GR 538128) is one of the natural wonders of Scotland. Beyond its huge entrance canyon on the shores below Glasnakille it forms a spectacular flowstone-encrusted passageway burrowing deep into the hillside. Its scale and formations are unprecedented, and the trip to its innermost recesses high in the roof of the passageway is breathtaking. No caving skills are required, but the route demands great care and the logistics of a visit should not be underestimated. Reaching the entrance canyon requires an awkward scramble along shoreline cliffs and over seaweed-encrusted rocks, and is possible AT LOW TIDE ONLY. Inside the cave itself the floor is in turn muddy, steeply ascending and pitted with transparent pools; the only way across the deep final pool is to swim. A torch is required. For the sake of those who come after you, please, please do not remove or interfere with the calcite formations.

The route to Spar Cave begins 100m south of the road junction in Glasnakille. On the left of the road is a stone byre; just beyond the byre a gap in the roadside fence marks the start of a path that descends right of the byre to trees at the edge of the shoreline cliffs; the latter part of this path may be waterlogged. At the trees, turn left on an initially unobvious path that winds down to a rocky inlet, then go left along the shoreline beneath the cliff face past a narrow flooded creek. The entrance to Spar Cave lies around the next headland; reach it by edging around rocky ledges at the cliff foot and clambering across seaweed-covered rocks at the tidal limit. This section of the route is passable for only a couple of hours each side of low tide.

The entrance canyon is about 60m (200ft) long and up to 30m (100ft) high, resembling 'some deep cathedral aisle' as John MacCulloch described it. The entrance itself lies at the landward end of the canyon, guarded by a 3m (10ft) high broken wall. This wall, complete with locked door, was built by an early nineteenth-century proprietor to prevent visitors robbing the cave of its long pendant stalactites ('spars'). Unfortunately, the wall did not serve its purpose (Sir Walter Scott, for instance, used a rope to climb it in 1814); the door was eventually demolished by a shot from an offshore gunboat. Today the cave is bereft of the stalactite formations for which it was once renowned.

Beyond the wall two passages lead off. That on the right soon degenerates into a narrow crawl. The main passage is on the left. It is muddy for some distance but then develops into a fantastic flowstone staircase some 50m (160ft) long, rising like a frozen marble cataract into the darkness of the roof high above. Everywhere — floor, walls, roof — is encrusted in creamy calcium carbonate ('spar'), which develops fine formations as it flows down the walls. The place has the aura and dimensions of a Gothic cathedral. There are no great stalactites left, and the roof is blackened from the smoke of ancient candles and torches, but it remains an awesome sight.

The corrugations in the flowstone provide a good grip, and the scramble up the passageway is not as bad as it looks. At the summit, high in the roof, care is required on a short level section lined with transparent, almost invisible pools. Then the flowstone passage descends again to a very deep pool some 5m (16ft) across, which marks the limit of exploration for those who do not wish to swim. The cave ends abruptly not far beyond the pool.

You will be loth to leave this magical spot, 'deep in Strathaird's enchanted cell', as Sir Walter Scott described it in *Lord of the Isles,* where 'dazzling spars gleam like a firmament of stars'. But make sure that you make the return trip while the tide is still low (Grade 5, $1^{1}/_{2}$+hr return).

In Gaelic, Spar Cave is known as Slochd Altrimen (Slochk *Altrimen*, Nursing Cave), after a tale of the ninth century. The son of the chief of Colonsay was shipwrecked on the Strathaird coast and found by Princess Dounhuila of nearby Dun Glass, whose father was the sworn enemy of the chief of Colonsay. Young Colonsay was imprisoned in Dun Glass, but Dounhuila fell in love with him and bore him a child, which, to ensure its survival, she had a trusty servant keep in Spar Cave. Dounhuila visited the cave to nurse the child, hence the cave's name. The story had a happy ending, for the chiefs patched up their feud and the lovers married.

The bays to the immediate south of Spar Cave are also worth exploring, and they too can be reached by steep winding paths if you can find them. The sandstone cliffs here are awesome, full of overhangs, caves and honeycomb formations; take care in their exploration.

Prince Charles's Cave
Unlike Rubha na h-Easgainne at the south-east tip of Strathaird, Suidhe Biorach (*Soo*-ya *Bee*rach, Pointed Seat) at the south-west tip is well worth a visit. It sports some exciting cliff scenery similar to that in the Spar Cave area and is easily reached by a good sheep path from Elgol. It was here that Prince Charlie ended his wanderings in the islands and quit Skye for the mainland on the night of 4 July 1746, and the cave in which he spent his last hours can be visited.

Begin at Elgol jetty. Go southwards above the beach and pick up a sheep path that climbs onto the cliff top and follows the cliff edge all the way out to the point, with superb views of Rum and the Cuillin. The cliff top in the vicinity of the point is complex and sports a number of deep creeks, fissures and other interesting rock features. Suidhe Biorach was so named because it used to be the custom for childless women to sit there in the hope of becoming fertile.

Prince Charles's Cave lies beyond the point beside a shoreline rock platform on the west side of the bay of Port an Luig Mhoir (Porst an _Looik_ Voar, Harbour of the Big Hollow). To reach it, continue beyond the platform in order to outflank the cliffs, then descend to the shore and return along the cliff foot. This is advisable AT LOW TIDE ONLY. The cave is a short but large 'through' cave floored by a pool, and it is not obvious until you have walked past it (Grade 2, 1½hr return).

Many seabirds nest on the cliffs of Suidhe Biorach and in the vicinity of the cave, and if your explorations are mistaken for aggression you may well have the unnerving experience of being dive-bombed. You have been warned!

5 minginish coast walks

Minginish (pronounced with a hard *g*, Great Promontory) is not only the Cuillin. In the shadow of those mighty mountains lies a coastline that in its own way is just as savage and spectacular. This is magnificent walking country, with dramatic cliffs, fantastic stacks and sweeping seascapes. In the south the entertaining coast walk from Elgol or Kilmarie to Coruisk is justly famed for its mountain scenery (5.1). North of Coruisk the steep seaward slopes of Gars-bheinn make coast walking impracticable, but the headland of Rubh' an Dunain beyond makes a pleasant stroll from Glen Brittle (5.2).

Between Glen Brittle and Fiskavaig is a great tract of wild and remote coastline that is virtually unfrequented and whose cliff top is as vertiginous and awesome as any Cuillin arête; walking here is a serious affair (5.3, 5.4, 5.5). Beyond Fiskavaig the gentler shores of Loch Bracadale provide some contrasting delightful short walks (5.6). In all, Minginish has walks of all kinds and grades to offer the coast walker, and adventure enough for many a day.

Note: the coastline from Elgol to Loch Brittle appears on the Outdoor Leisure map.

5.1 ELGOL TO CORUISK

To those underprivileged souls who never venture far from the roadside, the view of the Cuillin horseshoe from the hilly village of Elgol is one of the most celebrated on Skye. In summer, boats ferry tourists from Elgol jetty across Loch Scavaig to Coruisk at the heart of the Cuillin, but perhaps the grandeur and remoteness of this unique mountain fastness are best appreciated out of season or on a stormy day when the boats are not running and Coruisk is at its wildest.

In terms of mountain scenery there is no finer coast walk in the British Isles than that around the shores of Loch Scavaig. Paths from Elgol and Kilmarie join at the lonely bay of Camasunary and continue all the way to Coruisk, but the route is not without its adventurous moments and should be left well alone by those unsure of their scrambling abilities. In particular there is at least one major river crossing that may be impracticable after rain, and towards Coruisk the renowned Bad Step provides a sting in the tail that will keep the adrenalin flowing throughout the walk.

The path from Elgol to Camasunary begins at the top of the steep hill leading down to the jetty, 20m uphill from Bayview House (GR 520549). A cart track on the north side of the road heads uphill past a few houses, and at the last house a Gaelic signpost (Ceum gu Coir' uisge — Footpath to Coruisk) points the way onward across the hillside below Bidein an Fhithich (*Beej*an an *Ee*-ich, Raven Pinnacle). The path descends to cross a stream and then wends its way across the grassy hillside of Ben Cleat (Clait, Cliff) some 60m (200ft) above the shore.

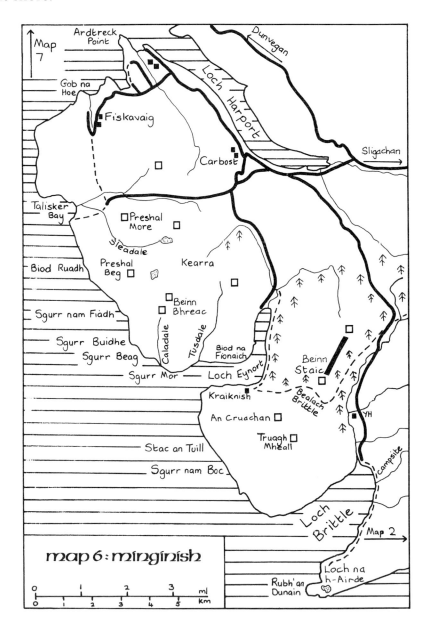

map 6: minginish

The walk is delightful, with Soay on one's left, the Cuillin drawing ever closer and the white house at Camasunary ahead acting as a homing beacon. Seals are not uncommon in Loch Scavaig, but you would have to be exceptionally lucky to see a sperm whale such as that which floundered ashore here in 1871 and whose teeth were collected and sold to tourists by Elgol crofters.

The path descends to the meadows at the foot of Glen Scaladal, then climbs around the slopes of Ben Leacach (*Lyachk*ach, Slabby) to 60m (200ft) again above vegetated cliffs at the water's edge. There is some exposure, but if you find yourself overlooking a precipice with no obvious way forward you have missed the true path a few metres back. Easier slopes are reached at Rubha na h-Airighe Baine (*Roo*-a na Harry *Ban*-ya, Point of the White Shieling), and from then on the path keeps low down by the shore to reach Camasunary (in Gaelic Camas Fhionnairigh, Cammas Ee-*oon*ary, Bay of the Fair Shieling). Camasunary is one of the most beautiful bays on Skye, its wide sandy beach backed by luscious green meadows, which are in turn backed by the savage rock faces of Sgurr na Stri and Bla Bheinn. This spot is well worth a visit even should you go no further (Grade 4, $3^1/2$ miles/ 6km, 2hr; 4hr return).

The route from Kilmarie to Camasunary begins just to the south of Kilmarie on the Broadford–Elgol road (GR 545172) and follows a Land-Rover track over Am Mam (Grade 2, $2^1/2$ miles/4km, $1^1/2$hr; 3hr return). The building of this track by the army in 1968 became a conservation *cause célèbre* when it was discovered that the intention was also to build footbridges across the Abhainn Camas Fhionnairigh and the River Scavaig and to dynamite the Bad Step. The track and bridges were built, but after a public outcry the Bad Step was left inviolate, and the bridges were soon destroyed by the elements.

The Kilmarie track is easier, drier and faster than the Elgol path, but it climbs higher, its stony surface is more uncomfortable and there are no views westwards until the summit of Am Mam is reached. The Elgol route is the more aesthetically pleasing for those who like the crash of waves and the rush of the wind, but because of its comparative ease and shortness the Kilmarie track has now become the major approach route to Coruisk.

Beyond Camasunary the route becomes more exciting. At the western end of the bay is a fine bothy, and then the first obstacle is encountered almost immediately in the form of the Abhainn Camas Fhionnairigh, which must be forded. The bridge marked on the OS map no longer exists. At low tide the river can be forded at its confluence with a smaller stream just upriver from the remains of the old bridge. At high tide the river is flooded beyond here at least as far as the island at GR 509191, and a longer detour will be necessary to ford it. In spate the river may become an impassable barrier all the way up to Loch na Creitheach and beyond.

On the far side of the river the path follows the shoreline around the craggy slopes of Sgurr na Stri. There is now gabbro underfoot (and also plenty of bog, but as your feet are wet anyway this is of no matter). At Rubha Ban (*Roo*-a Bahn, White Headland) Gars-bheinn comes into view across Loch Scavaig, and the increasing wildness of the scenery spurs you on with new vigour to the next headland (Rubha Buidhe, *Roo*-a *Boo*-ya, Yellow Headland), where the path cuts through a defile right of a rocky knoll isolated from the main hill-side. The top of this knoll provides a spectacular view of Loch na Cuilce (*Cool*-kya, Reeds), the rocky inner basin of Loch Scavaig, with the waters of Loch Coruisk just visible beyond. On a stormy day there can be few wilder prospects than this, with the turbulent waters of Scavaig crashing against the many islets, and the Cuillin wreathed in swirling cloud beyond.

Coruisk looks close at hand now, but chaotic terrain on the western slopes of Sgurr na Stri makes the going painstakingly slow. At two points boiler-plate slabs curve into the sea. The path rises over the top of the first but can find no way around the second — the infamous Bad Step, the negotiation of which is a moderate scramble with some exposure above deep water.

To cross the Bad Step, follow cairns down to the water's edge and clamber over huge blocks of rock that have fallen from the overhang above. Scramble round a corner and up a sloping crack, using finger holds on the slab above the crack for safety. Halfway up the crack go left along another horizontal fault onto easier ground (the temptation to continue straight on up the crack is what gets people into difficulties). The Bad Step is enjoyable or nerve-racking depending on your point of view; if in doubt leave it for another day and journey to Coruisk by a different route (see page 77).

Once past the Bad Step it is only a few minutes' walk to the shores of Loch Coruisk (Grade 5, 2½ miles/4km, 2hr from Camasunary; 8hr round trip from Elgol, 7hr from Kilmarie). Note that to reach the JMCS Hut and the west side of Loch Coruisk it is necessary to cross the River Scavaig (see page 75 for a description of the area).

For the sake of variety it would be preferable to walk out of Coruisk by a different route, either to Sligachan or Glen Brittle, if transport arrangements make this practicable. It may also be possible in summer to arrange for a lift back to Elgol by boat. If walking back to Elgol or Kilmarie, evening light on Rum will ease the journey homeward.

5.2 RUBH' AN DUNAIN

Rubh' an Dunain (Roo an Doonan, Headland of the Dun) is the headland on the south side of Loch Brittle. From Glen Brittle campsite its low-lying moors do not appear as inviting as the majestic Cuillin which tower above them, yet the path to the point provides a pleasant coastal walk with fine views of Rum, Canna and the southern Cuillin corries, and with many sites of historical interest to explore. Wellingtons are the best footwear, but if the rivers are in spate the route is best avoided altogether.

Begin at the campsite behind the toilet block and take one of the two paths that go right along the coast, one beginning above and one below the water storage tank. Use one path for the outward journey and the other for the inward; at the head of Loch Brittle the lower path passes close to rocky creeks, which are well worth exploring. The Allt Coire Lagan can usually be crossed on stepping stones, but if in spate there is a footbridge (not marked on OS map) just upstream from the lower path and downstream from the upper.

Beyond the Allt Coire Lagan a single path continues to the stream just before Creag Mhor (Craik Voar, Big Crag), where it divides again. Take the lower path beneath the 15m (50ft) basalt crags of Creag Mhor (1hr). Soon the first of the area's many ruined habitations will be seen in the wide depression known as the Slochd Dubh (Slochk Doo, Black Pit), a fault line that cuts right across the headland. The path peters out, but keep going on easy ground around the north and west slopes of Carn Mor (Big Cairn) to reach the north side of Loch na h-Airde (*Harja*, Point, 2hr). From here at least one more hour should be allowed for exploring the headland itself.

In front of the wall beside the loch is a well-preserved chambered cairn, with a 3m (10ft) long, 1m (3ft) high passageway leading into the central chamber, now roofless. When the chamber was excavated in 1931 and 1932 the remains of six adults and pieces of pottery were unearthed, dating its use to the Beaker and Neolithic periods. From here walk out to the point of the headland, where a cairn caps small sea cliffs and there are fine views of Rum (only 8 miles/13km away across the Cuillin Sound) and northwards along the Minginish coast to Stac a' Mheadais north of Loch Eynort.

From the point continue around the coastline to the southern shore of Loch na h'Airde. At the mouth of the loch is a channel that was built long ago to link the loch with the sea and enable it to be used as an anchorage. The waters of the loch are only just above sea-level, and tradition has it that MacLeod galleys used to shelter here (whether for safety from a stormy sea or for more warlike purposes is unclear). The dun after which the headland is named crowns a knoll on the far side of the channel, its landward wall still 4m (13ft) high, its seaward side guarded by cliffs.

Viewing the land from the vantage point of the dun, the attractions of the Rubh for habitation become apparent — look-out points, fresh water, hidden anchorages, flat land for farming and the sea for fishing. The many ruins in the area bear witness to centuries of occupation. In recent historical times the area was held by the MacAskills, a family of Norse origin who offered their services as coast watchers to the MacLeods after Norse rule was effectively ended at the Battle of Largs in 1263. When clan battles ended in Skye, at the beginning of the seventeenth century, the MacAskills turned to farming and fishing.

The Clearances of the nineteenth century effectively put an end to life at the Rubh. In 1811 Kenneth MacAskill and a large party of tenants emigrated to North and South Carolina; his son emigrated to New Zealand in 1847. The MacAskill farm was amalgamated with Glenbrittle farm and the MacAskill home abandoned. Nevertheless, in 1883 there were still twenty or more families living in the area. Today nothing remains but ruins:

East of Loch na h-Airde a shallow cave can be seen on the hillside. More of an overhang than a cave, it nevertheless revealed Beaker pottery and an Iron Age forge during the 1932 excavation. By following the stream left of the cave up towards a smaller lochan the ruins of Rhundunan House (the old MacAskill home) can be seen. To return to Glen Brittle campsite from here, recross the headland via the Slochd Dubh and rejoin the coastal path (Grade 3, 7½ miles/12km, 4½hr round trip).

Adventurous walkers may prefer to extend the walk along the shores of the Soay Sound to An Leac (An Lyachk, The Flagstone), the old ferry point for crossings between Skye and Soay. Note, however, that the route is much rougher than the stroll out to Rubh' an Dunain and will give you some small indication of the hardiness of the old islanders. The return journey back across the moor from An Leac to Glen Brittle is very rough and boggy and, in spate, rivers such as the Allt na Meacnaish may be impassable.

As far as An Leac the going is extremely pleasant. Beyond the Slochd Dubh an excellent sheep path follows the edge of 110m (350ft) sea cliffs along the Soay Sound. The northern coast of Soay is less than 2 miles (3km) away, and soon it is possible to see into Soay Harbour, the narrow inlet that almost cuts the island in two. From the Cuillin Soay looks flat and dull, but from here its sea cliffs and hills, reaching 141m (464ft) at Beinn Bhreac (*Vrai*-achk, Speckled), look much more interesting.

After crossing the Allt na Meacnaish, which forms a fine waterfall as it enters the sea, descend to the broad rock platform of An Leac below (4½hr from Glen Brittle). An Leac is the only landing place on the Soay Sound, but even here landing is not always easy; when the sea was high, travellers of yesteryear had to watch the wave and jump for it. Travellers arriving from Glen Brittle would light a fire to let the ferryman on Soay know they were waiting to be picked up. At one time each Soay family had its own allotted fireplace on the hillside, so that the ferryman would know exactly who required to be picked up. This practice had its other uses; it was not unknown, for example, for the minister's fire to go unnoticed.

The headland on the west side of the Allt na Meacnaish is known as Suidhe na h'Inghe (*Sooya* na *Hin*-ya, The Maiden's Seat), though who the maiden was and why she sat there is now lost in the mists of time. From the vantage point of An Leac the coastline to both left and right looks extremely interesting, with impressive cliffs and a number of caves. A continuation of the walk beyond An Leac to Loch Scavaig and Coruisk cannot be recommended, however, as the coastline becomes increasingly difficult to follow and eventually the walker is forced onto awkward high ground around Ulfhart (Howling) Point (see coast route from Glen Brittle to Coruisk, page 78).

The best route back to Glen Brittle contours around Ceann na Beinne (Kyann na *Bain*-ya, Head of the Mountain) and holds to the line of the Allt na Buaile Duibhe (Boola *Du*-ya, Black Fold) to regain the coastal path. The moorland crossing provides fine views into Coir' a' Ghrunnda, but the going is rough, boggy and tiring; in wet weather it might even be preferable to return via the Rubh' an Dunain route (Grade 4, 11 miles/17km, 6½hr round trip).

(right) *The beautiful double arches near Brandarsaig Bay*
(page 140) *Biod an Athair, the highest sea cliff on Skye*
(page 141) *Bearreraig Bay*

5.3 GLEN BRITTLE TO EYNORT

North of Loch Brittle are the first great sea cliffs of the west coast, rising to a high point of 217m (712ft) at Sgurr nam Boc (Bochk, Buck) and offering stunning views of the southern Cuillin across the loch. Here also is perhaps the most fantastic sea stack on Skye — Stac an Tuill (Stachk an Tuyl, Stack of the Hole). The walk, however, is a serious one, as the convex, crumbling cliff edge is one of the most dangerous and the return across the Minginish moors is rough.

The route begins near the foot of Glen Brittle, at the sharp bend where the road turns left to run alongside the River Brittle (GR 409210). Take the path that crosses the river (footbridge) to the former Post Office, but leave it for the rocky shoreline below the fields and fences until you can pick up another path that runs along an obvious grass shelf above the shore. Keep to this shelf until it crosses a stream that cascades from the moor above and begins to peter out on increasingly steep slopes, then make a steep rising traverse onto the moor, aiming for the top of an open gully seen ahead.

Once onto the cliff top, continue out towards the headland at the mouth of Loch Brittle, passing two fine lochans. The first, carpeted with reeds and water lilies, lies hidden in a basin a short distance from the cliff edge. The second is an attractive round lochan perched right at the cliff edge but having no outlet.

At the headland the coast turns north-westwards and the cliff edge becomes undulating and complex. To save time and energy it is probably best to keep well back from the edge, aiming for the rocky high point of Dunan Thearna Sgurr that can be seen some distance ahead; numerous choices of path indicate that the sheep have not yet decided upon an optimal route.

Beyond Dunan Thearna Sgurr the cliffs become more awesome and you are immediately faced with a major obstacle — the deep gorge of the Allt Mor and its waterfall. To negotiate the gorge, contour into the glen above the waterfall and ford the river (this can normally be done dryshod). From the far side of the river the waterfall is worth a closer look; it has an impressive free fall of some 15m (50ft) and is flanked by great fissures in the rock.

Beyond the gorge the cliff-top terrain is excellent — turfed with short grass and honeycombed by rabbit burrows whose inhabitants dash around with enviable alacrity. The very edge of the cliff, how-

Pinnacles of the Sanctuary, the Storr. The Old Man is on the right

ever, is extremely dangerous; its convex nature makes views over the edge impossible, and in places crumbling earth perilously overhangs the abyss. Fortunately, numerous headlands provide spectacular views without the need to get too close to oblivion.

The cliff top reaches its highest point at Sgurr nam Boc, whose summit is an uncairned ridge of grass that affords a view of the coast all the way from Rubh' an Dunain to Stac a' Mheadais north of Loch Eynort (4½ miles/7km, 420m/1,400ft, 3hr from Glen Brittle). The advice to avoid the temptation to peer over the edge will be appreciated once you reach the next headland beyond Sgurr nam Boc, from where the plunging cliff face is seen in all its glory. This headland is probably the best viewpoint of the whole walk, for from here also can be seen the fantastic Stac an Tuill beneath the next headland.

Few visitors to Skye today are even aware of the existence of this remote and curious stack, yet few creations of nature combine such symmetry of form with such intricacy of design, the complete sculpture resembling a gothic cathedral, complete with spire and vaulted window (the 'hole'). When Sarah Murray sailed past here on her way from Rum to Loch Eynort in 1802 she had a more common-place vision of the stack: 'like a lady dressed in a monstrous sized hoop and petticoat, such as are worn at the court of St James's, having a very large hole quite through the middle of the hoop.' For a closer view of the stack continue to the headland above it (but do not attempt to view it from here) and descend to the next headland beyond.

Beyond here the cliffs diminish in size towards Loch Eynort and a choice of routes presents itself. The descent around the coast to Loch Eynort is something of an anti-climax that involves a long walk back to Glen Brittle, but it does make a satisfying denouement to the walk if transport awaits at Eynort. The route continues around the coast, past a dun at the mouth of Loch Eynort, to Kraiknish, from where a path leads to a forestry road and so to Eynort. Note that another forestry road climbs from Kraiknish to the Bealach Brittle, from where Glen Brittle can easily be reached (see page 82).

Alternatively, a return from the cliff top to Glen Brittle can be made over An Cruachan and Truagh Mheall to prolong the views over Eynort and the Cuillin, but the tramp across the wet tussocky moor to these two unimposing tops will not appeal to many. As viewpoints they are best approached from the Bealach Brittle.

The shortest return route from Sgurr nam Boc goes past the marshy shores of wild Loch an Leth–uillt (Lai Oolt, Half Stream) and across the Bealach na h-Airigh Mhurain (*Byal*och na Harry Voorin, Pass of the Bent-grass Shieling) right of Truagh Mheall. Although the bealach is only 40m (130ft) higher than Sgurr nam Boc, the tramp across the moor is very rough; it seems a long time before the long flat bealach is reached and the Cuillin burst into view once more to beckon you homewards (Grade 4, 7$^{1}/_{2}$ miles/12km, 490m/1,600ft, 6hr round trip).

5.4 EYNORT TO TALISKER

Unlike its neighbours Glen Brittle and Talisker Bay, Glen Eynort is not noted for its dramatic scenery. Once into its confines, the Cuillin hidden from sight, its featureless grassy hillsides seem a world away from rock peaks and vertical sea cliffs. On a wet day, with rain sweeping across the moors, it can be a dreich place indeed, but when the sun shines on the still waters of Loch Eynort it is a green and peaceful haven in the wild Minginish landscape.

The east side of the loch is forested, and a forest road at the foot of the glen (GR 384271) gives access to some fine waterfalls (marked on the map). The head of the loch is also the unspectacular starting point for the most serious of the Minginish coast walks. The route to Talisker is a major undertaking, passing through some of the loneliest country on Skye and involving the crossing of steep grass slopes on the edge of awesome cliffs. It should be done only in good footwear, in good weather and when the ground is dry, and will not be appreciated by those who suffer from vertigo. For those prepared to meet its challenges, however, it provides a sensational cliff-top walk that will linger long in the memory.

The route begins at the end of the surfaced road in Eynort village (GR 379264). Continue straight on along an unsurfaced road to a farmyard, and then on a path past a ruined church to the ruined buildings on the small peninsula of Faolainn (Fœlin, Sea-gull). Beyond here follow a good sheep path along a grass shelf above small waterside crags and then take to the beach beyond.

Rounding the point beyond Faolainn (GR 374247) the hillside above the shore (Biod na Fionaich, Beet na Fee-onich, Shaggy Cliff) steepens, but the shoreline continues to provide good going on boulders and rock pavement. It is a curiously exciting promenade, for the sensation is one of clinging to the edge of the land, leaving behind the sheltered safety of the deeply indented loch for the wide horizons of the open sea. When Sarah Murray sailed into Loch Eynort from Rum during her tour of the islands in 1802 she described the mood of the place exactly: 'as silent and forlorn as an uninhabited island.'

As far as the point beyond Biod na Fionaich (GR 368244) it is necessary to leave the shoreline only once to bypass a small crag, but then the character of the route changes as cliffs begin to bar the way and it is necessary to take to higher ground. At the point itself at certain states of the tide the sea makes a deep gurgling sound as it penetrates a narrowing orifice in the rock. To outflank the cliff beyond here it is necessary to climb the steep grass slope above to a height of 30m (100ft). The first few metres are very steep indeed, and unless you are sure of your adhesion retrace your steps along the shoreline until less steep slopes present themselves. Once height is gained the Cuillin come into view, forming a black wall beyond Loch Eynort.

Keep well away from the crumbling cliff edge as you are forced up-wards on short turf to a height of 90m (300ft) at the headland above the sea caves marked on the map. From here descend into the hanging valley of Tusdale, a grassy bowl backed by a fine waterfall and drained by a series of smaller waterfalls, then keep high around the headland at the mouth of Loch Eynort (to avoid a descent and re-ascent) and regain the coast at Glen Caladale (2½hr from Eynort).

Between the Caladale river and the next headland of Sgurr Beag (Skoor Bake, Little Peak), a fine wide bay backed by a line of 90m (300ft) vertical cliffs gives a taste of the excitement to come, for the route now develops into a wonderful cliff-top stravaig to Talisker Bay. Short grass and good sheep tracks make excellent going, and numerous headlands provide excellent safe viewpoints, so avoid the temptation to go too near the cliff edge, which is crumbling, often overhanging and honeycombed with rabbit burrows. Rabbits will be seen diving for their burrows with seemingly suicidal speed, to be saved at the last moment only by pinpoint accuracy. Brinksmanship in the real sense of the word.

As you progress, the coastal architecture becomes increasingly im-pressive. Back towards Glen Caladale from Sgurr Beag a huge cave (not marked on OS map) can be seen holing the cliff face. Beyond Sgurr Beag the great grass-topped stump of Stac a' Mheadais (Stachk a *Vait*ish) is passed en route to the airy viewpoint of Sgurr Buidhe (Skoor *Boo*-ya, Yellow Peak). From here the next 2 miles (3km) of coastline, a line of unbreached cliffs soaring up to 280m (900ft) at Biod Ruadh (Beet *Roo*-a, Red Cliff), can be studied in detail; an iron fence-post provides security for the nervous.

It takes longer to reach Biod Ruadh than anticipated as the route un-dulates across the slopes of Beinn Bhreac (*Vrai*-achk, Speckled), over the huge cliff face of Sgurr nam Fiadh (*Fee*-a, Deer) and around crag-girt Preshal Beg. Preshal Beg is one of the most outstanding of the many hidden surprises of the route. It crowns the moor like an impregnable rock fortress, a dun fit for a giant. Its south-west face, remote and rarely viewed, is ringed by fluted basalt pipes in comparison with which the similar formations at the Giant's Causeway in Antrim seem but an inferior imitation.

The summit of Biod Ruadh, the highest point on the walk, has no cairn, not even one solitary rock. There is simply an airy tuft of grass teetering on the edge of the abyss (6½ miles/10km, 410m/1,350ft, 6hr). Beyond here the cliffs diminish in height towards Talisker Point, and if you do not wish to continue it is possible to turn inland into Sleadale for the return journey to Eynort (indeed the route can be shortened at any point by heading inland). The continuation to Talisker, however, holds much interest.

Descend along the cliff edge, detouring around one or two rock bands, to reach the headland above Stac an Fhucadair at Talisker Point. From this eagle's viewpoint the stack looks very impressive and the bay extremely attractive, with Atlantic rollers breaking on its wide strand (see next section). The cliffs prohibit a direct descent to the bay, however, and you need to turn right and head eastwards. Access to the bay is possible further along, down the steep grass slopes of Leathad Beithe (Lyat *Bay-a*, Birch Slope), but unless transport awaits at Talisker make a rising traverse into Sleadale. In front of you is the impressive prow of Preshal More, whose columnar basalt supports mirror those of Preshal Beg. While staying at Talisker in 1773 Boswell climbed Preshal More, and on seeing the hill from this angle one's admiration for him increases.

If your map reading is good you will aim for the ruined broch (Dun Sleadale) on the western slopes of Sleadale, surely one of the loneliest on Skye. Sitting among its ruins above the bleak moors of Sleadale, it seems unimaginable that anyone would ever wish to live there. From Sleadale the return route to Eynort takes a long but surprisingly level route through the hills, with the Cuillin occasionally soaring into view to beckon you homewards.

Follow the Sleadale Burn up to remote Loch Sleadale, hidden deep on the moor, then descend across the broad basin of Kearra and continue through the curious grassy corridor of the oddly named Clachan Gorma (Clachan *Gorrama*, Blue Stones). When the river begins to descend into Tusdale, contour left onto the Bealach na Croiche (*Croich-ya*, Gallows) and descend to the ruined church at Eynort to regain your starting point (Grade 5, 13½ miles/21km, 440m/1,450ft, 10hr round trip).

Approaching Talisker Point

5.5 TALISKER TO FISKAVAIG

Of all the bays on the Minginish coast, Talisker is the most exquisite. It lies at the foot of Gleann Oraid in a flat-bottomed U-shaped trench dominated by the prow of Preshal More, its beautiful sandy beach hemmed in by cliffs and given counterpoint by Stac an Fhucadair (Stachk an *Uchk*adair, The Fuller's Stack) at Talisker Point on the south side of the bay.

The public road to Talisker ends about 1 mile (1¹/₂km) from the bay, but the beach can easily be reached by two paths that make a fine short round. From the road-end (GR 326306) continue straight on along the private road through the grounds of Talisker House. On the far side of the house fork right on a path along the wooded right bank of the Sleadale Burn to reach the beach; return via the cart track on the south side of the bay. The stack can be reached AT LOW TIDE ONLY and is well worth investigation, although its ascent must be left to rock climbers. It has some impressive overhangs and a fine rock pavement beneath it (Grade 1, 1+hr round trip).

The northern part of the Eynort–Talisker walk described in the previous section can also be explored from Talisker, including ascents of Biod Ruadh, Preshal Beg and Preshal More. The prow of Preshal More is avoided by an ascent from either the Carbost road to the east or from Sleadale to the south.

North of Talisker the cliffs of the Minginish coastline continue to Fiskavaig before they give way to the less severe scenery of Loch Bracadale. The walk from Talisker to Fiskavaig is shorter and less vertigo-inducing than its two neighbouring coast walks to the south (5.3 and 5.4), but the coastal scenery is equally spectacular. Moreover, a cross-country cart track makes the return journey easy.

Begin at the end of the public road, going right through a farmyard and past a cottage to pick up the cart track to Fiskavaig. Follow the track to the first hairpin bend then leave it and climb diagonally across the hillside on good sheep paths to reach the plateau above the glen. Follow the edge of the plateau until above the beach, where the cliffs begin. There is a stunning view from here around the next cliff-girt bay to the 120m (400ft) headland of Rubha Cruinn (*Roo*-a *Croo*-in, Round Headland), with a fine waterfall dropping from the plateau into the centre of the bay. It is not uncommon for this waterfall to be lifted and blown far back onto the plateau by eddies of wind at the cliff edge, to fall as an umbrella of spray that can be disconcerting to passing walkers on a bright sunny day.

Rubha Cruinn is an excellent viewpoint for the cliffs of Biod Ruadh and then the coastline turns northwards away from Talisker Bay. Just beyond Rubha Cruinn an easy descent to the flat shore beside McFarlane's Rock is possible, but there is no shoreline route onwards, so it is best to stay high over Sgurr Mor (Skoor Moar, Big Peak). Beyond Rubha Dubh a' Ghrianain (*Roo*-a Doo a *Gree*-anin, Black Headland of the Sunny Place) a huge cauldron carved by the sea can be seen on the shore; a descent for a closer look is possible, but again you would have to climb straight back up.

At the headland just beyond Geodh' an Eich Bhric (Gyo an Yich Vreechk, Cove of the Speckled Horse) a short diversion away from the cliff edge is required to outflank lines of small crags and a strangely deep-cut gorge carved out of the plateau by a small stream. There are waterfalls marked on the map, but only a foolhardy person would attempt to get close enough to the cliff edge to view them.

At Rubha nan Clach (*Roo*-a nan Clach, Stony Headland) the coastline turns eastwards, leaving the open sea for the inner recesses of Loch Bracadale (2½hr from Talisker). The view over Loch Bracadale is stunning from any of the high vantage points around its shores and Rubha nan Clach is no exception. The southern cliffs of Wiay and Oronsay are especially impressive from here, and beyond Loch Bracadale MacLeod's Maidens and Tables are prominent.

Beyond Rubha nan Clach the cliff top becomes more complex and route-finding more interesting; small crags dot the moor and there is another substantial gorge to negotiate. The easiest going is to be found far back from the cliff edge, which is cut deeply by a number of streams. Again, you should not attempt to view any of the waterfalls marked on the map.

As you approach Gob na h-Oa (Gope na *Hoe*-a, Beak of the Cave) a broch can be seen in a superb position crowning an eminence on the right. You can take a short cut back to Talisker via the broch, but it is worth continuing to the headland above the Gob for the fine view back along the coast to Rubha nan Clach. This view includes the numerous waterfalls dropping from the plateau, which can at last be viewed in safety. Note that the caves marked on the map cannot be reached on foot and are best seen from Oronsay (see page 153) (4hr).

Beyond Gob na h-Oa, at the entrance to Loch Harport, stark cliffs give way to the more serene scenery characteristic of that loch, and the sandy bays and lines of cottages at Fiskavaig seem oddly out of place after the wildness of the preceding coastline. The route back to Talisker lies directly southwards. Contour onto the Fiskavaig road and walk up to a hairpin bend, then keep straight on along the excellent cart track that descends Huisgill to your starting point. Talisker is surprisingly less than 2 miles (3km) distant from Fiskavaig, and with Preshal More to draw you on it is soon reached (Grade 4, 7½ miles/ 12km, 290m/950ft, 5hr round trip).

5.6 BRACADALE SHORT WALKS

With its sweeping vistas and varied scenery Loch Bracadale is considered by many to be the most beautiful of all Skye lochs. In its inner recesses between Idrigill Point to the north and Rubha nan Clach to the south are a number of photogenic islands and promontories which interlock in such a way that from every angle they form a perfect composition, their landscapes so intricate that each turn in the coastline reveals some new surprise. At any time of day the sun illuminates something of interest, and there is often sunlight on these low-lying shores when there is cloud elsewhere in Skye.

The student of Skye history will find much of interest around Loch Bracadale, for its sheltered shores have long been coveted by both inhabitants and invaders. It was here, when the loch was known as Vestrafjord (Western Fjord), that Haco's beaten fleet took shelter in 1263 on its return north from the Battle of Largs. When Pennant came in 1772 he judged it to be the best site on Skye for a town, although that honour later went to Portree, surprisingly only 8 miles (13km) away as the eagle flies on the opposite coast of the island.

From the walker's point of view the outstanding features of Loch Bracadale are its five major peninsulas, on all but one of which there is something special to see: the extraordinary caves of Harlosh Point and Meall Greepa, the three-dimensional rock maze of Roag Island and the cliff scenery of Oronsay island. The peninsulas are described here from south to north.

Ardtreck Point
This stub of a peninsula is the least attractive of the Loch Bracadale peninsulas. The walk to the point passes a dun and a lighthouse, and there are good views of Oronsay and the Fiskavaig coastline, but the going is very rough and only the dedicated need read on. From the Portnalong–Fiskavaig road follow the road signposted 'Ardtreck' until it bears left across the peninsula and becomes unsurfaced (GR 338354). Begin walking here; continue a short distance along the unsurfaced road then turn right alongside a fence and head across the

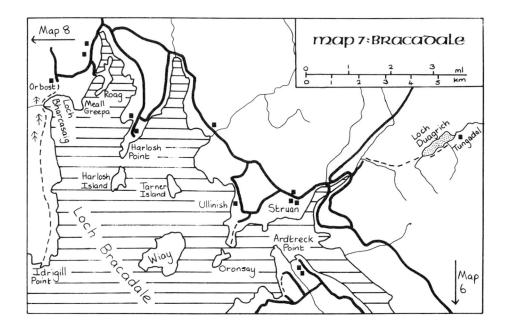

moor towards Dun Ardtreck, which can be seen ahead on the west coast of the peninsula. Keep close to the fence so that you can cross a transverse fence by a stile of stones at the fence junction, then aim for the cliff top on which the dun stands.

The walls of the dun are only 2½m (8ft) high, but they are equally as thick, and remains of the gallery between inner and outer walls can still be seen. Beyond the dun, descend to a small bay and continue along the bouldery shore beneath cliffs to reach the lighthouse at the point. A return route via the east coast of the peninsula is prevented by steep vegetated slopes and seaweed-encrusted rocks, and as the backbone of the peninsula is also very rough, it is best to return via the outward route. A sheep path along the cliff top from the lighthouse to the dun gives some slight variation (Grade 3, 1½ miles/2½km, 1+hr return).

Oronsay

The island of Oronsay consists entirely of the finest stretch of greensward on Skye, sweeping up from the shore at the mainland end of the island to vertical 72m (236ft) cliffs overlooking Loch Bracadale. The ground soon dries out after rain, making the walk to the high point of the island a pleasant excursion even when the going elsewhere may be heavy. On a sunny day the walk around the cliff top gives wonderful views over Loch Bracadale, and there are some delightful spots for simply pausing to enjoy the peace and solitude.

Like its namesake in Sleat, Oronsay (Ebb-tide island) can be reached by a beach causeway AT LOW TIDE ONLY. To reach it, take either of the minor roads to Ullinish that leave the Sligachan–Dunvegan road just north of Struan. A few hundred metres east of Ullinish Lodge Hotel, take the road to the south (now surfaced, although not marked as such on OS map) and park just before the last house (GR 322374). Go through a gate in the fence on the right and follow a cart track (becoming a path) past the house to Ullinish Point and the causeway.

Once onto the island follow the left-hand (south-east) cliff top above fine small creeks and crags until forced up to the highest tuft of grass at the end of the island, where the cliffs form an imposing wall. Beneath the high point is a wave-lashed skerry where two stacks hold out against the elements. To the south there are fine close-up views of the Talisker–Fiskavaig coastline. Westwards MacLeod's Maidens peer over the island of Wiay, while north-westwards there is a perfect view of the natural arch at the south end of Tarner Island. To complete a circuit of Oronsay return via the north-west coast (Grade 2, 3 miles/5km, 1½+hr return).

Harlosh Point
The Piper's Cave at Harlosh Point is the longest sea cave on Skye, and its exploration requires a torch. Reaching it on foot is an exciting excursion in itself, to be attempted AT LOW TIDE ONLY. The existence of the cave is an open secret; it does not appear on the OS map, yet it was famous as long ago as 1773, when Johnson and Boswell visited it, and the tale of the eponymous piper is one of the most famous in Skye folklore.

To reach Harlosh Point take either of the minor roads to Harlosh that leave the Sligachan–Dunvegan road just north of Caroy. Beyond Harlosh a road (now surfaced, although not marked as such on OS map) continues to Ardmore, where the walk begins. Aim just left of the spine of the peninsula initially to reach a gate in the double fence that crosses the peninsula. Beyond the gate, on the rise immediately to the right, are the almost imperceptible ruins of an old chapel.

The direct route to the Piper's Cave goes south along the cliff top, but it is worth making a detour via the north-west coast in order to view Dun Neill. The walls of Dun Neill are barely discernible, but then Neill hardly needed any — his dun crowned a promontory surrounded by sea cliffs on three sides, while on the landward side any attacker would need both hands to scramble up. In the bay beyond Dun Neill are further signs of habitation, and beyond here is the most westerly point of the peninsula, from where there are fine views of the Idrigill Point coastline and the beautiful sandy beach on the north coast of Harlosh Island.

Continuing around the coastline, Harlosh Point is soon reached, and here the excitement begins, for the sea cliffs along the south-east coast soon reach a height of about 20m (65ft). Beyond a deeply cut inlet a 10m (30ft) finger of basalt points the way to the Piper's Cave. From the cliff top directly opposite the pinnacle a well-worn simple scramble leads down to the shoreline, and AT LOW TIDE ONLY it is possible to scramble left along the cliff foot to the cave entrance. Beyond the huge arch that forms the entrance a 3m (10ft) square tube burrows into the hillside. With a torch it is possible to follow it to its abrupt end (watch your head!) some 50m (160ft) from the entrance. Without a torch you will readily appreciate the feelings of the piper, who was heard to mutter as he entered: 'I doot, I doot, I doot I'll e'er come oot!'

The Piper's Cave must have been longer in the days of the piper. Having been given the gift of music by a fairy queen, he was finally called to task and, having passed on the gift to his son (thus founding the hereditary school of piping at Borreraig), he entered the cave with his dog, pipes blasting. Followers above ground followed the sound of the pipes as far as Fairy Bridge, where the music stopped. The piper's dog reappeared, hair completely singed off, at the Uamh Oir. The complete tale can be read in the Piping Centre at Borreraig.

Beyond the cave it is possible to scramble a short distance further along the shoreline, but the only route back to the cliff top is the route of approach. The grassy walk back to the roadside takes about 15min (Grade 2 excluding scramble to cave, 2 miles/3km, 1¹/₂+hr return).

Roag Island

Roag Island is not really an island as it is connected to the mainland of Skye by a causeway that carries a road. Nevertheless, it feels like an island, and that is good enough. It is mostly flat except at its southern end, where a large table-like rock bastion is separated from the rest of the island by a short stone causeway making it almost another island in itself. This table is bounded by crags up to 10m (30ft) high and is a delightful playground for all who enjoy clambering around on shoreline rocks.

To reach Roag Island take the road to Roag village that leaves the

Sligachan–Dunvegan road at Roskhill south of Dunvegan. From Roag take the road to Ardroag (now surfaced, although not marked as such on OS map). Park on the landward side of the causeway, as parking is not allowed on the island itself. Follow the road across the causeway and around the bay until it turns sharp left into the centre of the island, then keep straight on along the shore to reach the causeway and the table top. The most interesting formations are at the south-west point, where the deeply fissured tangle of rock is like giant eroded crazy paving. (Grade 2, 1¹/₂ miles/2¹/₂km, 1+hr return.)

Meall Greepa (Mell Greepa, Precipice Hill)
At the headland of Meall Greepa is one of those exciting surprises of which Skye seems to have an unending store, in this case the largest archway cave on the island. The walk to the cave should be attempted AT LOW TIDE ONLY, and to be appreciated to the full it should be saved for the evening of a fine day, when the sun irradiates the cliffs.

Access to Meall Greepa is as for MacLeod's Maidens (see page 161). Leave the road at the eastern end of Loch Bharcasaig and follow a de-lightful rock platform out along the cliff foot. At one point the cliffs fall directly into the sea, but at low tide this can be crossed dryshod on stepping stones to reach the mouth of the cave (Grade 3, 1¹/₂ miles/ 2¹/₂km, 1+hr return).

Only now is the cave revealed in its true glory as a huge archway cave tunnelling right through Meall Greepa, forming a beautifully arched cavern some 40m (130ft) long by 10m (30ft) high, in whose dark recesses echo the swirling waters of Loch Bracadale. Brave souls who do not fear the prospect of a wetting can cross the channel at the cave's entrance and scramble some distance up the centre of the chan-nel on large blocks, which have fallen from the roof, but be warned that a slip would be very serious. Beyond the cave is a natural arch visible from certain angles during the approach walk but not reachable on foot.

Historical Bracadale
Anyone interested in the history of Skye will find many ruins to explore around the shores of Loch Bracadale, especially if using the OS 1:25 000 map as a guide. To the non-specialist two of the most in-teresting ruins are undoubtedly Dun Beag (the best preserved broch on Skye) and Tungadal souterrain (the best preserved souterrain).

Dun Beag (GR 339387) stands right beside the Sligachan– Dunvegan road immediately north of the Ullinish turn-off, and it is easily reached by a path (car park and signpost). As recently as 200 years ago its walls still stood 6m (20ft) high; local reuse of the stones over the centuries has reduced that height to only 4m (13ft), but between inner and outer walls can still be seen a cell and sections of gallery, complete with access steps. The site was excavated earlier this century and the stonework restored to give some indication of its former glory. If you stand inside the central enclosure today you will have some idea of the security afforded when the building was intact (Grade 1, ¹/₂hr return).

The remarkable Tungadal souterrain (GR 407401) lies hidden beneath the bleak moors that form the heartland of Skye between Bracadale and Portree. There is a good path most of the way, but the going is very rough and marshy in the vicinity of Loch Duagrich, and the featureless landscape will not appeal to all. The souterrain was excavated in 1988 and is now on public display; a torch is useful for its exploration.

The route begins at the foot of Glen Bracadale (GR 371395), reached by a minor road (signposted Amer) that leaves the Sligachan–Dunvegan road just south of Struan. Take the cart track on the right up Glen Bracadale to Loch Duagrich. Halfway along, when the glen turns left, some ruined buildings can be seen on the right, and behind the first is an ancient earth house, like a miniature souterrain.

At Loch Duagrich cross the extremely marshy mouth of the loch to gain a path along the south-east shore (note that the connecting path shown on the map does not exist). Once onto the lochside path, the going is good until the path ends two-thirds of the way along at a stream, beyond which marshy terrain is again encountered as far as the end of the loch. When cattle wade through the shallows here the landscape is more like the Camargue than the Scottish Highlands.

The souterrain is located as follows. Viewed from the end of the loch, the brow of the hill that forms the skyline on the right descends steeply and levels off over a grassy knoll just above the rim of the flat moor. The souterrain lies in the middle of this knoll, about 150m from the loch end (2hr). The entrance opens onto an 8m (25ft) long by 1m (3ft) square tunnel that runs under the earth like an ancient subway line. Light at the far end filters through what might have been a ventilation shaft. Such a remarkable construction in such a desolate landscape evokes a sense of wonder and curiosity about its builders. Return by the outward route (Grade 3, 6 miles/10km, 4hr return).

Note: at the time of writing afforestation is taking place in the Loch Duagrich region. The above access route remains open and it is intended that any fences erected will be crossed by stiles.

6 Ouírnish

Duirinish (*Joorinish*, Deer Promontory) in the north-west of Skye is fringed by mile after mile of some of the most spectacular coastal scenery in the British Isles. Inland the unusual flat-topped hills of MacLeod's Tables provide good hillwalking (6.1), but it is the coastline that is the major attraction. Here are to be found Skye's tallest stack (6.2), Skye's most beautiful cliff-top walk (6.3) and Skye's highest sea cliffs (6.4). In addition, the shores of Loch Dunvegan provide a number of interesting shorter walks (6.5).

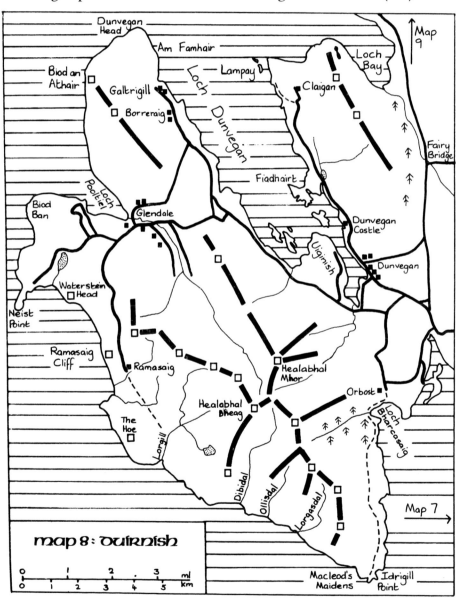

map 8: Ouírnish

6.1 MACLEOD'S TABLES

Healabhal Bheag (488m/1,601ft, *Hella*val Vake, poss Little Holy
    Mountain after its altar-like appearance)
Healabhal Mhor (468m/1,535ft, *Hella*val Voar, Big Holy Mountain)

Healabhal Bheag and Healabhal Mhor are curious truncated hills
whose appearance has given rise to their more familiar name of
MacLeod's Tables. It is as though their summits have been lopped off
by some supernatural force, and legend has it that this is precisely
what happened, in order to provide a bed and table for St Columba
when he was turned away from the door by a local clan chief.
Geologists have a more prosaic explanation: the shape of the hills
reflects the horizontal stratification of the basalt lavas of which they
are composed.

If legend is to be believed the name 'table' is doubly apt, for it was
on Healabhal Bheag that a MacLeod chief once dined his guests. The
story goes that on a visit to the King's court in Edinburgh he tired of
hearing of the splendours of Holyrood Palace and boasted that on
Skye he had a more spacious banqueting hall, a finer ceiling, a larger
table and finer candelabra. To prove the point he invited a number of
mainland lords to Skye and spread an evening feast on the summit of
Healabhal Bheag. With the flat summit as his table, a starry sky as his
ceiling and clansmen with flaming torches to light the proceedings,
one may assume that the point was proved.

Of the two Tables, Healabhal Mhor is the one more often climbed,
having the larger summit plateau (hence its name, although of lesser
height) and being more accessible from Dunvegan, but Healabhal
Bheag is the more interesting hill in all other respects. If climbed
separately, Healabhal Mhor is best ascended by its north-east ridge
from the track to Osdale (GR 243463), while Healabhal Bheag is best
ascended from Loch Bharcasaig (for access see page 161), following a
track up the right bank of the Abhainn Bharcasaig through forestry
plantations to the Bealach Bharcasaig.

If climbed together, the best starting point for the round is some-
where between the two hills on the Orbost road, eg the sharp bend at
GR 256445. From here head westwards across the moors of Glen
Osdale to gain the broad east ridge of Healabhal Mhor and follow it to
the summit. The ridge is enlivened by one or two rock bands and has
fine views over Loch Dunvegan, but its most appealing attribute is its
brevity (2hr).

Healabhal Bheag from Beinn na h-Uamha

The uniform steepness of the grassy upper slopes of Healabhal Mhor accentuate the flatness of the mossy summit plateau. The summit cairn, surprisingly large considering the lack of building material, lies at the far right-hand corner. The view is notable for its non-existence, for the edges of the table form a truncated horizon. On a hazy day you could be in the sky on a platform that has no visible earthly support.

To continue the round, descend to An Sgurran (An *Scoo*ran, The Rocks), cross Beinn na h-Uamha (Bain na *Hoo*-aha, Mountain of the Cave, GR 217429, not named on OS map) and climb steep grass slopes to the summit of Healabhal Bheag (3¹/₂hr). The summit plateau is not as vast as Healabhal Mhor's, but it is equally table-like, and the view over Loch Bracadale is stunning, especially when evening light picks out the headlands and islands.

The highest point on the plateau appears to be a grassy mound in the far south-west corner, beyond which the south ridge descends interestingly to the moor, with some opportunities for scrambling. Few would wish to continue southwards, however, for the featureless low hills of southern Duirinish are no more than excrescences on the moor and must be among the least frequented in Scotland.

To complete the round, descend Healabhal Bheag via its north-east ridge. This soon narrows onto the top of an impressive buttress, which in the evening casts a perfect pyramidal shadow onto the moor below. Circumnavigate the buttress on steep broken slopes to the left and continue down the ridge past one or two rises. Go over Beinn Bhuidhe (*Voo*-ya, Yellow) or bypass it on the right, with good views of Meall Greepa, to reach your starting point (Grade 4, 7 miles/11km, 750m/2,450ft, 5½hr round trip).

6.2 MACLEOD'S MAIDENS

At the southern tip of the Duirinish peninsula, just around the corner from Idrigill Point, stand the three most famous sea stacks on Skye — MacLeod's Maidens, the tallest of which (the tallest stack on Skye) reaches a height of 63m (207ft). The delightful walk to the dramatic viewpoint on the nearby cliff top is one of the classic coast walks of Skye. For most of the way there is an excellently contoured path, which makes the going extremely pleasant, and in addition a short detour (missed by most people) enables a stunning view to be had of the unique double arches south of Brandarsaig Bay. Although the path is easy, good footwear is essential in the vicinity of the Maidens, where the airy cliff edge requires great care.

The route begins on the shores of Loch Bracadale at Loch Bharcasaig (*Var*kasaig, Castle Bay), at the end of the Orbost road south of Dunvegan. The surfaced road ends at Orbost House but, depending on the state of your car, it is possible to continue along a very rough road to the lochside and the bridge over the Abhainn Bharcasaig (GR 252422). Loch Bharcasaig is a lovely bay bounded on the left by the headland of Meall Greepa (see page 156). Camping is possible with permission (enquire at the farm — GR 256431).

The path to the Maidens begins at the bridge and follows a clearing through forestry plantations. Beyond the trees the view over Loch Bracadale opens up as the path climbs onto the low bealach between Beinn na Boineid (*Bonn*aj, Bonnet) and Beinn na Moine (*Moan*-ya, Bog) and traverses high above Brandarsaig Bay. The complex contortions of the coastline around Brandarsaig Bay can be explored by those with an excess of time and energy; there is no other access to the shore en route.

The path continues over the next rise, past the abandoned village of Idrigill and through the Glac Ghealaridh (Glachk Yallery, Defile of the White Shieling, ie the level defile between Steineval and Ard Beag

MacLeod's Maidens

not named on OS map). From the near end of the defile a short pathless detour (requiring care) leads to one of the most stunning coastal views on Skye. Leave the path and climb up to an obvious clearing at the cliff edge halfway up the slopes of Ard Beag (Ard Bake, Little Height). The view from here back across Camas na h-Uamha (Cammas na *Hoo*-aha, Bay of the Cave) includes caves and stacks galore, but what makes it exceptional even by Skye standards are the remarkable double arches on the headland beyond, here seen in profile one behind the other, the waters of Loch Bracadale surging through both.

Returning to the path, continue through the Glac Ghealaridh to reach more ruins, beyond which the path loses itself among sheep tracks. The path marked on the map as continuing all the way around the coast is a figment of the mapmaker's imagination. Leave the ruins to your left and, using the map as a guide, head straight across the moor to the headland above the Maidens (Rubha na Maighdeanan, *Roo*-a na *Ma*-ijanan, the Maidens' Headland, not named on OS map).

The terrain is complex, with many knolls that make it difficult to hold to a direct line. You are most likely to reach the cliff top just before the Maidens, in which case follow the cliff edge until they come into view (Grade 3, 4½ miles/7km, 240m/800ft, 2½hr). If you reach the cliff edge at a very large bay with cliffs rising westwards, this is Inbhir a' Gharraidh (Inyir a Gharry, the Cove of the Walled Enclosure) beyond the Maidens.

The coastline between Ard Beag and the Maidens has some spectacular caves, which can unfortunately only be viewed by boat. They include the Candlestick Cave, named according to some after a large formation at its entrance and according to others after the candles needed to explore it, and Lady Grange's Cave. The tragic Lady Grange was abducted from Edinburgh in 1730 after overhearing a Jacobite plot and made to eke out the remainder of her life in sometimes appalling conditions on St Kilda, the Uists and many places on Skye, including this cave, until her death in 1745.

The crumbling cliff edge at Rubha na Maighdeanan demands extreme caution. The setting is dramatic. The cairn on the cliff top is perched some 70m (230ft) above the crashing waves below. The tallest Maiden (the Mother) stands close by; beyond stand her two daughters, one a dumpy pinnacle, the other seen from most angles as a thin rock blade. The best view of the Maidens is obtained from further round Inbhir a' Gharraidh, from where the three stacks appear in profile, the leaning summit block of the Mother resembling a head nodding to the two daughters. From this angle, and from the sea, the Mother has a truly human appearance that has been likened to a statue of a seated Queen Victoria. Across Loch Bracadale the Cuillin rear above the Minginish coastline to complete a picture of nature at its grandest.

If you fancy your chances at climbing the Mother stack (a Severe rock climb first completed by I. S. Clough and J. McLean in 1959), you must first abseil from the Rubha to the shore below (preferably leaving the rope in place). The only other approach is from the sea, and this is often made treacherous by the heavy swell and current around Idrigill Point.

The Maidens have a notorious reputation for shipwrecks, not helped by smugglers' false lights on the Black Skerry (see next section). In the light of this, Sir Walter Scott's evocative description of the Maidens as 'The Choosers of the Slain' in *The Lord of the Isles* seems apt. The Choosers of the Slain were the Norse Valkyries who, after a battle, chose the best and bravest of the slain to take their place in Valhalla.

After a sojourn at the Rubha the pleasant walk back to Loch Bharcasaig awaits. If it is late in the day, this is best taken at a leisurely pace in order to enjoy the view over Loch Bracadale and its islands at its best, warmed by slanting evening light (Grade 3, 9 miles/14km, 390m/1,300ft, 5hr return excluding time spent at the Maidens).

6.3 IDRIGILL TO LORGILL

The walk from Idrigill Point to Lorgill Bay is the finest cliff-top walk in the British Isles. The coastal scenery is breathtaking, the terrain is excellent and every headland reveals some new exciting surprise to spur the walker ever onward towards the westering sun. The route guards its secrets well, however, for it begins 4¹/₂ miles/7km from the nearest road-end (Loch Bharcasaig, GR 252422) and ends 2 miles/3km from the nearest road-end (Ramasaig, GR 165442). The walk therefore demands a certain amount of pre-planning.

The best way to complete the walk in a single day is to arrange for transport at both ends (Loch Bharcasaig to Ramasaig: 14 miles/22km, 720m/2,350ft, 8hr). Failing this, it will be necessary to camp at Lorgill or Ramasaig Bay at the end of the walk (a tent could be pre-pitched) and on the following day return across country to your starting point via the Bealach Bharcasaig south of MacLeod's Tables; note that a path descends the right bank of the Abhainn Bharcasaig through forestry plantations. On a long summer's day the complete circuit could be done in a single day by the super-fit. Other shorter return trips from Loch Bharcasaig to various points on the Idrigill–Lorgill coast are also possible, as a glance at the map will indicate.

The walk is described here from south to north, beginning at MacLeod's Maidens, although it has merit in both directions. Note that the cliff-top path marked on the map does not exist, but there are plenty of sheep paths and the going is excellent. Good footwear is essential and all the usual coast-walking precautions apply. Photographers should take plenty of film.

From MacLeod's Maidens (see previous section for access from Loch Bharcasaig) continue around the cliff top above Inbhir a' Gharraidh and across the slopes of Ben Idrigill, reaching a height of 200m (650ft). Descend slightly across a stream to reach the next headland, where there is a pinnacle low down on the cliff face. From here the route ahead stretches to Lorgill Bay and beyond, the cliff top like a bowling green — wonderful walking country.

Descend further into Glen Lorgasdal to reach perhaps the finest stretch of coastline on the whole route, studded with stacks and pinnacles. The first pinnacle passed clings to the cliff face like a huge Cleopatra's Needle that seems ready to peel away into the sea. Next comes an arête that is topped by two pinnacles, and on the cliff top above is a perfect green that would make an idyllic (though precarious) campsite.

From the small promontory just beyond the arête the view back is stunning. The arête is seen to be holed at sea-level, forming the natural arch marked on the map (GR 222380). Beside the arch are two stacks, one a wedge with a knife-edge summit ridge. Between the stacks the Lorgasdal river plunges into the sea. The scene is the epitome of all that is best in Skye coastal architecture ($1\frac{1}{2}$hr from MacLeod's Maidens).

Beyond here continue around the next headland to Glen Ollisdal at the foot of Healabhal Bheag, and then around the next headland to Glen Dibidal (Deep Glen) (3hr). Across the Geodha Mor (*Gyo*-a Moar, Big Cove) at the foot of Glen Dibidal is a lovely cove whose sandy beach and crystal clear waters are inaccessible on foot.

As its name implies, Glen Dibidal forms a deep gorge through which the Dibidal river tumbles to the sea, and it is necessary to lose height and take a diagonal line down across the hillside to cross the river above the gorge. For the first time en route it is possible to reach the shore here by a short scramble.

Beyond Glen Dibidal the coast becomes increasingly awesome, the map noting a number of caves and natural arches. The caves are massive, reaching almost the height of the cliff, and great care is required on the overhanging and crumbling cliff edge above them. The arches are similarly on the grand scale, being in reality enormous archway caves that tunnel through headlands. None of the arches or caves can be reached on foot from the cliff top. Adding to the fearsomeness of the scene is the treacherous An Dubh Sgeir (An Doo Skerr, The Black Skerry) offshore, where the wrecker and smuggler Campbell of Ensor lit false beacons to lure ships to their doom.

From Glen Dibidal regain the cliff top and reach the stream that drains Loch an Fhridhein, from where the first archway cave can be seen cutting through the headland beyond. Beyond here a fence leads on along the cliff edge above another deeply recessed cave (unviewable) and then the second archway cave comes into view — an enormous tunnel some 30m (100ft) long through which the sea pounds mercilessly. On the next rise the cliffs reach 90m (300ft) and MacLeod's Maidens can be seen for the last time. Continuing along the cliff edge, descend to the Scaladal Burn to view the largest cave of all, cutting deep into the cliff face ahead. Beneath your feet, but not visible until you reach the far side of the Scaladal Burn, is the third archway cave — another huge tunnel some 15m (50ft) long.

The crossing of the Scaladal gorge requires care; follow the edge of the gorge a short distance inland until you find a sheep path that descends into the gorge above a waterfall and climbs back along a rock ledge on the far side. Follow the far side of the gorge down to the cliff edge to view the third archway cave, then climb the steepest slope of the day to reach the vertiginous grassy summit of Biod Boidheach (Beet *Baw*-yach, Beautiful Cliff, GR 176408, not named on OS map). An iron fence-post provides security for the nervous (4½hr).

Beyond Biod Boidheach lies tranquil Lorgill Bay, whose beach and verdant pastures are balm to the eyes after the ferocity of the southern Duirinish coastline, and beyond the bay rise the cliffs of the Hoe (see next section). Descend to the bay, which is the first bay of easy access this side of Loch Bharcasaig, and stroll through the pleasant pastures beside the river to Lorgill shepherd's bothy (5hr).

If continuing to Ramasaig, pick up a path heading north-westwards past the ruins of Lorgill village onto the moor. The ten families who lived at Lorgill were summarily evicted in 1830 and forced to emigrate to Nova Scotia. The path becomes an excellent cart track across the moor to Ramasaig road-end (Grade 5, 7½ miles/12km, 390m/ 1,300ft, 6hr from MacLeod's Maidens).

6.4 NORTH DUIRINISH SHORT WALKS

The northern reaches of Duirinish contain the highest sea cliffs on Skye, culminating in the giddy 313m (1,028ft) summit of Biod an Athair near Dunvegan Head. For mile after mile the cliffs present a more or less vertical wall whose purity of line is unbroken by caves and stacks, and this gives them a fearsome appearance that is quite different from that of the southern Duirinish coastline described in the previous two sections. A network of minor roads facilitates access to the cliff top and enables the best viewpoints to be reached without too much effort, but good footwear is required and great care is essential at the cliff edge.

Lorgill Bay to Neist Point
North of Lorgill Bay the road from Glendale to Ramasaig runs close to the cliff top, and nowhere else on Skye are such magnificent cliffs so readily accessible. There are three high points along the cliff edge:

Neist Point

The Hoe, Ramasaig Cliff and Waterstein Head, each of which lies only a short distance across the moor from the roadside. Once onto the cliff top, the going is good and the views are superb.

The Hoe (233m/764ft)
The Hoe stands immediately north of Lorgill Bay and is reached via the cart track from Ramasaig to Lorgill Bay described in the previous section. From Ramasaig follow the track as far as its high point, then bear right to gain the Hoe's mossy summit plateau, which is set well back from the cliff edge (1hr). There are fine views along the coast in both directions — northwards across Ramasaig Cliff and Waterstein Head to Neist Point, and southwards over MacLeod's Maidens to the distant Cuillin.

For a magnificent return route descend northwards along the grassy cliff top to Ramasaig Bay. The going is excellent and the view across the bay is superb, especially if Ramasaig waterfall (GR 159438) and Loch Eishort waterfall (GR 155458) are in full flow. The headland of Hoe Rape halfway along makes a fine vantage point, but beware the aggressive seabirds that nest on its northern face. Descend to Ramasaig Bay to view the waterfall, then cross the meadows back to Ramasaig (Grade 3, 4¹/₂ miles/7km, 240m/800ft, 3hr round trip).

Ramasaig Cliff (247m/811ft)
North of Ramasaig Bay the cliffs rise steeply again to Ramasaig Cliff, whose summit lies only 400m from and 30m (100ft) above the high point of the road. From the roadside aim directly for the summit; the cliff edge lies just beyond (Grade 3, 1hr return).

Waterstein Head (296m/970ft)
Between Ramasaig Cliff and Waterstein Head the cliffs are continuous. The easiest approach to Waterstein Head begins at a high point on the road immediately east of Beinn na Coinnich (*Coan*-yich, Moss). Go over Beinn na Coinnich to reach the cliff edge and then walk along the cliff top to the summit of Waterstein Head, whose cliffs are the highest and most awesome on this stretch of coastline. Rocks at the cliff edge make it possible to lie down and peer over at the crashing waves far below (Grade 3, 2¹/₂ miles/4km, 140m/450ft, 2hr return).
   Ramasaig Cliff and Waterstein Head are easily combined into a fine round with a return walk along the road. The inclusion of The Hoe makes a more interesting but much longer circuit involving loss of height at Ramasaig Bay.

Neist Point (originally An Eist, An Eesht, The Horse)
Across Moonen Bay from Waterstein Head the curious appendage of Neist Point juts out into the sea like a giant knobbly arm, ending in rocky fingertips between which the surf pounds. There is much to see in the area, and a splendid surfaced access path, complete with concrete steps and hand rail, makes it a popular excursion.
   The path begins at the car park at Neist Point road-end (GR 133478), descends through a break in the cliffs and contours around the craggy lump of An t-Aigeach (An Tag-yach, The Stallion, GR 129475, not named on OS map) to reach Neist Point lighthouse, a beautiful inhabited building perched on the cliff top above the sea. Between the lighthouse and the point a vast cleanly-faulted three-dimensional rock pavement provides delightful scrambling. There are magnificent views southwards across Moonen Bay to Waterstein Head, Ramasaig Cliff and The Hoe and westwards across the Little Minch to the Outer Hebrides (stunning at sunset) (Grade 2, 1¹/₂+hr return).
   The east coast of the Neist Point peninsula is relatively flat, but on the west coast cliffs reach a height of 90m (300ft) at An t-Aigeach, and beyond here a two-tiered cliff reaches 120m (400ft). This latter cliff

top can be reached from the road-end by a path that affords good views of the point as it heads westwards along the cliff edge. The walk can be extended along the cliff top to the ruins of a coastguard lookout station, beyond which can be seen the top of Biod Ban (Beet Bahn, White Cliff), a stupendous mural precipice 196m (645ft) high. For an unimpeded view of the whole cliff face of Biod Ban, continue across the plateau past the lookout to the edge of Oisgill Bay. Return to the car park from the lookout by a path that goes straight across the moor (Grade 2, 1+hr return).

Loch Pooltiel and Glendale
It is possible to walk all the way along the cliff top from Neist Point to Loch Pooltiel, the cliffs gradually diminishing in height beyond Biod Ban to the flat shores at the head of the loch. Here is green and populous Glendale, whose water mill and craft shops attract many summer visitors. In 1882 Glendale crofters were at the forefront of resistance to the Clearances, and a gunboat was dispatched to Loch Pooltiel to intimidate them. A roadside monument (GR 197497) commemorates their achievements.

Loch Pooltiel to Loch Dunvegan
The extreme northern spur of Duirinish between Loch Pooltiel and Loch Dunvegan forms a large subsidiary peninsula in its own right, whose entire western coastline is one continuous line of cliffs from Glendale all the way to Dunvegan Head. This coastline makes a fine long walk, but as there is a road up the east side of the peninsula the highest cliffs at Biod an Athair near Dunvegan Head can be reached more conveniently from the road-end at Galtrigill (see below). From Dunvegan Head the cliffs continue along the east coast as far south as Borreraig and Galtrigill, and beyond here the low-lying shores of inner Loch Dunvegan become less interesting.

Borreraig and Galtrigill
Borreraig's main claim to fame is as the site of the former MacCrimmon Piping School. The MacCrimmons were hereditary pipers to the MacLeods for at least ten generations and operated the school from the early sixteenth to the late eighteenth century. A prominent monument stands on the hillside north-west of the village, and the Piping Centre, full of historical artefacts, is well worth a visit.

In order not to incur the wrath of their neighbours the pipers used to practise in sea caves, which can be visited in combination with an exploration of the coastline. The shore can be gained by walking down from the roadside to the bay north of Gob na Hoe (Gope na Hoe, Beak of the Hoe), and in the cliff face north of here are two caves which would seem ideal for bagpipe practice (Grade 3, 1+hr return). The most famous pipers' cave is still further north at Galtrigill Bay (GR 184548, not named on OS map), but the shoreline route to it is blocked by overhanging cliffs just short of the cave.

The cliffs of Gob na Hoe contain no sizeable cave, but climbers who do not mind using limpets for footholds may find a sea-level girdle traverse here more than exciting (a slip would be serious); note that the complete traverse is blocked by an impassable vertical section opposite a small rock islet.

The east coast road ends at the ruined village of Galtrigill, which was abandoned to the elements when its inhabitants gave up the hard struggle of supporting themselves off the land. Not far from the road-end is the Manners Stone, a large flat 1m square stone on which, according to tradition, you sit in order to find your manners. The stone is located as follows: just below the road-end is a ruined cottage with a prominent chimney, and just beyond this is an old fence and wall; follow the fence down for 100m and you will see the stone 20m to the left.

To reach Galtrigill Bay follow the edge of the gorge of the Galtrigill Burn down past the Manners Stone to a point above the bay, from where a rocky path meanders down to the beach. The prominent pipers' cave is at the south end of the beach (Grade 2, 1+hr return).

Biod an Athair (313m/1,028ft, Beet an *A*-hir, Sky Cliff)

Galtrigill road-end is the starting point for the shortest route to the summit of Biod an Athair, the highest sea cliff on Skye. From the road-end the gently rising moor and seemingly inconsequential summit make the ascent appear deceptively simple, but the airy cliff edge demands great respect and the usual coast walking precautions apply, especially if the continuation to the natural arch of Am Famhair (Am *Fahv*ir, The Giant) is included.

The best route across the heathery moor goes through the green fields above old Galtrigill village and along the banks of the Galtrigill Burn, veering right to reach the cliff edge and the summit. The best way to view the cliff face at the summit is to lie down on the grass and peer over the edge at the miniature Atlantic breakers far below, but such is the scale of the face that its dimensions are hard to take in. The views across to the Outer Hebrides are superb (Grade 4, 4 miles/7km, 250m/800ft, 2½hr return).

A worthwhile but rough extension to the ascent of Biod an Athair is to continue around the cliff top towards Dunvegan Head and return via the natural arch of Am Famhair. From the summit a good sheep path initially leads northwards along the cliff top, but as you progress the cliff edge becomes less well delineated, the going becomes heathery and tough and the struggle to reach the undistinguished point of Dunvegan Head is hardly worthwhile. It is better at this point to aim straight across the moor to Am Famhair — an interesting exercise in navigation! Am Famhair is one of the most remarkable natural arches on Skye, for it stands high and dry on the beach, completely unconnected to the cliff face and abandoned long ago by the sea, stranded like some megalithic sculpture.

To reach Galtrigill from Am Famhair it is best to take a direct line slightly away from the cliff edge in order to avoid the gorge of the Galtrigill Burn (4½ miles/7km, 270m/900ft, 3½hr round trip). For those wishing to visit only Am Famhair from the road-end, keep straight on to cross the Galtrigill river above its gorge, then trend right to reach the cliff edge (Grade 4, 2hr return).

6.5 DUNVEGAN SHORT WALKS

With its castle, hotels, shops and restaurants, Dunvegan has developed into the main tourist centre for Duirinish and north-west Skye. Popular haunts such as Glendale and Neist Point are only a short drive away, while in the immediate vicinity are a number of less well known places where you can wander the shores of Loch Dunvegan far from the madding crowd.

Dunvegan Castle
Dunvegan Castle is the most celebrated building on Skye. Its origin is lost in the mists of time, but the MacLeods have certainly lived there since the mid-thirteenth century. It is Skye's one remaining castle that still looks as sturdy and turreted as a castle should (although much of it dates back only as far as the nineteenth century).

It is open to the public and is well worth a visit, for inside are to be found all manner of treasures, including Rory Mor's Drinking Horn (a twelfth-century ox-horn that each chief had to drain at a draught to prove his manhood), the Dunvegan Cup (a fifteenth-century wooden cup covered with ornamental silverwork) and the Fairy Flag. The Fairy Flag dates back to the eleventh-century Crusades and is said to have magical powers, including the ability to avert disaster when unfurled. The flag can only be unfurled three times, however, and it has already been used twice (once at the Battle of the Spoiling of the Dyke — see page 177).

From beside the castle in summer boats leave to visit the Loch Dunvegan seal colonies.

Uiginish Point (Point of the Promontory of the Bay)
The best view of Dunvegan Castle and the offshore islands of Loch Dunvegan is obtained from across the water at Uiginish Point (GR 235491). The route to the point crosses rough moorland in places, but it is a fine peaceful tramp a world away from busy Dunvegan.

Begin at Uiginish Lodge Hotel (GR 243483), reached by a minor road from the Glendale road. Continue straight on through a gate left of the hotel and follow a track right through the hotel grounds. Pick up a sheep path on the grassy hillside above the east shore of the Uiginish peninsula and follow it out to the lighthouse at the point; there is some slight exposure towards the point as some shoreline crags are negotiated. The point is so surrounded by islands that it feels like an island itself.

Return via the west coast, cutting inland to avoid shoreline crags and aiming for the cart track that runs from Ob Dubh (Op Doo, Black Bay) back across the peninsula to the hotel. Note that the two duns marked on the map are completely dilapidated (Grade 3, 2 miles/3km, 1½hr round trip).

Fiadhairt (*Fee*-achursht, Grassland)
The small Fiadhairt peninsula north of Dunvegan Castle is completely surrounded by water except for a narrow isthmus that connects it to the rest of Skye. Because of its isolation and its rough-looking moorland approach it is rarely visited, and as a consequence it boasts one of the best preserved brochs on Skye and a shoreline frequented by Loch Dunvegan seals.

Although the peninsula itself is quite rough, the approach walk from the south-west corner of Loch Suardal (GR 239509) is surprisingly pleasant. From the roadside follow a short dirt track up the hillside, then bear right to some ruins ahead. At the ruins pick up an old cart track that contours right of the high point of the moor to reach the isthmus.

On the moor just beyond the isthmus stands the broch, whose inner and outer walls, although only 2m (6ft) high, are complete, with steps leading down between them to a partly covered gallery. The broch is unusual on two counts: it has two entrances (one a channelled passageway from the moor) and its excavation in 1914 uncovered a Roman artefact — a terracotta model of a bale of hides or fleeces. The shores of the peninsula can be explored at will, from the vegetated sea cliffs at the northern end to the low-lying rocks at the complex southern tip. If there are seals on the rocks, approach quietly, for they are easily disturbed (Grade 3, 2½ miles/4km, 1½+hr return).

Claigan Coral Bays
The popular coral bays of Claigan are easily reached and well worth visiting, even though you are unlikely to be alone there during the summer months. Note that the sand is not true coral but sun-bleached bits of a red alga called *Lithothamnion calcareum*.

The route to the bays begins at the sharp right-hand bend just beyond Claigan (GR 232537). A signposted cart track leads down to the shore and along to the first bay (GR 224544), beyond which a path continues to the more extensive second bay opposite the island of Lampay (Grade 1, 2½ miles/4km, 1½hr return). From here it is possible to continue all the way around the coast, on grass slopes between the shore and the cliffs of Sgurr a' Bhagh (Vagh, Bay), to Loch Bay in Waternish (if undertaking this route, note that it involves the fording of the Bay river).

Claigan Souterrain
Claigan souterrain makes an unusual objective for a short walk. Although not as impressive as Tungadal souterrain (see page 157), it remains a considerable construction and is much easier to reach. *Note:* the interior is muddy and dark, and a torch is required.

Begin at the sharp left-hand bend just beyond the start of the Claigan Coral Bays walk (GR 233538) and follow the cart track that goes straight on. The souterrain will be found about 500m along, not far beyond where the track bears right; its exact position is about 20m beyond the bend and 15m to the left, at the back of a small depression. The entrance is a low, lintelled burrow that leads to a narrow rising tunnel almost 10m (35ft) long. The souterrain was probably used as a refuge, and an excellent hiding place it is (Grade 1, 1hr return).

7 waternish

Waternish (pronounced Vatternish, Water Promontory) is the central of the three peninsulas of northern Skye that jut out into the Little Minch. Narrow, pointed and bent like a crooked finger, it has neither the mountain scenery of Trotternish to the east nor the coastal scenery of Duirinish to the west. It is, however, fine walking country, a remote, unfrequented and untamed land of wide horizons still echoing to the clash of claymores. Nowhere else on Skye has such an air of spaciousness, loneliness and timelessness.

For the walker the main features of interest lie on either side of the low-lying moors that form the backbone of the peninsula, where a number of notable stacks and duns dot the crag-girt coastline.

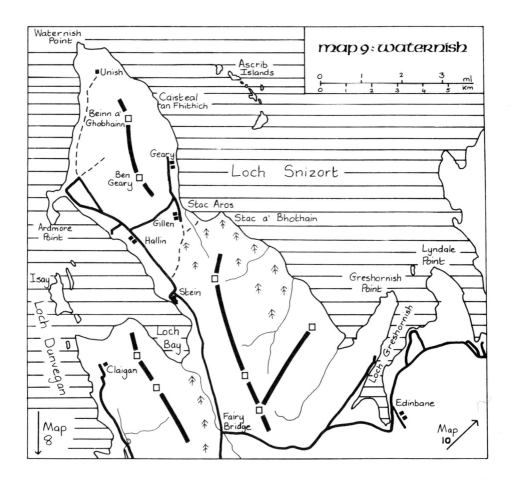

Coastal scenery at Rubha nan Brathairean

7.1 WATERNISH WEST COAST

The Waternish road leaves the Portree–Dunvegan road at Fairy
Bridge and runs up the west coast of the peninsula past Loch Bay to
Stein. The landscape is gentle, green and populous. At Loch Bay the
omnipresent basalt has been eroded by the sea to expose the limestones and sandstones beneath, and fossils abound. From Loch Bay it
is possible to walk all the way around the coast to Loch Dunvegan.

Beyond Stein a minor road continues up the west coast to Hallin
and Ardmore, and from Hallin another road cuts across the peninsula
to Geary (Gyarry, Enclosure) and Gillen on the east coast. On a conspicuous grassy knoll above Hallin stands Dun Hallin broch, reached
by a short tramp through the heather from the Geary road (Grade 1,
1/2hr return). The circular wall of the broch is 4m (13ft) high in places
and more or less complete, and there are fine views from here over
Loch Dunvegan and its islands. In former times the surrounding area
(as at Trumpan and elsewhere in Waternish) used to contain wolf
traps — rectangular pits up to 8m (25ft) long by 1m (3ft) wide, but
these are now filled in.

The west coast begins to get more interesting at Ardmore. There
are sizeable cliffs at Rogheadh (*Roe*-a, Noisy or Splashing Place) and
Ard Beag (Ard Bake, Little Height), but they lie on the private
property of Ardmore estate and access is discouraged. On a windy hill
above Ardmore Bay stands Trumpan Church, classified as an Ancient
Monument but currently, like so many of Skye's historical buildings,
in a dangerous state of disrepair. Among the graves is that of Lady
Grange (see page 163). At the back of the church is a stone stoup that is
reputed never to run dry.

One of the most infamous acts in the history of clan warfare took
place here in 1578 when the MacDonalds of South Uist anchored at
Ardmore and, knowing the church to be full of MacLeods, burned it
to the ground. One mortally wounded girl escaped to raise the alarm,
the Fairy Flag was unfurled and MacLeods from Dunvegan and round
about fell upon the MacDonalds at Ardmore Bay, killing them almost
to a man.

The MacDonald bodies were lain alongside a stone dyke that was
then tumbled over them to bury them. The battle has ever since been
known as the Battle of the Spoiling of the Dyke. The MacDonald

Sgurr a' Ghreadaidh from Sgurr na Banachdich
Coruisk and the Cuillin from Sgurr na Stri

attack was itself a reprisal for an equally infamous act, when the MacLeods discovered 395 MacDonalds of Eigg hiding from them in a cave and suffocated them by lighting a fire at the cave entrance. Those were bloody times.

The road ends just north-east of Trumpan, and beyond here the coast presents a continuous line of cliffs all the way to Waternish Point. The shore is accessible at Sgoir Beag (GR 225617), but there is no shoreline route from here either southwards to Ardmore or northwards to Waternish Point.

7.2 WATERNISH POINT

The march of time has left the northern tip of Waternish untouched, and here, more than anywhere else on Skye, there is a feeling of being far from civilisation, of being part of the great sweep of nature and of history. The traces of man that do exist merely add to this impression. The unmanned lighthouse at Waternish Point and the ruined brochs and memorials to long-forgotten clan battles that dot the now untrekked moorland seem to add to the feeling of a land abandoned.

The walk from Trumpan to the point is made easy by an excellent track, but the continuation along the east coast (the 'raven's coastline') is a much more serious proposition, involving rough going and an airy cliff-top walk. The route begins just north-east of Trumpan at a right-angled bend in the road (GR 229616). From here a Land-Rover track goes left through a gate to follow the cliff top all the way to the ruined house at Unish. The cliffs reach a height of 80m (250ft) but they cannot be viewed until beyond Unish as the track lies well back from the cliff edge.

To compensate for the lack of views of the cliffs there are glorious views westward across the sea to the hills of South Uist, North Uist and Harris, strung out like beads on the horizon. In addition you can make some interesting short detours along the way to view a number of sites of historical significance. The first of these is a prominent cairn on the moor on the right. This is a memorial to John MacLeod of Waternish, who was killed on the moor c1530 during the Second Battle of Waternish (contested by the MacLeods and the MacDonalds, naturally). Further along on the left a second cairn commemorates the death of his son Roderick MacLeod of Unish, who fell in the same battle.

It is not difficult to imagine these windswept moors ringing with the sound of battle and haunted by the ghosts of the slain, but as at

The 'raven's coastline', Waternish Point

Trumpan and elsewhere in Skye one feels appalled, angered and saddened by the senseless loss of life in clan society. The cairns, with inscriptions in both Gaelic and English, were restored by the Clan MacLeod Society USA as recently as 1985, yet already the elements have begun to erode them, as time has eroded memories of that long ago battle.

Just beyond the second cairn stands Dun Borrafiach, one of the most beautifully constructed brochs on Skye. It is remarkable both for the size of the stones used (up to 1m square) and for the quality of their placement, which is almost worthy of an Inca construction. Further along stands Dun Gearymore, a more dilapidated broch abandoned to sheep and rabbits but still worth exploring.

Beyond Dun Gearymore the track bears right away from the coast to the ruins of Unish House; to leave the track when it turns right and go left to reach the coastline at the pinnacled stump of An Camastac (The Stack of the Bay). The going along the cliff top from here to Waternish Point is excellent, and there are fine coastal views (Grade 2, 4 miles/6km, 2¹/₂hr; 5hr return).

It was at Waternish Point that Prince Charlie and Flora MacDonald first touched Skye after their journey across the Little Minch from South Uist in 1746. They tried to land at Ardmore Point but were fired on by soldiers stationed there. The oarsmen managed to row out of musket range and the small party sheltered awhile in a cave at

Waternish Point before crossing Loch Snizort to land on the coast of Trotternish.

By far the easiest return route from the point is by the outward route, but keen coast walkers may wish to continue around the east coast of the Waternish peninsula to explore the 'raven's coastline' and return across the moor. This extension involves much more serious terrain than the outward journey.

Heading eastwards from Waternish Point, the next point reached is Creag an Fhithich (Craik an *Ee*-ich, The Raven's Crag), where the coastline turns southwards into Loch Snizort and views of the outer isles are replaced by views of the Ascrib Islands and Trotternish. Beyond Creag an Fhithich a good sheep path through the heather clings to the cliff edge on the seaward side of an old fence. Composure is required; if in doubt stay further inland.

Approaching the headland of Biod a' Choltraiche (Beet a *Choltrich*-ya, Razorbill Cliff) the going deteriorates and it is best to stay away from the cliff edge altogether, keeping to the moor until Caisteal an Fhithich (*Cash*-tyal an *Ee*-ich, The Raven's Castle) comes into view. This is a grass-topped stack that is almost as high as the cliff itself and which is connected to it by a short beach causeway. Great care is required when trying to see or photograph the stack; the most dramatic and safest view is obtained from just beyond it, where it can be looked at across a waterfall (4½hr). The crag and castle are not named arbitrarily, as ravens do patrol this stretch of coastline.

The shortest route out from Caisteal an Fhithich, if transport can be prearranged, is to Geary road-end (GR 264625), using a track (not marked on OS map) from the Abhainn a' Ghlinne (see next section) (5½hr complete trip). Without transport at Geary you must cross the backbone of the Waternish peninsula to complete the circuit back to your starting point. Head diagonally uphill, aiming for the low point on the skyline between Beinn a' Ghobhainn (*Gho*-in, Blacksmith) and Ben Geary (Gyarry, Enclosure). The going is rough, but as height is gained the views open out to compensate. Descend to pick up the grassy cart track marked on the map at GR 240624, which provides a pleasant end to the day (Grade 4, 9½ miles/15km, 220m/720ft, 7hr round trip).

7.3 WATERNISH EAST COAST

The east coast of Waternish presents an almost continuous line of cliffs stretching southwards along the shores of Loch Snizort from

Waternish Point to the Greshornish peninsula. The northern cliffs are most easily approached from the Unish track (see page 178). Further south, the road from Hallin runs along the coast between Geary and Gillen, two lovely villages strung out along the cliff top above Aros Bay. From Geary road-end a cart track continues to the Abhainn a' Ghlinne (*A*-win a *Ghleen*-ya, River of the Glen) and can be used for access to the stack of Caisteal an Fhithich (see previous section) (Grade 3, 2hr return).

South of Aros Bay, shoreline access is possible at Loch Losait, where two stacks deserve investigation (see below). South of Loch Losait it becomes impracticable to walk the coastline as forestry plantations reach the cliff edge. Even after the trees stop at Creagan Dearga, the whole coastline as far as Loch Diubaig (*Joo*-bake, Deep Bay) is composed of steep broken dangerous cliffs that have no clearly defined cliff top, while the terraced hillsides above are rough and complex; not recommended.

Beyond Loch Diubaig the waters of Loch Snizort reach like fingers into the land, forming a number of narrow peninsulas. The first of these is Greshornish Point, a wild cliff-girt peninsula that is well worth exploring (see below). Next comes Lyndale Point, a stubby thumb alongside the thin finger of Greshornish (see below), and then the smaller peninsulas of Rubha nan Cudaigean and Aird Point, whose easily accessible low-lying fields attracts point baggers only.

Loch Losait (Lossaitch, Small Stream or Hollow)
The shore of Loch Snizort is easily reached at Loch Losait using the forestry road that begins at Gillen road-end (GR 268597); there is no parking at the road-end, but parking spaces can be found further back along the road. The forestry road continues past the last house at Gillen to a fork; take the left branch, which cuts back left past a ruined building and zigzags down to the shore.

The shoreline can be followed in either direction, westwards to Stac Aros (*Arrus*, House) or eastwards to Stac a' Bhothain (*Vaw*-in, Bothy). Of the two stacks, Stac Aros, a fine lump of rock some 10m (35ft) high, is the nearest and the most interesting; to reach it boulder-hop along the beach. The far side of the stack yields an exposed scramble up through thick vegetation to a guano-encrusted summit platform. Ten minutes further along the beach is a fine 30m (100ft) deep sea cave, which can be reached AT LOW TIDE ONLY by a short scramble. Unfortunately, there is no way beyond to the rock platforms of Aros Bay.

To reach Stac a' Bhothain go round the point east of Loch Losait. The going is initially good, on level grass above the beach, but eventually it degenerates into a boulder-hop along the shore. The 15m (50ft) stack appears grassy and uninteresting at first, but the vertical cliff face on its far side is very impressive. The stack is connected to the shore by a high neck that yields a straightforward if vegetated and exposed scramble.

Grade 3 (excluding scrambles). Allow 1hr to visit Loch Losait, plus 1hr for Stac Aros and cave, and 1¹/₂hr for Stac a' Bhothain.

Greshornish Point (Point of the Pig Promontory)
The Greshornish peninsula is wild, remote and rarely visited. The trip out to Greshornish Point makes a fine tramp, with an interesting dun and a number of stacks and caves to be viewed en route.

The walk begins at Greshornish House Hotel, reached by a minor road that leaves the Portree–Dunvegan road at Upperglen. Fifty metres beyond the hotel's entrance drive is a sharp right-hand bend; the route begins here, on a cart track that goes through a gate on the left. The track bears right to a clump of trees and forks. Take the left branch, which becomes a path, across the neck of the peninsula to a small bay on Loch Diubaig. Across the loch the map marks a natural arch, but it is indistinguishable by eye, and the long walk around the head of the loch to attempt to view it from above is unrewarding.

From the bay follow good sheep paths along the cliff top towards Greshornish Point. In the next bay are a number of caves and a 15m (50ft) finger of basalt, and in the bay beyond that stands a broader, grass-topped stack. The cliffs gradually increase in height and force the coast walker up to the high point of the peninsula at 97m (319ft), from where there are fine views across Loch Snizort and Loch Greshornish. Loch Greshornish is a long way from the open sea, yet there have been stories of icebergs and walruses here, and it is recorded that in one summer long ago it was so full of sharks that no one dared bathe in it. Another curious incident occurred in World War I when the loch was bombed by a plane that suspected a U-boat of lurking in its depths; this must have been a truly surreal sight.

Beyond the high point the cliffs diminish in height towards Greshornish Point, where small crags fringe an area of lush green moss. Turning southwards along the east coast, the next feature of interest is ruined Dun na h'Airde (*Harja*, Point), which occupies a fine position on a rock promontory surrounded on three sides by 15m (50ft) sea cliffs. AT LOW TIDE ONLY it is possible to clamber along the shoreline beneath the dun, where water–worn holes in the rock give some indication of the power of the sea.

The east coast is mainly flat and good going above the beach soon leads back to Greshornish House. On reaching the grounds at Greshornish aim for a gate in the wall and a track that leads back to your starting point (Grade 3, 4 miles/6km, 3hr round trip).

Lyndale Point (Line–dale, Flax Dale)
The Lyndale peninsula does not match Greshornish for rugged scenery, in fact much of it is uninspiring farmland, but its length makes its furthest reaches quite remote, and those who enjoy a wild moorland tramp will find the walk to the point a rough and rewarding excursion. The obvious approach on the map is from Lyndale House, but this should be avoided as the access road is private and leads into the heart of the farmland. The best starting point is on the minor road that leaves the Portree–Dunvegan road just west of the Suladale turn-off (dun baggers should note the presence of Dun Suladale broch, slightly less ruinous than most, just west of Suladale). When the road bears left to rejoin the main road a cart track beside a wood on the right (GR 377542) gives access to the east coast of the peninsula.

The east coast is vegetated and not particularly appealing, but good sheep paths make the going pleasant. On the shoreline is a flat stretch of rock named Seal Rock, but you will be fortunate to see any seals there. Lyndale Point itself is a short grassy promontory beyond which lies Eilean Beag (*Ailen* Bake, Small Island), alive with noisy seabirds (1hr). Turning southwards from here along the west coast, the shoreline becomes craggier and more interesting. Follow sheep paths along the cliff top, with Eilean Mor (*Ailen* Moar, Big Island) and Greshornish Point coming into view, then aim for the summit of Torr a' Chruidh (Torr a *Croo*-y, Horseshoe Hill, 65m/214ft) to obtain the best going and the best views.

From Torr a' Chruidh the return route is rough. Quit the west coast to avoid the farmland around Lyndale House and head straight down the middle of the peninsula past the large loch seen ahead. The sheltered shores of this reedy loch harbour trees and rhododendrons, oddly out of place in the moorland landscape. Continue past the loch through the shallow defile beyond, using the roadside wood as a navigation aid in otherwise featureless country, and bear right at some ruins to reach your starting point (Grade 3, 4½ miles/7km, 3hr round trip).

8 trotternish

Trotternish (meaning obscure) is the largest and most northerly of the peninsulas of Skye. Along its length runs an undulating mountainous ridge that reaches its highest point at The Storr (719m/2,358ft). The walk along the crest of the ridge, known as the Trotternish High Level Route, is one of the finest backpacking expeditions in Scotland, with pleasant terrain and magnificent coastal views. The western slopes of the mountains are tame and featureless, but on the east there is an almost continuous line of cliffs. Beneath the cliffs landslips have formed some of the most remarkable landforms on Skye, the most famous of which is the 50m (165ft) pinnacle of the Old Man of Storr. The mountains are described below from south to north (8.1 to 8.4).

Only one road crosses the ridge, from Uig to Staffin via the Bealach Ollasgairte (260m/850ft, *Byaloch Olla-skarr-stcha*, GR 440679, not named on OS map), but a coast road completely encircles the peninsula (47 miles/75km round trip from Portree) to give easy access to both the mountains and the coast. The coast has mile after mile of stacks, caves, natural arches, waterfalls and other coastal features, which cannot be seen from the road but which provide endless opportunities for rewarding short walks. The coastline is described below in an anti-clockwise direction (8.5 to 8.9).

8.1 THE STORR

The Storr (719m/2,358ft, Pillar or Stake)

It is at The Storr that the backbone of the Trotternish peninsula begins to erupt into the contorted forms for which it is renowned. The view of The Storr from the Storr lochs (Loch Fada and Loch Leathan) on the coast road north of Portree is one of the most famous and photographed on Skye, with the summit cliffs of the mountain given scale by the Old Man, which stands at their foot. The Old Man is only one of a number of extraordinary pinnacles that ring the basin known as The Sanctuary, and the walk up to The Sanctuary is one of the most popular excursions on Skye.

There is a car park just north of Loch Leathan at the foot of The Storr (GR 509529), but the muddy path that climbs from here through forestry plantations directly to The Sanctuary is closed because of erosion. Alternative routes climb each side of the woods. The path on the south-west side is the normal approach; it begins beside a small stream at the bend in the road near the north end of Loch Leathan (look for a stile; GR 503525) and follows the stream up through the woods to enter The Sanctuary (Grade 3, 2½ miles/4km,

310m/1,000ft, 2+hr return). There is also a longer path from the south side of The Storr car park that joins this path and is worth a detour on descent (signposted 'car park') as it passes a fine lochain hidden deep in the woods.

The array of pinnacles that guard the secluded interior of The Sanctuary give it the aura of a prehistoric site. The Old Man in particular is like a megalithic stone; John MacCulloch wrote of it in the early nineteenth century: 'Had this rock been on the plains of Hindostan instead of the mountains of Skye, it would have been an object of greater devotion than the Jaggernaut pagoda.' It rises 50m (165ft) from its plinth and is undercut all round; the rock is so flaky that it comes away in one's fingers. One can well sympathise with the famous Victorian climber Harold Raeburn, who remarked after a visit here: 'The Old Man may be climbable but we didn't make an attempt.'

Don Whillans made the first ascent in 1955. The route is graded Very Severe and begins on the north-west face near the right-hand end of the overhang. A second route, graded Extremely Severe, climbs the prominent pillar at the foot of the Portree face, and good luck to all who venture thereon. Nearby, and prominent among the other pinnacles of The Sanctuary, is the improbable Needle — a fragile wedge of rock with two 'eyes' left by fallen blocks.

Behind The Sanctuary tower the 200m (650ft) summit cliffs of The Storr, split into five buttresses by deep dark gullies. It is worth continuing to the summit for close-up views of these cliffs and for the summit panorama. The normal ascent route takes the path that goes through The Sanctuary and around the northern end of The Storr cliffs to a shallow basin above the cliffs of Coire Scamadal (Short Valley). From here climb back left above The Storr cliffs and up a grassy corridor through the small rock band that guards the summit plateau rim to the north. From the summit there are fine views over Raasay and south across The Storr lochs to the Cuillin. Great care is required if venturing near the crumbling cliff edge (Grade 4, 4 miles/7km, 580m/1,900ft, 4hr return).

The route down may be difficult to locate in mist. A short distance from the summit a cairn marks the top of the grassy corridor through the rock band. Descend the corridor into the shallow basin; at the low point of the basin, at the very edge of the Scamadal cliffs, the path goes right, outflanking the cliffs of The Storr and leading back into The Sanctuary.

Admirers of landslip scenery may wish to vary their return route by a detour along the north ridge, at the end of which the castellated rocky eminence of Carn Liath (Carn *Lee*-a, Grey Cairn) thrusts up boldly from the moor. The impressive northern cliffs of Carn Liath, hidden on approach, sport the cleanest climbing rock on The Storr, and beneath them is perhaps the most chaotic terrain in all Trotternish. The rarely visited summit is a simple scramble from the south. The best return route is back along the north ridge above the Coire Scamadal cliffs until it is possible to contour across to rejoin the normal route (allow 2hr extra).

The normal route can be combined with either of two rougher routes to the summit plateau to make a circuit. One route leaves the southern end of The Sanctuary and climbs the stone shoot at the back of Coire Faoin (*Fœ*-in, Empty). The going is steep and rough, but a cairn at the top confirms that you are not the first to ascend it. Whether the gully is best tackled on ascent or descent is a matter of personal taste.

A more interesting route climbs to the Bealach Beag (*Byaloch Bake*, Little Pass) south of Coire Faoin. The ascent is mostly on grass, with some simple scrambling beside the stream higher up. At the bealach turn right up pleasant grass slopes to reach the summit. Perhaps the best circuit is to ascend via the Bealach Beag, bypassing The Sanctuary on ascent, and descend via the normal route through The Sanctuary (Grade 5, 4 miles/6km, 580m/1,900ft, 4hr round trip).

8.2 THE CENTRAL TROTTERNISH RIDGE

North of The Storr the gentle western slopes of the Trotternish ridge contrast with an almost continuous line of cliffs on the east. As far as The Quiraing few walkers give the hills more than a passing glance, for the western approaches are mostly dreary and the eastern cliffs are guarded by miles of boggy moorland. The best way to tackle this part of the ridge is as an end-to-end walk, if transport can be arranged at both ends, beginning at The Storr and finishing at the Bealach Ollasgairte at the high point of the Staffin–Uig road. A few of the hills, however, make worthwhile objectives in their own right for shorter day trips.

Heading northwards from The Storr, the next peak reached is the second highest in Trotternish — Hartaval (668m/2,192ft, Hart Mountain), most easily climbed in combination with The Storr despite the low bealach between them. Then comes a long flattish section culminating in Baca Ruadh and Sgurr a' Mhadaidh Ruaidh, two peaks that make an interesting round from the east (see below).

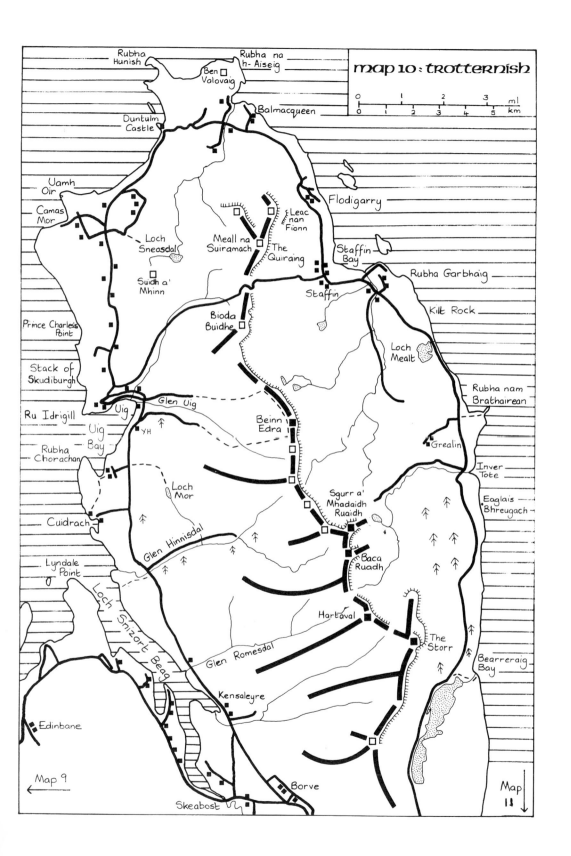

map 10 : trotternish

Rubha Hunish
Rubha na h-Aiseig
Ben Volovaig
Balmacqueen
Duntulm Castle
Uamh Oir
Camas Mor
Loch Sneasdal
Meall na Suiramach
Leac nan Fionn
Flodigarry
The Quiraing
Staffin Bay
Suidh a' Mhinn
Staffin
Rubha Garbhaig
Prince Charles's Point
Bioda Buidhe
Kilt Rock
Loch Mealt
Stack of Skudiburgh
Ru Idrigill
Uig
Glen Uig
Rubha nam Brathairean
Uig Bay
YH
Beinn Edra
Rubha Chorachan
Loch Mor
Grealin
Inver Tote
Sgurr a' Mhadaidh Ruaidh
Eaglais Bhreugach
Cuidrach
Glen Hinnisdal
Baca Ruadh
Lyndale Point
Loch Snizort Beag
Hartaval
The Storr
Glen Romesdal
Bearreraig Bay
Kensaleyre
Edinbane
Map 9
Borve
Skeabost
Map 11

Beyond Sgurr a' Mhadaidh Ruaidh the ridge undulates over a succession of tops to Beinn Edra, the most northerly 600m (2,000ft) hill on Skye, whose summit is easily reached by paths from the west (see below). North of Beinn Edra a low point of 280m (900ft) is reached before the ridge rises steeply again to Bioda Buidhe (466m/1,530ft, *Beeta Boo*-ya, Yellow Point) and descends to the Bealach Ollasgairte (260m/850ft). Bioda Buidhe is easily climbed from the car park on the bealach and is worth the outing for the cliff-top views of the landslips below, where the huge lump of Cleat (Clait, Cliff) towers over Loch Cleat.

Sgurr a' Mhadaidh Ruaidh (593m/1,945ft, Skoor a Vatty *Roo*-y, Hill of the Red Fox)
Baca Ruadh (637m/2,089ft, *Bachka Roo*-a, Red Bank)

These two peaks are unusual for Trotternish in that they thrust out steep stubs of ridges to the east around Coir' an t-Seasgaich (Coiran *Tchays*-kich, Corrie of the Reeds), such that the round of the corrie skyline makes an interesting and problematical route with plenty of opportunity for scrambling. Access is by an unsurfaced road (GR 517606; rough but drivable) that runs past Lealt to picturesque Loch Cuithir (*Coo*-hir, Cattle Fold) at the foot of the massive eastern buttress of Sgurr a' Mhadaidh Ruaidh.

This road was built to enable exploitation of the diatomite that floored the loch (diatomite is a siliceous earth with many industrial applications). The diatomite deposit was originally more than 13m (40ft) thick and over 20 acres in extent, and has been mined several times, most recently for a short time after World War II.

To permit mining Loch Cuithir had to be drained (the drainage channel around the loch can still be seen), and the group of reedy lochs that exist today are only the remnants of what was once one large loch. The diatomite was transported by rail to Inver Tote for drying (see page 204); what remains now lies under water again, and little of the mining operation is apparent except for some old brickwork and the line of the railway. The land has reverted to its former state and now only an occasional fisherman or walker passes this way.

From Loch Cuithir the route to the summit of Sgurr a' Mhadaidh Ruaidh goes left of the cliffs on good grassy terrain to the ridge that forms the skyline. This ridge abuts against rotten cliffs that offer no way up, but on the far side of a shallow corrie is another ridge whose broken slopes provide a simple, if sometimes earthy, scramble to the

Sgurr a' Mhadaidh Ruaidh

summit. The summit is perched airily at the cliff edge above Loch Cuithir and offers grand views of the undulating Trotternish ridge and the vast flatlands of eastern Trotternish (1¹/₂hr from Loch Cuithir).

Baca Ruadh is easily reached by a pleasant stroll around the curving plateau rim above Coir' an t-Seasgaich (2hr), and then things become more exciting again. To descend from the summit of Baca Ruadh, go eastwards straight over the edge down steep grass slopes to reach the top of the eastern buttress. Crags bar a direct descent from here, but they are easily negotiated by a gully a short distance along on the right. Lower down, another hidden line of crags bars the way, but these again are easily outflanked a short distance along on the right, by a shelf that slants down right to easier ground.

To avoid all problems on descent, keep to the steep grass slopes that descend from the summit to the right of the buttress, then contour round the foot of the buttress. From here cross the mouth of Coir' an t-Seasgaich, contour round the foot of Sgurr a' Mhadaidh Ruaidh and recross the moor to Loch Cuithir (Grade 5, 4 miles/6km, 520m/1,700ft, 3¹/₂hr round trip).

Beinn Edra (611m/2,006ft, Bain *Et*tera, The Between Mountain)

Beinn Edra's craggy eastern face and gentle western slopes do little to distinguish it from many another Trotternish hill, but the approach from the west is eased by two paths that make the ascent more appealing than most.

West of Uig, Glen Uig cuts deep into the hills to the foot of Beinn Edra, its upper basin fringed by crags and waterfalls. Roads penetrate the glen high up on both the north side (signposted Glen Conon) and the south side (signposted Sheader) and, from the end of each, paths continue to the summit of Beinn Edra. The northern path continues straight on from Glen Conon road-end and climbs to the Bealach Uige, from where it hugs the cliff edge southwards to the summit.

The southern road up the glen passes through a strange landslip of 'fairy hills', like giant anthills, in the midst of which the fortress-like rock of Castle Ewen towers over a picturesque roadside lochan. Glen Uig is sometimes called the 'Fairy Glen'. The path to Beinn Edra from the road-end is shorter than the northern path and has better views of the waterfalls on the north side of the glen. It begins as a cart track midway between the last house and the turning circle at the road-end and climbs to the Bealach a' Mhoramhain, from where it hugs the cliff edge northwards to the summit (Grade 4, 6 miles/10km, 500m/ 1,650ft, 3¹/₂hr return).

It is tempting to combine the two paths into a circular route, but this would involve crossing the moor above the crag-fringed upper basin of Glen Uig and is less appealing than it first seems.

8.3 THE QUIRAING

The Quiraing (*Kwi*-rang, Round Cattle Fold, ie The Table)
Meall na Suiramach (543m/1,781ft, Mell na *Soo*ramach, Maiden Hill)

North of the Bealach Ollasgairte, beneath the summit cliffs of Meall na Suiramach, stands a ghostly labyrinth of rocky spires that is one of the natural wonders of Scotland: The Quiraing. Visitors have come here to be thrilled or terrified for a century or more; in the heyday of Victorian tourism fifty to sixty visitors a day were guided around the narrow corridors between the spires. On a dreich day, with the wind shrieking around the rocks, it can be a terrifying place indeed, but when the sun shines there are few more exciting and inspiring places to explore.

The easiest and most pleasant route into The Quiraing begins at the car park at the Bealach Ollasgairte, at the high point of the Uig–Staffin road. From here a fine path that is almost Alpine in character clings to the hillside beneath the crags of Maoladh Mor (*Mœla* Moar, Big Bare Hill) and takes an almost level route into the heart of The Quiraing. After a pleasant half-hour walk you arrive at a basin that is reminiscent of The Storr Sanctuary. On its left soar the complex pillars and buttresses of the main cliffs, among which the 36m (120ft) Needle is prominent, while on the right rises the castellated rocky eminence known as The Prison.

The summit ridge of The Prison gives some enjoyable moderate scrambling. A path goes off to the right around the back of the crags to reach the ridge between the southern rock tower and the central wall, both of which provide short, fairly exposed scrambles. Climb the tower from the left (east) side, then return along the ridge and gain the top of the wall by a scramble on the right. Beyond the wall another leaning tower at the north end of the ridge looks impregnable, but again a path contours around the back to find a moderate exposed scramble to the top in a superb situation.

From the northern tower it is possible to regain the basin at the foot of The Prison by a direct descent of the north ridge, but the steep grit-covered rocks are not recommended. It is better to return to the dip between the central wall and the northern tower, then follow a path that contours beneath the tower around the foot of the rocks.

The main path from the Bealach Ollasgairte continues through the basin past The Prison, but the most fantastic formations in The Quiraing lie hidden on the hillside above The Needle; cairns mark the start of routes up the steep slopes of grass, stones and earth. The impressive but rotten crags of The Needle have yielded a rock climb graded Hard Very Severe. The path goes left of and behind The Needle, crosses the gully on its right and squeezes between two rock pillars to emerge into a fantastic pinnacled defile.

The path meanders up this secret, claustrophobic sanctuary and deposits you on the curious Table, a 36m (120ft) by 18m (60ft) flat expanse of grass beneath the summit cliffs of Meall na Suiramach. In former times an annual midsummer shinty match was played here, but today The Table is left to sheep. Looking back from The Table, the view down the defile, with pinnacle crowding upon pinnacle, resembles nothing less than a Chinese print; it is a unique and marvellous prospect. The path continues a short distance beyond The Table but unfortunately there is no breach in the crags that guard the summit plateau of Meall na Suiramach above.

The Quiraing

The north tower of The Prison,
The Quiraing

The shortest route back down to the basin is the route of ascent, but just below the final scramble onto The Table a path down a gully on the far side enables an alternative descent. Further down this gully there are a number of routes around various rock towers; all are straightforward and all rejoin the main path at the far side of the basin.

The path through the basin continues northwards along the foot of the main cliff face through complex country. After passing a reedy lochan it forks; the right branch descends to another lochan and eventually to Loch Hasco (see next section). The left branch crosses the neck of land at the foot of the south-west ridge of Leac nan Fionn and reaches the plateau north of Meall na Suiramach at a break in the cliffs (GR 449705).

From here a return route to the Bealach Ollasgairte can be made along the plateau rim, where grassy going makes for a fine cliff-top walk with magnificent views over the spires of The Quiraing to Staffin Bay and the offshore islands. Away from the cliff edge the plateau becomes mossy and yielding, and is best avoided except for the easily reached summit of Meall na Suiramach. Beyond The Quiraing the cliff edge becomes less well delineated and it is best to keep high, contouring along sheep paths, until a way can be made down the steep grass slopes of Maoladh Mor to the car park.

Return trip to basin: Grade 3, 2 miles/3km, 1+hr. Round trip via plateau: Grade 4, 4½ miles/7km, 340m/1,100ft, 3hr excluding time spent at Quiraing. Exploration of The Quiraing from the basin: Grade 5, 2+hr. The equally interesting hill of Leac nan Fionn can also be included in the route without too much extra effort (see below).

8.4 LEAC NAN FIONN AND THE NORTH END

To the north and east of The Quiraing landslips have created an astonishingly contorted terrain, full of knolls, crags, pinnacles and hidden lochans; some of the knolls make fine vantage points and are crowned by duns. The most interesting features occur around the flanks of Leac nan Fionn and its neighbour Sron Vourlinn, which from Staffin appear as a single table mountain fringed by vertical cliffs. Good paths approach the area from The Quiraing in the south and from Loch Langaig in the east.

Leac nan Fionn (373m/1,225ft, Lyachk nan *Fee*-on, Fingal's Tombstone)

The ascent of Leac nan Fionn presents some enjoyable scrambling problems (easily avoided if necessary) and enables the exploration of one of the unsung wonders of Trotternish — Pinnacle Basin. The Loch Langaig approach route begins on the coast road just south of Flodigarry (GR 464710). There is a small lochan on the east side of the road and a cart track leading to Loch Langaig on the west; park at the start of the track or at a parking space just to the north.

Loch Langaig lies in a hollow barely 100m from the road and commands an impressive view of the precipices of Leac nan Fionn's east face. The track circles the loch on the right and continues as a path to Loch Hasco, another fine lochan that nestles at the foot of the steep hillside beneath the cliffs. Note the rock tooth that projects from the hillside up on the right.

Southwards from Loch Hasco a defile climbs to another hidden loch (Loch Fada), but the route to the summit of Leac nan Fionn continues straight on, following a fence up to the foot of the prominent left (south) buttress of the east face. It is possible to climb the steep grass gully on the right of this buttress, but a more pleasant and interesting route goes left, following a path below the crags of the complex south-west ridge. Note the rock needle high up on the crest of the ridge. Breaks in the crags enable short cuts to be taken up to the ridge, but it is better to continue to the neck of land where the end of the ridge abuts against the cliffs of Meall na Suiramach.

From here double back and climb the ridge to the summit; gentle grass slopes on the left enable all obstacles to be easily bypassed. The first obstacle is a rock tower that provides a short sharp scramble to the clump of grass crowning its summit. Above here grass rakes rise between crags, right of which is the rock needle that was seen from below. The needle goes direct, providing a simple scramble, but good luck to anyone who dares to place more than a hand on its airy top.

Beyond here lies the level grassy summit of Leac nan Fionn, at the edge of the east face (2hr from Loch Langaig). The cliffs are split into four buttresses of approximately equal height. The rightmost (south) buttress is separated from the rest by a shallow notch whose negotiation involves a moderate exposed scramble.

A descent northwards enables a magnificent circular route to be made via Pinnacle Basin. Make for the saddle that separates Leac nan Fionn from Sron Vourlinn; the direct descent is barred by cliffs that are easily outflanked on the left (west). Once onto the saddle, aim for the lochan and the wall just beyond, and then descend over the lip of the saddle into one of the secret hollows of Trotternish. This is Pinnacle Basin, where pinnacles rise from the hillside like prehistoric standing stones, each with an individual character that gains from its group

Leac nan Fionn

setting. The most impressive pinnacle of all is undercut all around and is reminiscent of the Old Man of Storr. There is plenty of climbing and scrambling to be done hereabouts.

On leaving the basin aim diagonally right down the steep hillside to rejoin the approach path above Loch Langaig. On the way you should pass the rock tooth seen during the approach walk, and this provides a simple scramble to round off a magnificent route (Grade 4 excluding optional scrambling, 3 miles/5km, 270m/900ft, 3hr round trip).

A second approach route to Leac nan Fionn is the path from the Bealach Ollasgairte via The Quiraing (see previous section). This approach seems longer on the map, but on the ground it provides delightful level going and passes through tremendous rock scenery. Follow the path through The Quiraing and beneath the cliffs of Meall na Suiramach until reaching the neck of land at the foot of the south-west ridge, then climb the ridge and descend to Pinnacle Basin as described above. From Pinnacle Basin contour round the foot of the east face to regain the path to The Quiraing (Grade 4 excluding optional scrambling, 5 miles/8km, 160m/500ft, 3hr round trip).

Both approaches have their attractions. The ideal route would combine both, using transport at both ends. The Quiraing approach enables The Quiraing and Leac nan Fionn to be combined into perhaps the most exhilarating round in Trotternish.

Sron Vourlinn (363m/1,192ft, Strawn Voorlin, Mill Nose)

A worthwhile extension to the ascent of Leac nan Fionn is the ascent of Sron Vourlinn, the cliff-girt hill to the north, which marks the end of the Trotternish ridge and provides superb views across the northern tip of Trotternish to Harris and Lewis. The saddle between Leac nan Fionn and Sron Vourlinn is flanked by cliffs on both sides; descend Leac nan Fionn's grassy western slopes to avoid these and aim for a breach in the cliffs to the left of Sron Vourlinn's southern wall. Once onto the cliff top the walk along Sron Vourlinn's summit ridge is wonderfully spacious; continue out to the north top, beyond which lie only flat moors and the sea (Grade 4, additional 1½hr return from Leac nan Fionn).

Sgurr Mor (492m/1,615ft, Skoor Moar, Big Peak)

The view westwards from Sron Vourlinn is blocked by the higher ridge of Sgurr Mor, whose grassy slopes are easily ascended but whose summit plateau is covered in yielding moss that makes tough going. The small summit cairn is almost impossible to locate in mist, and in fine weather the views are curtailed by the hill's convex slopes. Not recommended except as a finish to the Trotternish High Level Route (Grade 4, additional 1½hr return from Leac nan Fionn or Sron Vourlinn).

8.5 THE BRAES TO PORTREE

The Braes

The Braes north of Loch Sligachan are more renowned for their historical associations than their walking potential, for it was here on 17 April 1882 that the Battle of the Braes was fought between local crofters and an imported police force. Braes crofters had reached the end of their tether when summonsed for grazing on land that had been taken from them, and when the local constabulary arrived with 48 extra policemen from Glasgow to arrest the ringleaders a running fight broke out, truncheons versus sticks and stones. The police were beaten back to Portree. Widespread newspaper coverage highlighted the grievances of Scotland's crofters and led indirectly to the Napier Commission of 1883 (see page 18). A roadside cairn commemorates the battle.

Nothing could be further removed from those hectic scenes of yesteryear than the tranquil Braes of today, isolated from the summer bustle of modern Skye by a long road from Portree or a path from Sligachan (see page 83). Few walkers come this way, for neither the map nor the view from the roadside gives any indication of the coastal playground to be found on the seaward side of the small wing-shaped peninsula that juts out into the Narrows of Raasay opposite the Braes. Here, in one short, exciting, cliff-fringed stretch of coastline, is one of the most amazing collections of secret caves, pinnacles and strange coastal formations on Skye.

There are two roads through the Braes: the B883 from Portree and a minor road to its immediate east. From any point on the minor road cross the neck of the peninsula and walk round to the ruined dun at its northern point. There is often sunshine here when the Red Hills and the Cuillin are in cloud, and the view across Loch Sligachan can be dramatic. The main area of interest lies southwards along the cliff top, beyond the cove formed by the dog-leg in the coastline.

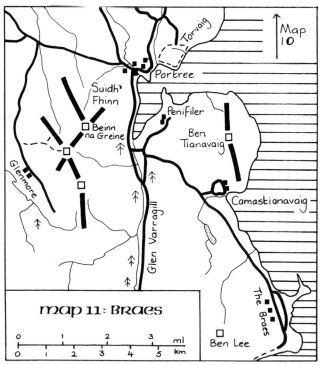

map 11: Braes

The first feature reached is a cave, which can be visited AT LOW TIDE ONLY. The entrance is a 30m (100ft) long canyon whose 10m (30ft) high walls are a trap when the tide comes in. Access is from the shore, which at low tide can be reached via a small bay just beyond the cave. Also of interest in this bay is a stack left high and dry on the beach.

In the next bay is a similar but even larger cave whose entrance canyon can be reached by a scramble down a gully on the far side. The back of the cave splits into three or four arched caverns, in the deepest of which it is possible to stand upright some 20m (65ft) from the cave entrance.

Beyond the far bounding wall of the entrance canyon is a deep hole into which the sea flows through a natural arch (which can be clambered over). Just beyond here is the most remarkable formation of all — a 3m (10ft) long concertina of rock that stretches across a canyon like a fragile bridge. Such is its advanced state of erosion that it seems to be suspended by unnatural forces. DO NOT ATTEMPT TO CROSS.

Next comes a 3m (10ft) tall gendarme that adorns the end of a short ridge. Brave souls can reach its table-top by a step across from the ridge and a mantelshelf manoeuvre. Beyond the gendarme the cliffs become smaller and provide bouldering problems galore (Grade 2 excluding optional scrambling, 1+hr round trip).

Ben Tianavaig (413m/1,355ft, Ben *Tchee*anavaig, Mountain of the Stormy Bay)

Ben Tianavaig forms its own peninsula to the immediate south of Portree and is a magnificent viewpoint for Raasay and the east coast of Skye. In appearance it has much in common with the hills of the main Trotternish ridge, with uniform, mostly unbroken slopes on the west (giving the hill an attractive pyramidal shape) and tiers of cliffs formed by landslips on the east. To the north the cliffs are holed at sea-level by caves such as Tom Cave and the Scarf Caves, which cannot be reached on foot but which can be studied through binoculars from across Portree Bay.

The upper slopes of Ben Tianavaig are composed of porous gravel, with large expanses of short turf that remains remarkably dry even in wet weather. The pleasant terrain and the summit views make the ascent far more rewarding than you would expect from such a lowly hill. The shortest route to the summit is from Camastianavaig on the Braes road to the south-west (GR 506396); a rock band at 250m

(800ft) provides sport for scramblers (Grade 4, 2 miles/3km, 360m/1,200ft, 2½hr return).

A longer and more interesting route combines an ascent of Ben Tianavaig with an exploration of the north coast. The route begins at Penifiler (GR 489417), reached by a minor road from the Braes road. From here cross the neck of the Vriskaig Point peninsula to lonely Camas Ban (Cammas Bahn, White Bay), a broad strand of almost black sand (despite its name) hemmed in by cliffs on each side. Ruins here reflect the bay's former importance as a source of lignite.

From Camas Ban follow a good path eastwards over small shoreline crags to a larger stony bay. At the end of this bay more crags force you up onto a broad grass shelf some 20m (65ft) above the sea, where another good sheep path provides excellent coast walking close to the cliff edge. Soon another bay is reached, enclosed by skerries that are a popular meeting place for all kinds of seabirds. It is worth descending to the bay to explore the rock pavement at the water's edge, where rock buttresses project seaward like fingers. There are a few small caves (1½hr).

Leave the coast at this point for the ascent of Ben Tianavaig. Although a long stony beach leads onwards towards the Scarf Caves, the shoreline route eventually becomes impracticable. At the end of the beach a nightmarish sheep path continues some distance along a perilous grass shelf above the sea, but it leads nowhere and can be recommended only to those who have cloven feet. Leave such exploits to guidebook writers who know no better; climb the hillside, following the line of a stream that comes down from Ben Tianavaig to the near end of the beach (GR 504427). Continue past some ruined dwellings directly to the summit of Ben Tianavaig; the going, as noted above, is excellent (3hr).

The summit is perched close to the edge of the broken cliffs of the east face, and in the basin below are a number of pinnacles similar to those on the main Trotternish ridge. The view is considerable, encompassing Portree huddled around its bay, the Trotternish ridge and east coastline, an incomparable panorama of Raasay, and to the south the Narrows of Raasay and the mountains of southern Skye. Descend directly to Penifiler down the steep western slopes, negotiating one or two rock bands. Plan your descent from the summit, aiming left of a line of small cliffs and Druim Loch, for once onto the flat moor navigation is difficult (Grade 4, 4½ miles/7km, 440m/1,450ft, 4hr round trip).

Portree short walks

As befits the capital of Skye, Portree is beautiful. The main street, Somerled Square and the harbour are obvious attractions, but the equally picturesque headland above the pier (known as The Lump) is less well known. To reach it take the road on the right of the Tourist Information Office for a short distance and then go left (gate) on a track. At the top of The Lump is a beautiful pine-encircled ring where the Skye Highland Games are held (Grade 1, $^1\!/_2$hr return).

Another fine path makes a girdle traverse of The Lump. This path branches right from the above track 30m beyond the gate and eventually comes out between the Tourist Information Office and the adjacent church. It can also be reached from the shore by steps from the end of Bayfield Road (Grade 1, 15min).

The north side of Portree Bay offers a pleasant shoreline walk on recently renovated paths. Leave town on the Staffin road then keep right along Scorrybreck Road to descend to the shore. From the road-end (GR 489438; parking space) a good path continues past a boat-house to the Black Rock (marked as Sgeir Mhor [Skerr Voar, Big Skerry] on OS map) at the entrance to the bay. This low-lying skerry can be reached AT LOW TIDE ONLY (Grade 1, $^1\!/_2$hr return from road-end).

Beyond the Black Rock the path turns northwards past the Wishing Well and the Battery Green and traverses steep grass slopes beneath the cliffs of Ben Chracaig (144m/474ft, *Chrachk*-aig, Bay of the Fissure). On the hillside above, just south of the summit and 6m (20ft) below the cliff top, lies MacCoitir's Cave (GR 495438), named after a sea-robber who used it as a lookout and a retreat. Today the danger-ously steep and loose slopes of Ben Chracaig make the 5m (15ft) slit that forms the entrance virtually inaccessible; abseiling from the cliff top is the best approach. The path negotiates a boulderfield and reaches a gate in a wall, where it forks. Both branches provide in-teresting circular routes back to the road-end.

The left branch zigzags up steeply beside a wooded gorge to reach another wall and then, after a short distance, doubles back to the sum-mit of Ben Chracaig (by continuing beside the wall you will reach the Fanks path — see below). Nearby is the pile of rubble that was once Dun Torvaig. Beyond the summit the path follows the cliff edge, with fine views over Portree Bay, and descends steeply to rejoin the shore path just east of the gate near the boathouse (Grade 3, $1^1\!/_2$hr round trip).

The right branch at the first wall goes through a gate and along the edge of a fine raised beach around farmed fields. Beyond the fields a cart track will be found that climbs back left to Torvaig road-end (GR 495446); if approaching from Torvaig, go left at the road-end then immediately right through a gate to find this cart track.

To return to your starting point go straight across Torvaig road-end on a muddy cart track (the Fanks path) that descends past sheep fanks to a road beside the Coolin Hills Hotel. Keep straight on past the hotel and take the path on the right to reach the shore road near a bridge a short distance west of your starting point (Grade 2, 1½hr round trip). If approaching the Fanks path from this side, continue past the hotel until the road bends sharp left, then keep right to find the path. Note that on the west side of the bridge a short path leads to a fine two-tiered waterfall and pool.

South of Portree the hills and forests of Glen Varragill are worth exploring. A Forestry Commission car park (GR 477425) is the starting point for a 2 mile/3km forest walk that is well maintained and has all streams bridged (Grade 1, 1hr). Halfway along, the path reaches a fire break and turns down left to return to the car park. By leaving the path here and climbing steeply up the fire break you will reach open hillside and the broad ridge that forms the skyline when viewed from Portree. Go left to reach the summit of Beinn na Greine (417m/ 1,367ft, *Grain*-ya, Mountain of the Sun), the highest point on the ridge, or right to reach the viewpoint of Suidh' Fhinn (312m/1,022ft, *Soo*-ya Een, Fingal's Seat), from where Fingal traditionally viewed a massive deer hunt in Glen Varragill below (Grade 4, 3 to 4hr return).

Suidh' Fhinn can also be reached from the B885 Bracadale road: leave the road at the cattle grid beyond the last house (GR 471438) and follow the left bank of the stream up the hillside. The two routes can be combined into a round trip. Beinn na Greine can also be reached easily from a high starting point on the Glenmore road to the west (GR 434412). A surfaced road (locked gate) climbs to the summit of Skriaig (396m/1,298ft), from where Beinn na Greine is only a short walk away.

South of the Forestry Commission car park a beautiful old path climbs over the Bealach Mor (*Byal*och Moar, Big Pass) south of Skriaig. It begins 200m north of the Braes turn-off at an inconspicuous gate in the forest fence (GR 474411) and winds its way mysteriously through the woods onto the open hillside. It reaches the Glenmore road at a bend south of Glenmore, just below a new bulldozed track (GR 441399).

8.6 PORTREE TO STAFFIN

North of Portree the coast consists of steep craggy hillsides that make a shoreline route impracticable. Prince Charles's Cave marked on the map is best approached from the sea and is unlikely to have been used by Charlie. The hilltops between the coast and the coast road appear as mere excrescences on the moor and are unappealing, although the most southerly tops are within easy reach of Portree.

Bearreraig Bay

Bearreraig Bay (GR 516531), at the foot of The Storr, is the first place north of Portree where access to the shore is easy, and it is worth visiting for its waterfall, its fossils, its views of Holm Island and its unique approach route — a descent of no less than 674 concrete steps. Begin at the Storr Lochs Dam access road, which leaves the coast road at the north end of Loch Leathan; cars can be parked at The Storr car park 500m further north. Walk down the road and across the dam to a cottage, from where a pulley-operated railway descends steeply to the electricity generating station on the bay 140m (450ft) below.

Descend the steps beside the railway to reach the curving beach. Go left to view the waterfall below the dam, still impressive although diminished by the hydro-electric scheme, then go round the corner on the right to view the craggy lump of Holm Island. There are many fossils to be found in the shoreline rocks, including abundant ammonites, curled up like Catherine wheels. There have been other finds here as well; in 1891 a Norse treasure hoard was discovered, including silver bracelets and rings, and coins from as far away as Samarkand. By fording the Bearreraig river, the equally fossiliferous north shore of the bay can be explored (Grade 2, 1+hr return).

Rigg and the natural arches

North of Bearreraig Bay the coastline erupts into a succession of natural arches and other coastal formations, none of which can be seen from the coast road above and some of which cannot be viewed from land at all. Shoreline access from Bearreraig Bay is not possible, but some interesting explorations can be made via a cliff-top route from near Rigg and a shoreline route from Inver Tote (see below).

From Rigg picnic area on the coast road (GR 520577) a broad grassy platform can be seen above the shoreline cliffs, with two old fishermen's huts on the right. To reach this platform, go through the gate at the far end of the picnic area and descend the grass hillside diagonally to avoid its steepest slopes. From the huts a path goes down to the shore, where a natural rock jetty (Leac Tressirnish) juts out into the sea.

Follow a sheep fence northwards along the cliff top to view the main features of interest; the cliff edge beyond the fence is dangerous. The most prominent feature, a respectable stack, is not marked on the map. The name Na Famhairean (Na *Fahv*iren, The Giants) on the map refers to some offshore rocks that are dangerous to boats (Grade 3, 1+hr return).

By continuing along the cliff top beyond the end of the grassy platform it is possible (with care) to obtain a view of the Eaglais Bhreugach, although this is more safely viewed from Dun Grianan.

Inver Tote south shore
Eaglais Bhreugach (*Ecklish Vree*-agach, False Church)

Inver Tote (GR 520605), at the mouth of the Lealt river, provides shoreline access to the Eaglais Bhreugach, an enormous boulder split by a churchlike archway. The route to Inver Tote begins just north of the last house on Lower Tote access road (GR 516602) and follows a cart track past some sheep pens and through a gate. For a cliff-top view of the Eaglais Bhreugach, continue straight on beyond the gate to the cliff edge and then go right to Dun Grianan, whose few remaining stones perch airily at the cliff edge (Grade 2, 1hr return).

To reach the south shore of Inver Tote, take the indistinct path that starts immediately beyond the gate and goes diagonally left to the edge of the gorge of the Lealt river, then follow a good path down the gorge beside an impressive waterfall.

The walk from here to the Eaglais Bhreugach can be done AT LOW TIDE ONLY, as the initial section is impassable at high tide; there is no alternative way back. The route goes right along the shore beneath Dun Grianan on rock pavement and large boulders. The Eaglais stands in a shallow bay 1 mile (1½km) along the beach. It is 12m (40ft) high and has a circumference of about 36m (120ft). Holing its centre is the huge arch that gives it its name, although according to tradition there is more to the name than mere appearance, for there are tales of pagan rites here, involving the roasting of cats.

Beside the main arch is another smaller passageway, still large enough to walk through, and on the beach nearby is an isolated pinnacle some 5m (16ft) high whose name adds to the legends, for this is the Cubaid (*Coob*aj, Pulpit) of Satan. The scramble up the landward or seaward end of the Eaglais looks tempting, but the vegetated higher slopes are steep and dangerous.

It is worth continuing a short distance further along the beach to a 20m (65ft) long sea cave whose near wall is holed by another large arch and whose entrance is guarded by deep ankle-grabbing seaweed. In some weathers a curtain of water falls across the entrance to give the place the air of a secret grotto, but beware the loose and water-logged cliffs above, which are prone to rockfall. This cave marks the limit of shoreline progress. The natural arch further along, which is prominent during the walk to the Eaglais, cannot be reached. Return to Inver Tote while the tide is low (Grade 3, 3hr return).

Inver Tote north shore
Lealt Waterfalls (Leth-allt, Lai-owlt, Half-stream)

The Lealt river drops steeply between the roadside and Inver Tote to form some impressive waterfalls. The two-tiered upper fall is best seen from the north bank of the river, where there is a car park (GR 516605). Go through the gate in the fence at the back of the car park and turn right to reach the top of the fall or left to view it across the Lealt gorge. In the gorge itself is a curious pinnacle, whose precariously balanced summit block seems about to topple.

To reach the north shore at Inver Tote, continue along the edge of the gorge through a quarry and pick up a path on the right that meanders down the steep grassy hillside. This path may be difficult to find from above. It eventually reaches some steep overgrown steps that lead down to the prominent chimney of the old diatomite workings, where diatomite from Loch Cuithir was dried and shipped (see page 188).

To view the impressive lower fall and its pool, follow the left (near) bank of the river upstream, but note that the fall can be seen equally as well from the right bank, reached by the path from Lower Tote (see above). Note also that in dry weather and at low tide the Lealt river can be forded near the river mouth (where there are remains of an old bridge), but at other times cross further up, at the edge of the pool below the lower waterfall. If climbing up to the car park from the north shore, do not be misled by sheep paths that go up the gully on the right (Grade 2, 1+hr return from car park).

From the north shore you can walk northwards along the beach,

The Eaglais Bhreugach

past an impressive needle-like pinnacle and Sgeir Dhubh skerry, to Rubha nam Brathairean.

Rubha nam Brathairean (*Roo*-a nam *Bra*-huren, Brothers' Point)

Rubha nam Brathairean (GR 528628) is one of the most delightful spots on the Trotternish coastline, yet good footwear is essential for its exploration as some unexpectedly exciting scrambling is involved on a narrow arête and on exposed paths. To reach the Rubha, begin opposite Glenview House just north of the Grealin turn-off (GR 516625). Take the cart track that goes past one house to the gate of another. Go through this gate and immediately turn right on a path that curves to the bay below, where there are ruined buildings and numerous creeks and small crags on which to scramble.

A somewhat exposed path goes right above the crags and around the bay towards the point, which is guarded by a curious dun-like knoll that cannot be circumvented. Moreover, the ridge that leads out to the knoll narrows to a sharp arête and sports two gendarmes. The scramble over the gendarmes is moderate but exposed; sheep paths contour below the crest for the less gymnastic. Care is required also on the scramble over the knoll to the green table-like pastures at the point beyond.

The knoll was at one time fortified. By tradition, in later times it was inhabited by Donald Mac Dubh Ruaraidh and his brothers, after whom the promontory is named. The brothers survived by remaining neutral in the many disputes between the MacLeods and the MacDonalds until they could see the likely outcome, when they would join the winning side to obtain any available booty. On the shore below the knoll is the Preas Dhomhnuill Dhuibh (Press=Cupboard), a deep opening where the booty was stored.

From the landward side of the two gendarmes an exposed path cuts diagonally down the cliff face to the shore, from where it is possible to walk out along flat shoreline rocks to Sgeir Dhubh (Skerr Ghoo, Black Skerry) at the next point. Sgeir Dhubh has a tragic history that testifies to the dangers of the Trotternish coastline. In 1812 sixteen people were killed here when a boat from Portree struck the rocks in darkness; winds drove the boat to Gairloch, and only one body was recovered. The cliff face south of Sgeir Dhubh boasts a slender pinnacle some 50m (160ft) high, behind which the Old Man of Storr forms a perfect backdrop. It is possible to walk along the beach all the way to Inver Tote (Exploration of the Rubha and Sgeir Dhubh: Grade 5, 2hr).

Kilt Rock

North of Rubha nam Brathairean high cliffs fringe the coast as far as Staffin Bay. The cliff edge everywhere is dangerous and best avoided except at Loch Mealt viewpoint (GR 509655), where a wooden barrier has been built beside the 52m (170ft) Mealt Waterfall to allow safe viewing of the famous Kilt Rock. This 90m (300ft) two-tiered cliff derives its name from its resemblance to a pleated kilt, with an upper half of vertical basalt columns and a lower half of horizontal sandstone beds.

Those interested in history will find many sites to explore along this stretch of coastline, as a glance at the map will indicate. There are several duns and cairns, including Dun Dearg, one of Skye's 'fire hills' on which beacons were lit to summon men to arms. From the north side of Loch Mealt juts the promontory of Rubha na Ceardaich (*Roo*-a na *Kyard*ach, Smithy Point), which was once an island; early inhabitants built a dun here and in later times it became a safe place for blacksmiths to make their weapons.

Staffin Slip

North of Kilt Rock the sea cliffs diminish in size towards the wide sandy shores of Staffin Bay, which look magnificent when the north wind fuels the crashing waves. On the south side of the bay a minor road from Stenscholl (GR 483680) cuts around the foot of the cliffs to Staffin Slip, where there are several interesting features.

At An Corran (The Point) and Rubha Garbhaig (*Roo*-a *Garra*vaig, Point of the Rough Bay) are some small shoreline crags, while on the landward side of the road an easily accessible cliff face provides good sport for rock climbers. Above the slipway a grass track, paved with rocks, meanders up through a break in the cliffs. This is the Cabhsair (*Cah*sair, Causeway), constructed in 1846 to provide work during the potato famine. It ends on the moor at a fence, and a short distance above is a collapsed chambered cairn.

The most fascinating place to explore is a giant crazy pavement south of the slipway, reached by walking across the flat marshy ground above the shore. The pavement is littered with huge boulders that have rolled down from the cliffs above, and in places the going is labyrinthine. A scramble around the boulders along the pavement edge above 5m (16ft) sea cliffs involves some interesting moves. Some of the cracks in the pavement are considerable, and it takes nerve to reach all the small promontories that jut out into the sea (Grade 2 excluding scrambling, 1+hr return).

8.7 STAFFIN TO DUNTULM

Creag na h-Eiginn (Craik na *Haigin*, Crag of Distress or Violence)

North of Staffin Bay the coastline is relatively flat and uninteresting until beyond Flodigarry Bay. The cliffs begin again at Creag na h-Eiginn, which is not as interesting as the cliffs further north but which provides a useful objective for a short moorland walk in the vicinity of Flodigarry. Take the Flodigarry Hotel road to a fork, then keep left above the hotel to a building at the road-end. Go through a gate in the fence and tramp across the moor to reach the Creag (Grade 3, 1hr return).

The north-east cliffs

Between Creag na h-Eiginn and Port Gobhlaig (Porst *Goalaig*, Forked Harbour) the coastline bristles with sea stacks and the cliff top is easily reached by a short (drivable) track from a high point on the coast road (GR 450737; an old building is at the roadside). The going along the cliff top in either direction is good and the views are exciting, but great care is required at the cliff edge, where sheep fences aid safety but inhibit viewing.

Southwards, the cliff top should be followed at least as far as the bay before Galta Mor (Big Pig), where there is some fine basalt piping. Beyond here the going remains easy as far as Steall a' Ghreip (Shtyowl a Ghrape, Waterfall of the Precipice), but neither the waterfall nor the cave marked on the map can be seen from the cliff top.

Northwards, the first features of interest are the outstanding twin stacks of Stacan Gobhlach (*Stachkan Goalach*, Forked Stacks), which are linked to the shore by a double line of great flat rocks like giant stepping stones. Around the next headland stands the great needle of Stac Buidhe (Stachk *Boo*-ya, Yellow Stack), with a precariously balanced boulder at its summit. Continuing along the cliff top, a small inlet hides a fine 20m (65ft) stack whose summit is only about 6m (20ft) from the cliff top and seems almost close enough to jump onto (the author disclaims all responsibility for failed attempts!). Beyond here the cliffs peter out into the rocky bay of Port Gobhlaig (Grade 2, 1+hr return).

Note that access to the cliffs from Port Gobhlaig, via the road through Balmacqueen, is awkward — there is no parking space on the shore road and sheep fences abound. The shore itself can be reached by a gate in the roadside fence at the near end of the shore road.

Rubha na h-Aiseig (*Roo*-a na *Hash*ik, Ferry Point)
Ben Volovaig (111m/364ft, Mountain of the Bay of the Steading)

After the cliff scenery south of Port Gobhlaig the flat moor of Rubha na h-Aiseig at the extreme north-east tip of Skye comes as something of a disappointment. This remote, desolate and featureless spot will be appreciated only by seekers of solitude and lovers of wild wave-lapped shores. Others may well prefer to venture no further than Stac Lachlainn (Lachlan's Stack) en route.

The rough tramp to the point begins on the shore at Port Gobhlaig, reached by a minor road that leaves the coast road just beyond the Connista turn-off (GR 434742). From Port Gobhlaig follow the shore round to sturdy Stac Lachlainn. Just before the stack is a deep enclosed pool, formed by a natural bridge through which the sea enters. On the seaward side of the stack is a natural arch visible only from further along the coast.

Beyond Stac Lachlainn keep close to the cliff edge and look for sheep paths that descend through a break in the cliffs to the shore. The cliffs continue inland along the face of Ben Volovaig to the north coast, almost cutting off the flat boggy north-east tip of Skye from the rest of the island. On the way to the point it is best to keep close to the rocky shoreline, where grass enables easy walking and where there are good views of the lonely island of Eilean Trodday.

Continuing westwards around the promontory beyond the Rubha, some ruined buildings on the bay of Lub Stac nan Meann indicate that the place was not always so deserted. The line of cliffs beneath Ben Volovaig is reached again on the far side of the bay. Stac nam Meann (Stachk nam *Mai*-un, Stack of the Kid) can be seen further along, but the going along the cliff top is very rough and only stack baggers will wish to venture there.

The best return route traverses Ben Volovaig, which despite its lowly height provides fine views over the northern reaches of Trotternish, including the stacks near Port Gobhlaig and Rubha Hunish. The ascent is rough but short. From the summit pick a route down the heather-clad slabs of the south face and walk back across the tussocky moor, following a fence to the right of the houses near Port Gobhlaig until a gate gives access to the road (Grade 4, 2¹/₂hr round trip).

If the walk to Rubha na h-Aiseig does not appeal, the viewpoint of Ben Volovaig is worth considering as an objective on its own. Begin at the end of the public road at Port Gobhlaig, where the road turns

Looking towards the cliffs of Meall Tuath from Rubha Hunish

right through a gate to the last house. Continue straight on towards a shed, pass through a gate and follow the fence around the house. Cross the moor and climb the slabby south face of Ben Volovaig (Grade 4, 1¹/₂hr return).

Rubha Hunish (Roo-a Hoonish, Bear Point)

Rubha Hunish is the most northerly point on Skye and a worthy end to the island. It is a long, grassy, crag-girt headland, lonely and breezy, fringed by beautiful stacks and almost completely cut off from the rest of the island by the 100m (330ft) cliffs of the appropriately named Meall Tuath (117m/383ft, Mell *Too*-a, North Hill). There is only one route down through the cliffs, and even this is difficult to find without prior knowledge.

The route to the Rubha begins at Duntulm Castle or Duntulm Castle Hotel (see below). From Port Duntulm walk northwards along the shore of Tulm Bay, picking up a good sheep path on the grass just above the rocks. At the far end of the bay shoreline rocks force you up the hillside, and at this point you should make directly for the summit of Meall Tuath. A coastguard lookout station at the summit has a fine view across Rubha Hunish to the Shiant Islands and Lewis, with the curiously shaped islet of Lord MacDonald's Table further left.

The cliffs of Meall Tuath fringe the coastline eastwards towards Rubha na h-Aiseig and westwards towards Rubha Voreven. There is no shoreline access from the east, and from Rubha Voreven chaotic rockfalls make shoreline progress awkward, especially at high tide. The only easy access to Rubha Hunish is from the dip between the summit of Meall Tuath and the south-west top. From the south-west side of this dip a rocky path disappears behind a large boulder and zig-zags down to the shore.

The most interesting features of the headland lie hidden on its north-east side, where there are some fine sea cliffs, stacks and deep creeks to explore. Near the neck of the peninsula is a fine blade-shaped stack, and further out towards the point stands magnificent Bodha Hunish (*Boe-a Hoon*ish, Bear Reef), a 30m (100ft) stack that is one of the most perfectly proportioned on Skye (Grade 3, 3hr return).

Duntulm Castle

The ruins of Duntulm Castle on a craggy headland overlooking the Little Minch are all that remain of a once grand building, the chief residence of the MacDonalds from the early seventeenth to the early eighteenth centuries. The castle was dismantled (and on one occasion blown up with gunpowder) so that its stones could be reused; the re-maining fragments of wall give scant indication of its former size and magnificence. This forlorn place has witnessed many scenes of glory and tragedy, revelry and bloodshed, and echoes with the ghosts of the past.

The castle is easily reached by a five-minute walk from the car park to the south (GR 411741) or from Duntulm Castle Hotel to the east. On the rocky shore of Port Duntulm below, reached by a path from the castle, is a long groove said to have been made by the keels of MacDonald galleys. Beside the ruins is a memorial to the MacArthurs (hereditary pipers to the MacDonalds), with an inscription whose poignancy is enhanced by the surrounding ruins: Thig crioch air an t-Saoghal, Ach mairidh gaol is ceol (The World will end, But love and music endureth).

8.8 DUNTULM TO UIG
The Uamh Oir (Oo-a Oa-ir, Cave of Gold)

West of Duntulm the low-lying shores of the broad bay of Lub Score are more suitable for roadside picnics than coast walks. At the end of the bay stands the headland of Ru Bornesketaig, which traditionally was the scene of yet another dispute between the MacLeods and MacDonalds. Both clans claimed ownership of the land, and to avoid bloodshed it was agreed that the dispute be settled by a race between their best war galleys, whosoever's hand touched land first being deemed the winner. When the race got underway the MacLeods gained the advantage, but a MacDonald cut off his hand with his dagger and threw it ashore, thus becoming the first to touch land.

Several caves are in the vicinity of Ru Bornesketaig, some of which were used by smugglers in former times; one in particular, the magnificent Uamh Oir, is the closest Skye comes to having a cave to rival the wonders of Fingal's Cave on Staffa. The cave's name derives from its legendary use for the secretion of valuables in times of trouble.

To reach the Uamh Oir from the coast road, take either the road signposted Camas Mor, keeping left at a fork and right at the next crossroads, or the road signposted Bornesketaig, going straight on at the crossroads. The road ends just beyond the last house (GR 376715). Begin walking here, keeping straight on along a cart track and then a path, to reach a gate in a fence. Beyond the gate aim for the first knoll on the left, which is near the cliff top and crowned by a completely dismantled dun whose stones have been reused for the many other ruined dwellings in the vicinity.

Continue along the cliff top until a break in the cliffs, just before the headland, allows a steep grassy descent to the shore (care when wet). The Uamh Oir lies just around the corner on the right, its hexagonal basalt columns forming a perfect rectangular entrance to the deepwater channel beyond. Beside the entrance is a crazy basalt pavement reminiscent of the Giant's Causeway in Antrim. You cannot enter the cave nor cross to the far side of the entrance. In the opposite direction from the cave, back along the shore towards Camas Mor, you can walk some distance along a fine rock pavement at the cliff foot well above the waterline, but there is no through route.

After exploring the shoreline it is worth wandering along the cliff top around Ru Bornesketaig, at least until a magnificent needle stack and natural arch come into view. Note that a short cut from here back across the fields to your starting point is beset with fences (Grade 3, 1+hr return).

Rubh a' Chairn Leith (Roo a Charn Lay, Point of the Grey Cairn)

The road to Camas Mor (Big Bay) continues as far as the slipway marked on the map (GR 370707), and from there an interesting short walk follows the cliff top to Rubh a' Chairn Leith and Dun Liath. Camas Mor itself is a fine bay enclosed by natural breakwaters at each side. From the slipway climb steep grass slopes to reach the cliff top and then walk out to the point, where an unreachable rock tower, vertical and lichen-encrusted, juts out from the cliff face.

Further along at the cliff edge stand the ruins of Dun Liath (*Lee*-a, Grey), beyond which the cliffs give way to a gentler coastline. The shore below the dun is easily accessible, and AT LOW TIDE ONLY it is worth returning this way to Camas Mor, for between the dun and the point are some interesting basalt causeways and pavements on which to clamber around (Grade 3, 1¹/₂hr return).

Eilean Chaluim Chille (*Ailen Chalum Keel-*ya, Island of St Columba's Chapel)

Seekers of antiquities will note that on the moor south of Dun Liath the map marks the chambered cairn of Carn Liath and a cashel at Eilean Chaluim Chille, which to the uninitiated will appear as mere piles of rubble. Eilean Chaluim Chille, as its name implies, was once an island in Loch Chaluim Chille, which was drained in 1824 to provide more farmland; today the island appears as a lighter-coloured stony patch on the moor. The loch was named after St Columba, who founded a monastery on the island; in later times the island became a refuge for Norse pirates.

Since the loch was drained, deterioration in the drainage scheme has caused much of the land to revert to treacherous marsh, which is everywhere dangerously deep and should be avoided. There is only one safe approach to the cashel, provided you do not deviate from the route, and even this has nothing to recommend it unless you are interested in ruins. It begins at the house 50m south of Kilmuir House in Linicro (GR 387683). A road goes right of the house to another house and from there a cart track crosses the moor, bridging some wide drainage ditches to reach the island south of the ruined cashel (Grade 2, 1+hr return).

Prince Charles's Point

South of Dun Liath the coastline is flat and uninteresting, given over to farming, as far as Skudiburgh. The area has many associations with Prince Charlie and Flora MacDonald, who landed here in 1746 at the

featureless spit of land now called Prince Charles's Point. This unremarkable spot is of historical interest only, but for those keen to visit
it the easiest approach is via Monkstadt Farm access road (GR 387675).

Ru Idrigill and Skudiburgh

The bold viewpoint of Ru Idrigill on the north side of Uig Bay is
easily reached by a fine little path from the coast road just north of
Uig. The path begins at the hairpin bend above Idrigill village (GR
383640; parking) and follows a shelf above the Idrigill road (the path
ends at the village, which forms an alternative starting point). At two
trees some distance along the path, take a small side path up to the
plateau and then turn left to reach the headland. The end point lies just
beyond the high point seen ahead (Grade 2, 1hr return).

To the north of Ru Idrigill the commanding vantage point of Dun
Skudiburgh can be seen atop a rocky knoll above the waters of Loch
Snizort. To reach it, return to the low point of the plateau above
Idrigill and follow a sheep path that descends diagonally down steep
broken slopes to the shore. This path requires care when used by
humans; at one point a small overhang under which sheep pass easily
must be negotiated on hands and knees or bypassed on steep earthy
slopes. On the shoreline below the dun is the 15m (50ft) rock finger of
the Stack of Skudiburgh, but it cannot be reached on foot because of
shoreline cliffs (Grade 3, 1hr return from Ru Idrigill). *Note:* avoid an
approach to Dun Skudiburgh from Totscore road-end (GR 380656)
as it crosses farmland and is beset with fences and ditches.

8.9 UIG TO SKEABOST

Uig is the ferry point for the Outer Hebrides and, with a connecting
road to Staffin on the east coast, a good base for exploring the Trotternish mountains and coastline. In the immediate vicinity are Glen Uig
(see page 190) and the two headlands of Uig Bay (Ru Idrigill (see
above) and Ru Chorachan), all of which are worth a visit.

Ru Chorachan (Steep Headland)

Facing Ru Idrigill across Uig Bay is the headland of Ru Chorachan,
which like its neighbour offers fine views across the bay and Loch
Snizort. The route to the Ru begins south of Uig at the crossroads in
Earlish where the surfaced road ends (GR 385612). From here follow
an unsurfaced road until it turns right, then go straight on over a stile,

and along a path through the fields. The path ends with a steep descent to the secluded bay of Camas Beag (Little Bay) at the foot of the gorge and waterfall of the Allt Yelkie. On the far side of the bay an excellent sheep path climbs back up to the cliff top and follows a level shelf all the way out to the point (Grade 3, 1½hr return).

The walk can be extended into an engaging circular route by continuing southwards along the seaward side of Ru Chorachan. The cliff top here is rough and complex, and its convex nature is such that the cliff face cannot always be seen, but sheep paths again ease the going and there are fine views across Loch Snizort.

The cliffs diminish towards the green pastures of Cuidrach, from where a lovely old path takes a wonderfully intricate route back to Camas Beag to rejoin the Earlish path at the top of the steep descent to the bay. From Cuidrach follow a sheep path around the fence of the house at GR 378596 to pick up the path alongside a drystone wall; it is very indistinct in places. Approaching Camas Beag, look for the little wooden bridge by which the path crosses the Allt Yelkie, then look for gates and stiles in order to keep to the path as it is very overgrown (Grade 3, 3hr round trip from Earlish). Even if you do not make the round trip to Cuidrach, this underused path is worth exploring from Camas Beag as far as the bridge.

Hugh's Castle

Hugh's Castle (GR 381583, Caisteal Uisdein on OS map) was built by Hugh MacDonald in the early seventeenth century. It was a strange construction in that it contained no door, entry being by ladder, and even today it is difficult to get inside the ruin. There are two ways to reach the castle: from Cuidrach to the north and from South Cuidreach to the south.

The minor road to Cuidrach leaves the coast road south of Uig (GR 389597) and ends beside the shore at the sheltered bay of Poll na h-Ealaidh (Pole na Haily, Pool of the Song). When the road bears right to the bay (park here), go left along a Land-Rover track to a cottage, then keep straight on beside a fence to the high point of the moor directly ahead; the castle crowns some sea cliffs immediately beyond (Grade 2, 1+hr return). The route to the castle from South Cuidreach (GR 385581) is shorter but goes through a farmyard, and permission should be sought from the nearby house.

The castle ruins form a sturdy rectangular enclosure some 16m (52ft) long by 10m (32ft) wide, with walls up to 5m (16ft) high and 3m

(10ft) thick. The easiest way in is through a narrow chest-high window aperture on the landward side, through which it is possible to squeeze sideways. Inside are only nettles and fallen stones.

Hugh built the castle as part of his plot to attain the leadership of the clan, then held by his uncle, Donald Gorm. He planned to invite Donald Gorm to his castle and then murder him. Unfortunately for Hugh, the invitation was inadvertently sent to an accomplice and the details of the plan to Donald Gorm. His end, in Duntulm dungeons, was a terrible one, given salt beef to encourage his thirst and then walled up to die in agony; the details are gruesome.

Inland lochs: Loch Sneosdal and Loch Mor

Inland from the west coast of Trotternish the extensive western slopes of the mountainous spine of the peninsula are generally boggy and dull. Lovers of wild moorland country will find plenty of rarely trodden ground here, including a number of remote hill tops such as Beinn Fhuar (423m/1,388ft, GR 427608) and Beinn a' Sga (452m/1,483ft, GR 437563). A number of long glens penetrate far inland, but the only one with any features of note is Glen Uig (see page 190). Two beautiful wild hill lochs hidden high on the moors, however, are worth seeking out. The routes to these lochs provide few views and few features of interest along the way but will be appreciated by lovers of wild places. Both lochs were formerly worked for diatomite and have good tracks to them.

Loch Sneosdal (GR 413692; *Snee*-osdal, Snow Dale) is cradled in a hollow beneath the dark precipices of Creag Sneosdal and is easily reached by a cart track that goes to within few hundred metres of it. The track begins at the sharp bend on the minor road south of Heribusta (GR 394701); it has a good surface as far as its high point and is drivable if the gate is unlocked (Grade 2, 2hr return from gate). Note that at the Peingown end of the Heribusta road are Flora MacDonald's grave and monument and the Skye Museum of Highland Life, both worth visiting.

The walk can be extended beyond Loch Sneosdal by a traverse across the top of Creag Sneosdal. Climb the grass slopes east of the crags and walk along the cliff top to Suidh a' Fhinn (*Soo*-ya Een, Fingal's Seat; Mhinn on OS map). Descend northwards down grass slopes west of the crags to rejoin the access track.

Loch Mor (GR 405603) lies on the moors east of Cuidrach. Like Loch Sneosdal it is easily reached by a cart track (Grade 2, 2hr return).

the track as ending here). The main track branches right to the head of the loch; the left branch soon peters out, and only the most dedicated bogtrotter would wish to continue beyond its end to the conspicuous trig point on Creag Chragach (324m/1,063ft) in the middle of the moor.

Loch Snizort Beag

The most southerly section of the west coast of Trotternish follows the shores of Loch Snizort Beag. One hundred metres south of the bridge over the River Hinnisdal, a cart track goes down past a house to a black sand bay at the mouth of the loch (GR 384568). The bay is not the most outstanding feature on the Trotternish coastline, but the track to it makes a pleasant walk and the cliffs on each side of the bay sport some shoreline crags on which to clamber (Grade 1, 1+hr return).

South of the bay the major features of interest are historical, as a glance at the map will indicate. The best preserved standing stone on Skye is Clach Ard, which stands beside the road at Peinmore (GR 421491). It is much weathered but it is still possible to make out the mysterious Pictish symbols: a 'V' rod at the top and double circles crossed by a 'Z' rod beneath. At Borve (GR 452480) are five standing stones beside the road in the shape of a cross, and in a field near Eyre (GR 414525), accessible by a gate in a fence, are two more prominent stones. The largest cairn is Carn Liath, a huge heap of stones on the banks of the River Haultin near Kensaleyre (GR 420514). It can be reached by a gate in a fence and a short marshy walk.

On an island in the River Snizort at Skeabost (GR 418485) is an interesting ruined chapel. The path to it begins at old Skeabost Bridge, on the short stretch of old road that runs from the junction of the Portree–Dunvegan road and the B8036. The path follows the right bank of the river and crosses to the island by a bridge of wire cages filled with stones. Among the overgrown chapel ruins is a fine carved headstone of a warrior with a claymore.

ACKNOWLEDGEMENTS

During the preparation of this book I have received generous help and support from many people. First and foremost I am indebted to Wendy Gibson, who eased the task of research and was there when it mattered. Mandy Millar provided motivation, lettering for sketch maps and many valuable comments about the text. Rory Macdonald uncomplainingly corrected my attempts at Gaelic pronunciation, although the phonetic guide in the text is solely my responsibility. Paul and Grace Yoxon of the Isle of Skye Field Centre were good enough to proof read the book and correct some errors. Cathy King helped with the photographic processing. I thank them all.

In addition I would like to thank all the friends I have made on Skye and all the companions with whom I have explored Skye over the years and who have contributed unwittingly to the content and spirit of this book.

index